Speaking French in Louisiana, 1720–1955

SPEAKING FRENCH IN LOUISIANA 1720–1955

LINGUISTIC PRACTICES OF THE CATHOLIC CHURCH

SYLVIE DUBOIS,
EMILIE GAGNET LEUMAS, AND
MALCOLM RICHARDSON

Louisiana State University Press Baton Rouge

Published by Louisiana State University Press

Manufactured in the United States of America
First printing

Designer: Barbara Neely Bourgoyne
Typeface: Arno Pro
Printer and binder: Sheridan Books

All maps and charts were drawn by Gabriele Richardson.

LIBRARY OF CONGRESS CATALOGING-IN-PUBLICATION DATA

Names: Dubois, Sylvie, 1963– author. | Leumas, Emilie Gagnet, 1958– author. Richardson, Malcolm, 1947– author.

Title: Speaking French in Louisiana, 1720–1955 : linguistic practices of the Catholic Church / Sylvie Dubois, Emilie Gagnet Leumas, and Malcolm Richardson.

Description: Baton Rouge : Louisiana State University Press, [2018] | Includes bibliographical references and index.

Identifiers: LCCN 2017019261| ISBN 978-0-8071-6844-8 (cloth: alk. paper) | ISBN 978-0-8071-6845-5 (pdf) | ISBN 978-0-8071-6846-2 (epub)

Subjects: LCSH: Catholic Church—Louisiana—History. | French language—Religious aspects—Catholic Church—History. | Language question in the church—Louisiana—History. | Communication—Religious aspects—Catholic Church—History. | English language—Religious aspects—Catholic Church—History.

Classification: LCC BX1415.L9 D83 2018 | DDC 282/.763—dc23

LC record available at https://lccn.loc.gov/2017019261

The paper in this book meets the guidelines for permanence and durability of the Committee on Production Guidelines for Book Longevity of the Council on Library Resources. ♾

CONTENTS

ACKNOWLEDGMENTS

This book would never have been written without the generous involvement of the Archdiocese of New Orleans, which permitted us to use their archive materials, records, letters, administrative documents, and directories. They also provided us much appreciated, comfortable working space to consult files and records.

Our deepest thanks go to Charles Nolan, retired archivist of the Archdiocese of New Orleans, and John J. Treanor, former vice-chancellor of the Archdiocese of Chicago, for their guidance in suggesting where we might find relevant material and for always being available to discuss Catholic Church history. We also owe much to the archivists who shared the research material at their institutions: Barbara Dejean at the Diocese of Lafayette, Kevin Allemand at the Diocese of Houma-Thibodaux, Ann Boltin and Renée Richard at the Diocese of Baton Rouge, and Monte Kniffen at the Provincial Redemptorist Archives in Denver.

We are grateful for the support of a number of institutions and individuals. In particular, the Center for French and Francophone Studies at LSU funded many long hours of fieldwork at the Archdiocesan Archives and provided financial support for archival research trips at international locations: the Centre des archives d'outre mer in Aix-en-Provence, France; the Archives Nationales de France in Paris; and the Sacred Congregation of the Propaganda Fide in Vatican City. We are indebted to the PhD graduate students enrolled in LSU French seminars in 2013 and 2014. They helped

Emilie Leumas and Sylvie Dubois to extract and catalog more than nine thousand letters to build the 1803–1859 Antebellum Correspondence database.

Special thanks to professor emeritus Jay Edwards of the LSU Department of Geography and Anthropology, for encouraging us to trace the linguistic history of the Louisiana Church from its colonial past; to Albert Camp, who read and commented on the complete manuscript; and to the anonymous reviewer who provided constructive criticisms on an earlier draft. Gabriele Richardson worked tirelessly to adapt and redraft our charts and maps, using ArcGIS and other sophisticated software to bring them to professional standards, while checking with painstaking care the statistical data on those figures. The completion and editing of the manuscript were facilitated by the Louisiana Board of Regents, which awarded a research ATLAS grant to Sylvie Dubois in the 2015–16 academic year.

Most of all, we are indebted to three hundred years of Louisiana Catholic priests who wrote sacramental records. Their patient attention to duty and, as our study will show, their attention to the language needs of the faithful unwittingly wrote an important chapter in Louisiana's sociolinguistic history.

Speaking French in Louisiana, 1720–1955

INTRODUCTION

"I am getting too old for my words to have any weight with you. What I say, instead of sinking in, slides off, leaving no impression. I deem it necessary that a younger man take charge of you, and perhaps his word may have more effect than mine," said the seventy-two-year-old pastor Father Joseph Subileau to his parishioners from his pulpit in the spring of 1913. Father Subileau had officiated faithfully for forty-eight years as pastor of St. Augustine Church in New Orleans. But his wistful farewell was the result not of age or debility or, despite what he said, the need for a more youthful pastor. As reported by the *New Orleans Times-Democrat* in 1913, "everybody in his parish understands French perfectly, but the younger generation is being taught their catechism in English; they make their confession in English, and they listen with more interest to sermons in English."[1]

A devoted priest, Father Subileau felt a profound responsibility toward his parish's survival. Since he did not feel sufficiently at ease with the English language to carry on his ministry, he stepped down to avoid losing some of his flock. In his last address, he gave his blessing to his successor, a young priest who spoke both languages fluently and who could minister to the congregation's language requirements. In a way, Father Subileau's departure encapsulates much of what is found in the following pages: a proudly francophone church carefully measuring the linguistic preferences of its parishioners and willing to make a painful change to retain its faithful.

Father Joseph Subileau, pastor of St. Augustine Church. (Courtesy of the Office of Archives and Records, Archdiocese of New Orleans.)

Social and economic influences from the turn of the nineteenth century to the mid-1950s created the necessity for Francophones to learn English in Louisiana, a necessity that was negotiated in different ways and at different paces by institutions and communities. Within the state government, the change, at least for official documents, was largely completed in the first decade following the Louisiana Purchase in 1803. Within the Catholic Church, in many ways a more powerful and stable social structure than the state in south Louisiana, the change was more long-term and cautious but also more sensitive to the language needs of the people. The fact that church parishioners in New Orleans could still attend Father Subileau's sermons in French on the eve of the First World War may surprise someone living outside of Louisiana (and some natives, too). Searching only the archives of the state government, scholars would naturally be persuaded that south Louisiana was an anglophone culture from the early nineteenth century. However, church writing practices from the eighteenth century until the 1960s offer another picture. A quick look at nineteenth-century church archival material is sufficient to appreciate the extensive use of both

French and English; the more measured look taken in this book shows that the church, like Father Subileau, was willing to go to greater effort than the state to make certain that Anglophones and Francophones were accommodated.

OVERVIEW OF THE CATHOLIC CHURCH IN LOUISIANA

"Louisiana," or La Nouvelle France, was a vast territory that ran from the mouth of the Mississippi River to the Great Lakes and as far west as present-day Montana. It was claimed for France in 1682 through the exploration of René-Robert Cavalier, Sieur de la Salle. Both the Catholic Church and the Louisiana Territory were very much tied to Canada for many years. New Orleans was founded in 1718 at the mouth of the Mississippi and in 1723 became the capital of French Louisiana. Slavery was introduced in 1719 and eventually became an economic key to the colonial Gulf Coast. The Catholic Church came with the French colonial administration, although it was weak and controlled from Canada. In terms of formal organization, the Louisiana Catholic Church in the early eighteenth century encompassed the Upper and Lower Louisiana territories. It consisted of a multiethnic population of faithful, clergy, and religious who attempted to preserve and nurture the faith by establishing parishes, schools, orphanages, hospitals, and other necessary institutions. Of course, there were enclaves of other linguistic groups, including Native American groups, during the French regime. But for the majority of the population, being a Louisianan was synonymous with being Catholic and a French speaker (or more accurately a speaker of one of the regional dialects of France, as discussed later).

In 1763, the Treaty of Paris officially ceded Canada and the eastern part of the Mississippi basin to Great Britain, and Louisiana—a vast area—to Spain. This change benefited the struggling Gulf Coast area economically. The treaty likewise boosted the coastal Catholic Church, which gained some independence from Canadian dominance in 1793 when the king of Spain and the pope created the Archdiocese of New Orleans, first known as the Diocese of Louisiana and the Floridas.

Spanish authority required the use of the Spanish language, especially for those who occupied civil and ecclesiastical positions, and thus created a bilingual space for written and spoken French and Spanish. The records from the Church and religious orders illustrate the day-to-day negotiation of this language choice, which was generally Spanish for formal correspondence and administrative records, French or Spanish for less formal use. However, this bilingualism in written records did not significantly diminish the strength and depth of the existing French culture, nor the need to speak French in daily interactions. There are many reasons why the French language did not weaken after forty years of Spanish rule, especially the lack of significant Hispanic immigration set against the migrant waves of French-speaking Catholics fleeing British rule as a result of the Treaty of Paris. The francophone "Acadians" were expelled from Canada and settled in Louisiana in large numbers in the 1780s. They were joined very quickly by white and black refugees from the revolt in Saint Domingue beginning in the 1790s and also by French people discontented with the 1789 French Revolution.

After the Louisiana Purchase (1803) and statehood (1812), however, major waves of immigration poured onto New Orleans's docks between 1809 and 1860, dramatically changing Louisiana's demographic profile. From the standpoint of the Catholic Church in Louisiana, immigrants could be divided into two distinct groups. The first cohort would be comprised of Catholics who swelled the already-established Catholic population, settled mostly in south Louisiana, and diversified the state's Catholic ethnic dimension (Italians, Germans, Irish, etc.) even more than it already was. The second, and less easily digested, group were the Protestant "American" immigrants. Settling at first mainly in the less-populated northern part of Louisiana, these Protestants created a clear religious geographic divide within the state, with the result that only a few new Catholic churches were established in north Louisiana. Being almost exclusively anglophone and moving into areas with sparse populations, the Protestants were quickly dominant in language and culture and did not experience the same kind of ethnic and language issues as in the south.

The waves of nonfrancophone Catholics prompted the Catholic Church

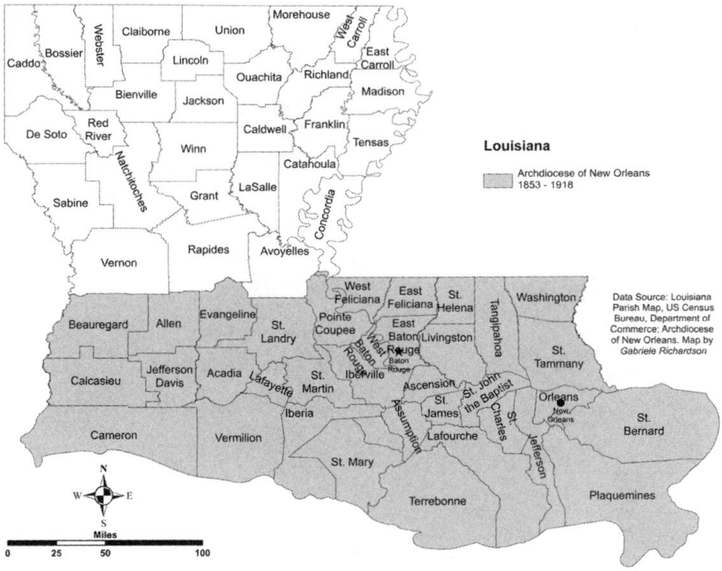

Figure I.1. The Archdiocese of New Orleans, 1853–1918

to restructure. As Jay Dolan observes, the ethnic diversity among Catholics led the Church in Louisiana to adopt "the concept of a national parish, or a congregation organized principally along the lines of language rather than territorial boundaries."[2] Therefore, the Catholic Church in south Louisiana differs from the Catholic Church in other areas of the United States in that it started from a French base and diversified into English and—in the nineteenth century, anyway—other languages, even Hungarian.

The term "Louisiana Catholic Church" in this book refers only to the dioceses situated in what was the geographical territory of the Archdiocese of New Orleans after 1853. Its boundaries after the Civil War up to the first half of the twentieth century are illustrated by Figure I.1. This area encompassed thirty-five civil parishes, totaling 23,203 square miles. "Civil parish" is the Louisiana equivalent of "county," whereas "church parish" refers to a community of the Christian faithful within the diocese that has its own place of worship under the authority of a pastor. All of the

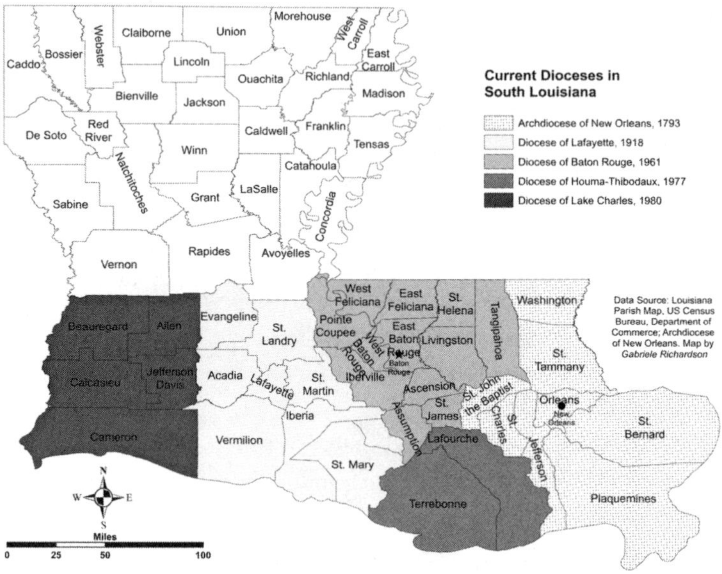

Figure I.2. Current dioceses in south Louisiana

parishes and clergy within these boundaries took their directives from the Archbishop of New Orleans. Today (Fig. I.2), five dioceses comprise this same geographical area: the dioceses of Lafayette (1918), Baton Rouge (1961), Houma-Thibodaux (1977), and Lake Charles (1981), as well as the Archdiocese of New Orleans.

CHANGE FROM FRENCH TO ENGLISH IN LOUISIANA

Two main objectives define this book: to document language change and maintenance over time in the Louisiana Catholic Church and to contextualize the switch from French to English within a broader Louisiana social and historic framework. Catholicism has always run deep in south Louisiana culture, and linguists have repeatedly proved that language and culture are profoundly intertwined. Their interaction creates emotions, values, ideals, and loyalties. Language maintenance is directly linked to a culturally dominant force at any point in time, and in the main years of this study the Church was a vital part of the Louisiana power structure. By contrast, language shift is a "by-product of unequal rates of social changes,"[3] a process whereby a particular language community gradually reduces its use of one language and replaces it with another language. The Louisiana Church weighed its language options continuously to deal with a shifting and decidedly unequal rate of social change. The archival records reveal a deep sense of concern and watchfulness within the church hierarchy about the most effective language to keep the layfolk in the confessionals. The haughty French prelate dismissing English services as a sign of decline is largely a myth.

Accounting for the maintenance of French and the overall development of English in Louisiana is a tortuously complex affair, with national, local, intra-city, family, and even intra-organizational aspects, and this book tells only part of the story, if an overlooked part. Contacts were complex among races, different levels of society, and ethnicities, and especially between English- and French-speaking groups. Ethnicity does not always align with concepts of race, race is not defined by language, and language is not to be confused with ethnicity. Moreover, ethnic frontiers, racial and linguistic, constantly modify themselves to adapt to a perpetually changing economic system, from a plantation system to a system of tenant farming, and from an industry based on manufacturing to one based on petroleum and chemical operations. Without a doubt, any neatly linear story of Louisiana linguistic reality is a misleading story.[4]

Until recently, few empirical studies were conducted on the introduction and evolution of the French and English languages among different social and ethnic groups in Louisiana. In fact, most authors who have commented on the decline of French in Louisiana and its progressive replacement by English in nineteenth-century Louisiana are travelers and plantation bookkeepers. Their reflections on the language are often highly generalized and present the introduction of English in Louisiana as a sudden historical phenomenon, akin to the abolition of slavery, in this way leaving us to suppose that Francophones decided from one day to the next to quit speaking and writing in French. Historians have often restricted their comments on language to the domain of the New Orleans elite.[5]

Also, until recently, the rare existing research done by trained linguists concerned mainly the second half of the twentieth century and was often built on more or less reliable data from the United States census. Theses and dissertations for the most part were lexicographical in nature and described one single ethnic group or one single location. They concentrated on the spoken French of the few, comparing the Louisiana variety of French with the standard French of France. In the last twenty years, however, there has been a remarkable improvement in both the quantity and quality of scientific studies.[6] In spite of these recent studies on language maintenance and shift, few empirical studies have looked at the early stages of language change in Louisiana, notably the protracted negotiation between the native variations of French and the encroaching English.[7]

The story of Louisiana English might be expected to start after the Louisiana Purchase or statehood because this was the time that government documents written in French switched quickly to English. But, for a linguistic study, this would grossly oversimplify what happened. Language shifts within the Church did not march in lockstep with major political changes such as the Louisiana Purchase (1803), statehood (1812), the Battle of New Orleans (1815), or even the Civil War (1861–65). In both colonial times and post-1803 Louisiana, while the Church made no centralized and formal decision about language, it adjusted on both the macro and micro levels; it adapted in varying degrees to the predominant culture's language but also adapted to the situation at the parish level.

Church officials' attitudes were also deeply affected by political and religious struggles far beyond "American" soil. The early colonists, although often French-born and mostly French-speaking and Catholic, were notoriously bad Catholics. Anticlericalism had a European history extending at least back to the late Middle Ages. Outright anti-Catholicism was not just a nineteenth-century American political and social issue and was especially virulent in America's "mother country," England. In France itself, besides the decapitation of a monarch and termination of church privileges, the French Revolution eventually led to the imprisonment of Pope Pius VI.

French revolutionaries profoundly undermined the Church's spiritual and secular authority and disrupted the missionary network, both in France and wherever Napoleon's armies conquered. These last significant political shifts happened while the Louisiana Church was under Spanish rule, and the influences of the Enlightenment on the Louisiana clergy were felt until 1814. Changes for the Church continued through the Civil War and Reconstruction to the twentieth-century oil industry juggernaut and beyond. Thus, to comprehend the language evolution within the Louisiana Church, one must take into account both local and global shifts that transformed Louisiana from the "failed state" of the early French colony to a post–World War II modern economy.

LOUISIANA CATHOLIC CHURCH ARCHIVES

During the nineteenth century, the Louisiana Catholic Church stood as the last vestige of French cultural dominance and the last powerful stronghold for the written French language in Louisiana, and fortunately for the study of the Church's shifting relationship to the francophone culture, the Louisiana Catholic Church has one of the largest holdings of written material in North America concerning church affairs. These important archival resources can add a critical chapter to the knowledge of language change in the linguistic gumbo that is south Louisiana. Considered as an organization, the Catholic Church had a structure extending back well over a millennium and systems of record keeping that reflected European practices dating from the Middle Ages. Continuity of material such as is found in the Louisiana Catholic Church is nevertheless uncommon in the United States as it covers not only a wide time span but also a large geographic area.

Until recently, these written records were an unexplored resource for the study of linguistics. Ironically, one of the worst natural disasters in US history opened an opportunity to research the archives. Following the devastation of Hurricane Katrina in August 2005, the Archives of the Archdiocese of New Orleans were temporarily relocated to the Diocese of Baton Rouge. Emilie Leumas, who worked as archivist for the Baton Rouge diocese at the time, gained approval from Louisiana church officials to access the extensive, well-maintained, and searchable archive collections of the archdiocese.

The Church's archives provide many genres of documents that represent language practices over a large geographic area. Though government records exist in the various civil parish and federal courthouses, they may not represent the language practices of the community over time.[8] Abundant Spanish records from the later eighteenth century reflect only the language practices of the Spanish colonial overlords and their priests, while the predominance of English in pre–Civil War records reflects an attempt to bring Louisiana in line with the dominant federal administrative and legal culture. Official pronouncements making English the language of the law also make the language shift to English appear more abrupt than it actually was. By contrast, the written documents of the Catholic Church in Louisiana are one of the richest but least explored sources of archival material available for research to language scholars interested in the tangled story of language changes in south Louisiana.

This book's primary source of archival material is sacramental registers, which record baptisms, first communions, confirmations, marriages, and burials of individual members of the church parish. Baptism, marriage, and burial registers were selected as the focus because these important moments in the Catholic faith are cataloged in the form of separate textual entries rather than simply as lists of names, as in the case of first communions and confirmations. Each entry is usually handwritten and signed by the priest and witnesses to the event. Depending on the style and handwriting of the priest, one register (or volume) may cover ten years of local history, while another fifty years.

Sacramental registers include information about families (parents, godparents, aunts, uncles, siblings, etc.), communities (witnesses at a marriage), and events. They tell a story far beyond one individual. The registers contain information about religious life (those entering the priesthood or becoming religious brothers or nuns), African Americans (including enslaved and free people of color), Native Americans, immigrants, yellow fever epidemics, natural disasters (hurricanes, tornadoes, and floods), mortality rates, and so on. The hypothesis for this study was that the language used in the sacramental registers reflected, to a large extent, the status of the French language in the Louisiana parishes. It also reflected the Church's different levels of perception of the language's utility in the local communities.

However, the registers are not a wholly dependable guide to language preferences within the parishes. The Louisiana Catholic Church's hierarchical structure, social constraints, and language attitudes also had to be taken into account to elucidate the speed and source of language change. Therefore, secondary archival collections were used to flesh out those influential constraints and attitudes only implied in the registers. The archdiocesan administrative records were the first such collection employed and consist of three genres of documents: annually published directories of archdiocesan officials; the Archiepiscopal Council Minutes from 1858 to 1921; and pastoral letters from the archbishop to the clergy and laity between 1844 and 1934. They give evidence of discussion at the administrative level of the need to accommodate English-speaking church members.

The second collection, the archdiocesan archives' Antebellum Correspondence, includes more than nine thousand personal letters written in French and English from individuals to New Orleans bishops and priests between 1803 and 1859. From that epistolary collection, a database was constructed of more than 1,500 letters with metalinguistic comments about language use in nineteenth-century Louisiana. The Antebellum Correspondence provides the voices of religious and laypeople, members of distinct religious congregations, priests and nuns, faithful men and women, highly educated writers and those with basic writing skills, who are writing spontaneously about their perception of real problems. The collection sheds light on French-language writing practices over more than sixty years, offering unparalleled continuity. Since learning how to write and spell in eighteenth- and nineteenth-century Louisiana was nearly always the result of a Catholic instructional system, there is a link, albeit of an indeterminate nature, between the Church's language practices and the faithful's written prose. At the same time, it's clear that most Louisiana Catholics did not write letters to the Church, and many were illiterate or functionally so, and therefore the letters do not represent a cross-section of who the priests saw sitting in their pews, especially in the more rural parishes.

The third collection includes church parish records and reports about local priest and parishioner membership from the five modern dioceses (New Orleans, Lafayette, Baton Rouge, Lake Charles, Houma-Thibodaux). The archives departments of these dioceses contain documents such as administrative correspondence, clergy files, wardens' minutes, church parish reports, diocesan newspapers, and financial files. Of these, by far the most valuable were the parish visitation records. From at least the 1880s, the Archdiocese of New Orleans was trying to keep a formal record of the languages used in the parishes. The effort was not particularly scientific and sometimes yielded contradictory results, but these records are critical evidence that the language preferences of parishioners were being monitored at the center of church administration. A final collection consists of the house chronicles and correspondence of the Redemptorist priests, who staffed several parishes in New Orleans.

COMMUNITIES OF PRACTICE

This is an empirical study that not only examines archival materials, but also borrows a methodological framework from the educational theorist Etienne Wenger to describe the intricate workings of an administrative entity and the internal pressures that created linguistic shift over time. The framework is based on linguistic realities rather than the traditional and rather monolithic way authority in the Church organization is usually described.

A traditional view of the Louisiana Catholic Church would look like a pyramidal structure with the archdiocesan administration led by the archbishop, entrusting ecclesiastical functions to the priests, who in turn supervise the local churches ministering to the faithful membership. Roman Catholic theologian Avery Dulles claims that the Roman Catholic Church views itself institutionally as a perfect society "that is subordinate to no other and lacks nothing required for its own institutional completeness."[9] Therefore, the Church is not a democracy or representative society in which all the faithful have the same rights, but one strongly rooted in a hierarchical concept of authority. It is a "society of unequals" wherein the power of God (to sanctify, teach, and govern) is attributed to a specific group of faithful (clerics). Regarding language change, however, the evolution did not filter down in this strictly hierarchical way. Instead, Wenger's notion of *communities of practice* better describes the Church's internal practices, guided by implicit relations, tacit conventions, subtle cues, untold rules of thumb, underlying assumptions, and shared worldviews held in common by the Catholic faithful in south Louisiana.[10]

A "community of practice" can be defined simultaneously by its membership and by the practices of that membership. It is "an aggregate of people who come together around mutual engagement in an endeavor."[11] The Louisiana Catholic Church might be considered as a network of communities of practice. Its membership is composed of the Catholic population at large, including priests and laity. The Catholic faithful share similar ideological representations, codified procedures, regulations, documents, and other signs of membership. Their mutual engagement is to practice, spread, and preserve the Catholic faith and its teaching among the local people. This engagement presupposes a sense of belonging; yet this sense of belonging potentially created for Louisiana parishioners a conflict between religious faith and language use.

The nucleus of the nineteenth-century Louisiana Catholic Church was the archdiocesan administration with its Archiepiscopal Council. This "community of practice" was composed of high-ranking clergymen and local priests who participated in its daily administration. Surrounding the archdiocesan administration was a constellation of different communities of practice represented by church parishes (Fig. I.3). They were served by appointed "secular" priests (also called "diocesan" priests) and "religious" priests who belong to an order (such as the Jesuits, Dominicans, Josephites, etc.) under the authority of the archbishop. The "faithful," or parishioners, were naturally essential members of these communities. While some participated in parish administrative activities (church wardens, council members, etc.), the social participation of most members can be uncovered to some degree through documents (correspondence, parish visitation re-

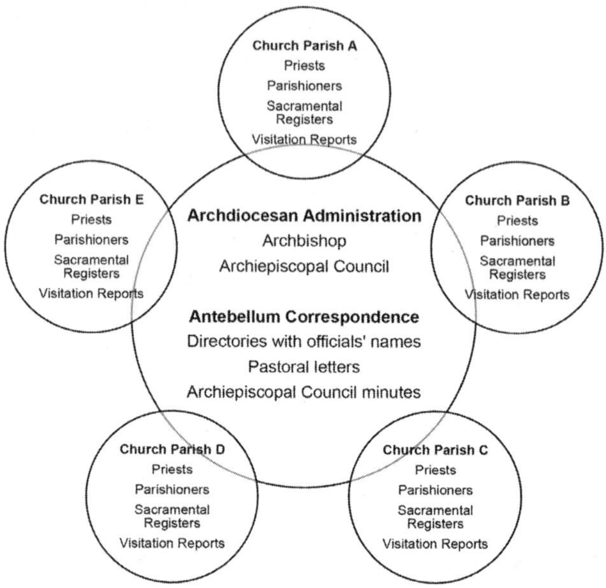

Figure I.3. Network of communities of practice in the Louisiana Catholic Church and their major documents

ports, and data collected in sacramental registers) that describe the profile of the local membership.

Each church parish and the archdiocese form a separate social enterprise with its own vision, strategies, and distinct membership. The negotiations within these enterprises (their local conditions, the number and origin of their members) and between them (who works with each other and against each other) orchestrate the practice of the faithful.

THE "LINGUISTIC TIP"

Exploring the domain of the Louisiana Catholic Church, this study seeks to uncover the pressures that created and stalled change from French to English within the Church's communities of practice. It attempts to explain and document the "linguistic tip" at the turn of the twentieth century and the long period of bilingualism found in archival written records. In doing so, it takes in a wide group of nineteenth-century individuals and ethnic groups inside and outside the Louisiana Church whose reactions to the sometimes violent social and economic changes in the state worked first to bring the two languages to an amicable working relationship and then reached a "tip" beyond which it was not possible to support the French language except in the most marginal parts of the state.

Father Subileau's retirement was precipitated by a complex set of factors affecting the Louisiana Church over time. It was also conditioned by local tensions within his own community of practice at a particular point of time. While Father Subileau considered his lack of fluency in English an impediment to his mission in 1913, parishioners from St. Joseph Catholic Church in Rayne, Louisiana, petitioned Bishop Jeanmard in 1941, urging him to find a priest who could celebrate Sunday Mass and deliver the homily and announcements in French. Not only did language shift in Louisiana occur unevenly throughout the Catholic population, it took several paths.

French can still be heard today in a few rural areas of south Louisiana, and it is the first choice of many of the older generation, a majority of them still devoted Catholics or descendants from a family originating from a Catholic tradition. Their language journey deserves to be chronicled; after all, it is Louisiana's story as well.

NOTE ON CITATION OF ARCHIVAL MATERIALS

Given the different sources and genres of archival materials that we frequently refer to and cite, we have adopted a reference system for archival documents that helps keep endnote references clearly defined but concise. Chapter 2 especially contains numerous references to letters and reports written by Crown officials and religious representatives in Louisiana to the Secrétariat d'État de la Marine in France (state secretary for the Navy). This correspondence originated from the archival Louisiana collection included in the Fonds des Colonies (Colonial Archival Collection) deposited at the Centre des archives d'outre mer in Aix-en-Provence, France. The Louisiana collection has several archival series (A, B, D, E, and F) comprised of different genres of documents. Relevant to our purpose is the epistolary collection entitled Correspondance à l'arrivée en provenance de la Louisiane, 1678–1807 (Correspondence sent from Louisiana to France). We have consulted only the biggest collection file, marked as C13-A, which contains letters from 1678 to 1753. See Menier, Taillemite, and De Forges, *Inventaire des Archives Coloniales,* 1976.

The Louisiana collection is available at the Archives Nationales de France, although a few microfilmed copies are found in Louisiana (Loyola University, University of Lafayette, among others). The reference system for these documents follows the model used by French archivists, with the name, the date, and the folio number, when provided. Therefore, an endnote reference to a letter from this collection will appear in the following way: AN (for Archives Nationales)-AC (for Archives Coloniales), C13A-12 (folio), March 8, 1713, Letter from Crozat.

Throughout the book, empirical evidence is also taken from three collections in the Archdiocese of New Orleans (AANO). References to the collection of the archdiocesan administrative business records (ABR), which comprises Catholic directories, Archiepiscopal Council's minutes, pastoral letters, and St. Louis Cathedral administrative documents, will be abbreviated as in the following example: AANO-ABR, 1789, St. Louis Warden's Minutes. The Archdiocese of New Orleans Antebellum Correspondence from 1803 to 1859 will be referred to as, for example, AANO-AC, 1840, Father Rousselon's letter to Bishop Blanc. For the last collection, which encompasses archival documents from Louisiana dioceses (church reports and administrative records), we will use the acronym AANO-DD. We also present empirical evidence from the Vatican archives, notably the Sacred Congregation of the Propaganda Fide. Established in 1622, this ministry of the Holy See in Rome was in charge of the missionary network throughout the world. Quoted letters are taken from two sources: the Series Congressi America-Canada of the Propaganda Fide and the *Annales de l'Association de la Propagation de la Foi,* published in Paris from 1816 to 1830 (Vols. I–IV), both abbreviated as VANT-PF. Luca Codignola's article “Guide des documents relatifs à l’Amérique du Nord française et anglaise” on the documents related to French and English North America in the Archives of the Propaganda Fide is extremely useful for anyone interested in religious documents. Of all letters related to North America, two-thirds were sent between 1760 and 1799, that is, a few years before the Louisiana Purchase.

1

THE CHURCH, LANGUAGE, AND POLITICS IN COLONIAL LOUISIANA, 1718–1803

THE FRENCH WAY OF REPRESENTING THE WORLD

While there are many good histories of colonial Louisiana,[1] the question of language preferences is rarely raised. The popular assumption is that everyone spoke French except a few Spanish administrators, and that view somewhat approaches the truth. It is also true that this Church was French, again with the exception of some Spanish administrators, and the Crown and Church worked as a team (although as very unequal partners). It is easy to sentimentalize a triumphant scene of a French cavalier landing on the Louisiana shore, proudly planting the French flag, with a robed priest standing close by, eyes heavenward. Unfortunately, historians and church records show that this romantic picture, although flattering to the French colonial self-image, disguises a number of hard realities about trying to establish a colony in the disease-ridden semitropics in the eighteenth century. When we look at language practices in colonial Louisiana, there are also realities that disturb a similarly romanticized image of colonists, laborers, and gentry gathered around a neat colonial church chatting with the priest in Parisian French. Church records show that this image is also a fantasy. For most of the period from the founding of New Orleans in 1718 to Louisiana becoming a state in 1812, both the Church and the French language were in some distress.

Two themes are particularly important in the colonial period concerning the Church as an organization, themes which affected its linguistic behavior subsequently. First, the Catholic Church in Louisiana was always dependent on and subservient to the political and especially financial support of the ruling elite to carry out its mission. The language changes of the nineteenth century were an extension of a hundred and fifty years of prior accommodation in the interest of the survival of its essential mission, the salvation of souls within the body of the Church. The Church's responses to linguistic, political, and social pressures were always intended to further that mission. But the nineteenth-century Church, freed from its connection to and dependence on any government, pursued that mission in a way that would have shocked the colonial administrators who so openly disdained it.

Second, the Church during the colonial period (and later) considered the native francophone population to be hopelessly poor Catholics as a whole, so that in a sense the exasperated Louisiana French higher clergy were awaiting the arrival of groups who might provide the slothful citizens with a Catholic "Great Awakening." After the Church found disappointment in immigrant groups such as the Acadians and Haitians, not to mention the Spanish and other European Catholics, the desired group of devout Catholics—the Irish—first put in an appearance in the colonial period in the form of the able Father Thomas Hassett and other Irish priests.

To return to the beginning, however, the French incursion into Louisiana was not exactly a religious crusade but the result of a Nouvelle France colonial adventure authorized by the French Crown, an adventure meant to make money and to thwart the enemies of France who were already operating in North America, notably the British and Spanish. As soon as the French religious wars subsided, the Crown threw itself into colonial expansion to fill its coffers. In the 1690s, colonial outposts were established along the Gulf Coast of the Louisiana Territory, which then spanned from the Gulf of Mexico and the Florida peninsula to the Canadian border. Politically and economically, the venture did not end well for France. In 1763, France was forced to cede Louisiana to Spain. The next half-century was also one of political instability. The Revolutionary and Napoleonic periods ended Spanish rule, but then Napoleon quickly sold the Louisiana Territory to the United States. The decade between the Louisiana Purchase in 1803 and its statehood was also turbulent. The Church therefore found itself repeatedly dealing with new, nonfrancophone ruling elites.

Despite such political changes, Louisiana remained markedly French until statehood. Perhaps because of shared Catholicism, the Spanish made only nominal attempts to make Louisiana Hispanic. The successive Spanish administrations were never able to challenge the numerical dominance of French-speaking Louisianans in any case, nor could they convince the founding population that a French identity was less prestigious than a Spanish one.

THE EARLY POLITICAL ADMINISTRATION AND THE CHURCH

Accommodation defined the interactions between church and state from the beginning, with the Catholic Church doing all of the accommodating. This weakness in the Church partly came from a failure of different interest groups within it to put together a united front. The early years of church missions were marked by infighting caused by a lack of formal supervision from distant Quebec and disagreements between Louisiana secular administrators and religious orders.

As was often the pattern, the secular authority had to step in to settle squabbles among colonial religious groups. A ruling from the state secretary for the Navy, dated June 29, 1716, allocated Louisiana colonial posts to the different religious orders that had been battling among one another for dominance.[2] But this territory allocation did nothing to encourage French priests to come to Louisiana. Their shortage was a constant lament from the colonial administrators up to the final days of the French regime, and the clergy, in their letters, were often irritable about frontier conditions and homesick. Louisiana's conciliator Martin Diron d'Artaguiette grumbled about the lack of women in the colonial posts; Governor La Mothe-Cadillac complained about the excessive severity of the missionaries toward the inhabitants; Father Francisco Hidalgo, a Recollet, bemoaned the misery and poverty of the colonial posts; La Mothe-Cadillac and his conciliator, Jean Baptiste Dubois-Ducloc, did not get along and voiced their complaints about one another in many letters.[3]

NEGOTIATIONS BETWEEN THE CHURCH AND THE CROWN: AN UNEQUAL PARTNERSHIP

The Church in Louisiana was not independent financially. The king's representative in Nouvelle France was the governor general who supervised, from Quebec, the entire territory divided into three regions: Canada, Acadia, and Louisiana.[4] Because of Louisiana's great distance from Quebec, in December 1712, the Crown created the Conseil Supérieur de la Louisiane (hereafter Superior Council of Louisiana). Its members acted as colonial councillors of the Louisiana posts and later of the city of New Orleans. They fixed prices, acted as a lender, and managed the budget and the land concessions. They also supervised the financial activities of religious congregations. As church historian Charles Nolan noted, "The crown purchased and erected [Louisiana] churches and schools, paid clergy, religious, and sacristan salaries."[5] As in France itself, the state and church powers in Louisiana had traditions, duties, and interests which sometimes intertwined, sometimes not.[6] As God's reflection on earth, the King of France established dioceses, nominated bishops, and authorized missionaries to serve in the colony. At other times, their traditions, duties, and interests opposed one another. Evangelizing the Indians and the slaves was not the duty of the government; trade exploitations did not involve the clergy's participation although tapping church income did: royal dispatches announcing new church levies were regularly sent to the local clerics.

An excellent example of the interrelationship among the civil administration, the Church, and language can be seen in the effects of the civil law on the culture of people of African descent, mostly slaves, with results quite different from those in other slaveholding areas of North America. The Superior Council of Louisiana created and ruled a complex society that included free, indentured, and slave labor and the relationship of all types of labor. To manage this slaveholding system, Louisiana's administrators and the Superior Council's members applied the Customs of Paris or Civil Laws, which set Louisiana apart from the British and anglophone colonies. They also implemented Louis XIV's "Code Noir," developed in 1670 to regulate the development of slavery in the French West Indies. The first six articles of the 1724 code concerned the authority of the Catholic Church over the treatment of slaves. The Code Noir mandated that slaves be converted to Catholicism by being instructed and baptized in the Catholic faith, permitted to marry (although they could not do so without the approval of their master, and marriage did not confer to them civil rights), freed from work on Sunday, buried in consecrated ground, and treated humanely. The small religious communities that owned slaves—Jesuits, Capuchins, and Ursulines—were faithful to these rules. But the humane care model displayed by these communities was not emulated by some secular slaveholders, especially those who saw slaves' transformation into Christian faithful as an impediment to the trading enterprise. Nevertheless, in spite of some planters' resistance, Christianization via the Code Noir became the most effective method of slave acculturation in Louisiana, as in other French colonial endeavors. Permitting slaves to marry, baptizing slaves and their children, and encouraging other slave owners to respect the rule tied a large number of Africans and their descendants, not only to their owners, but, more importantly, to the French culture, language, and official religion, although in an oblique way.

However closely the Church worked with the Crown, one important fact (noted especially in Charles O'Neill's *Church and State in French Colonial Louisiana*) must be kept in mind. From the very start, the Catholic Church was a subordinate element in Louisiana. Local secular authorities viewed the missionaries as frontier diplomats whose role was to facilitate the fur trade and make alliances with the Indian tribes. Restraining "the unruly and licentious *habitants* and making sober, industrious, and profitable citizens out of them" was also considered the duty of the parish clergy.[7] The Church was thus an agent of social control in the service of economic development while having to accept a certain degree of religious

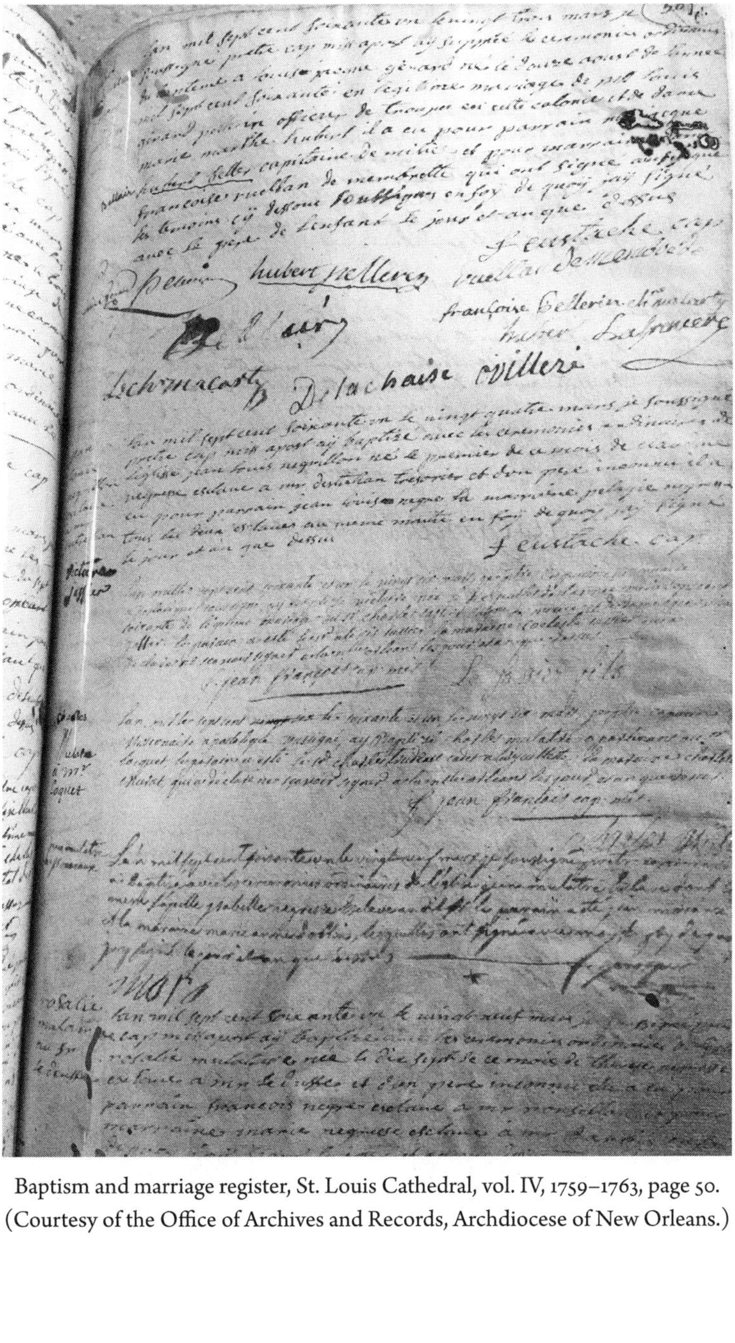

Baptism and marriage register, St. Louis Cathedral, vol. IV, 1759–1763, page 50. (Courtesy of the Office of Archives and Records, Archdiocese of New Orleans.)

inconsistency demanded by the secular authorities. Economic opportunity trumped strict adherence to the rules of the Crown or the Church. According to O'Neill, this opportunistic attitude explains why religious conversion to Catholicism was not enforced in Louisiana. Commercial companies recruited Swiss Reformed soldiers and German Protestant farmers to Louisiana, despite explicit and repeated but unenforced prohibitions from the king. So we see from early on that the Louisiana Catholic Church learned to live side-by-side with those outside the French Catholic culture (a significant departure from the French Crown's practice) and make the best accommodation it could to retain the financial support needed to maintain the faith. If it took living with German speakers whose grandfathers had savagely oppressed Catholics, so be it.

THE LOUISIANA POPULATION: A SOCIOLINGUISTIC PORTRAIT

Again, it might be assumed by those unfamiliar with the history of the French language that everybody in Louisiana spoke "French," meaning what today might be called "school French" or the French as (supposedly) spoken and written in Paris. Thus it might be assumed that all Francophones in Louisiana understood each other perfectly, regardless of their place of origin. Crown officials rarely discussed language issues in their letters, and when they did, they emphasized the importance of native languages. For example, Governor Perier wished that the governor and post commanders would learn how to speak local native languages. Bienville insisted upon the need to learn them in order to improve the colony and to develop bilinguals by sending orphan boys into Indian villages, a practice established in Nouvelle France by Jacques Cartier and Samuel de Champlain.[8]

In reality, Louisiana colonists were neither culturally nor linguistically homogenous. The first censuses of the founding population between 1705 and 1760 illustrate this diversity, and with regard to the linguistic composition they show two important facts about the social makeup of south Louisiana.[9] First, the first African slave population, which was clearly not francophone in origin, came mostly from West African countries such as modern Senegal and Guinea and was brought to Louisiana between 1717 and 1731, at the very beginning of the colony.[10] A copy of a census conducted around 1727 by De Chavannes, secretary of the Superior Council of Louisiana, indicates 1,952 inhabitants, 276 indentured servants, 1,540 African slaves, and 229 native Indian slaves. But in New Orleans, the number of African slaves (35%, or 450 out of 1,540) surpassed the white population (31%) and increased further over the next decade.[11]

As to the white population, the censuses indicate a small population characterized by class and linguistic diversity. Before the founding of New Orleans, only a few hundred settlers, mostly soldiers and slaves, lived on colonial posts. From 1721 to the end of the French colonial period in 1763, fewer than one thousand people from all social ranks came to Louisiana. Among those with financial means, we find planters sponsored by magnate investors in France and in Canada, colonial administrators, clerks, and artisans working for the companies (Crozat's or Law's) or for the Crown. Of the great majority below the moneyed classes, soldiers were considered by the planters and administrators to be a low class of inhabitants. Aside from a small group of officers, most were part of a large low-status group of young and illiterate recruits. Besides the planters, administrators, and soldiers, the population had a large contingency of unskilled and skilled indentured settlers. Deportees from France (convicts and indigents) were the dregs of the colony.

These censuses highlight the population's heterogeneity in origin and language. The majority of Louisiana inhabitants had a mother language other than French. Slaves spoke African languages; settlers from Spain, Italy, and non-French regions that were ultimately annexed by France spoke other languages. But even among the francophone settlers, some spoke mutually unintelligible Gallo-Roman dialects, such as the Franco-Provençal, the Poitevin, the Béarnais, and the Savoyard. Within the French-speaking population, then, many knew nothing of the Ile-de-France dialect (the King's French).[12] One additional fact is relevant: with the exception of the elite, the majority of these Francophones were illiterate, so the relative linguistic unity sometimes imposed on a polyglot population by a common standard written language was absent.[13]

This standard written language was, however, used by the small group of educated elite in charge of the colony, who wrote and probably spoke the French of the Ile-de-France in order to communicate with the French administration in Paris. Still, even Louisiana administrators spoke a regional dialect as a mother tongue. Quebec French was Governor Bienville's and Governor Dugué de Boisbriand's dialect; Governor La Motte-Cadillac spoke Toulousian French, whereas Commissioner De La Chaise's first language was Auvergnois French. Governor de L'Epinay's dialect was Breton French but he probably spoke Quebec French as well, having served many years in Canada. Only the small number of French aristocrats was likely to have spoken "pure" French exclusively, but since even in the swamps of Louisiana no respectable aristocrat would ever do office work, colonial endeavors were in the hands of the so-called *tiers état,* or bourgeoisie, also relatively few. This population never intended to mingle with the settlers, even though their mission was to attract as many as they could. So it appears that the social classes had little social interaction outside of strictly business transactions, and the development of a common dialect was made even more unlikely by this de facto segregation.

Among the Louisiana colonists of modest origins, a large part came from Canada. In fact, letters written by both Louisiana governors and conciliators during the French regime regularly mentioned the presence of French Canadians, who were sought after for many reasons. Unlike immigrants directly from Europe, they had valuable experience with the Indian trade and, consequently, were accepted by many Indian tribes.[14] They also knew their way around the vast American interior and, if provided with a wife and a means of subsistence—according to the administrators, anyway—would stay and increase the number of inhabitants. Many did, but the impoverished state of the colony and the unhealthy climate encouraged a high level of outward migration among these resourceful men, who knew where to move when better possibilities appeared.

From this sociolinguistic portrait, several observations can be made. First of all, there was not one original variety of "Louisiana" French during the colonial period. The varieties of spoken French during this era were numerous and were a continuation of those being spoken in France and Nouvelle France. These varieties of French dominated the Louisiana countryside as well as New Orleans. This linguistic situation would scarcely seem upsetting to arriving French colonists, of course, because Louisiana's linguistic situation did not really differ from that of France, where bidialectalism and multilingualism were the norm.[15] The majority of the colonists left France before its real linguistic unification efforts, certainly before these efforts had time to take effect in France and elsewhere.[16] Therefore, the colonists were used to living in a linguistic environment where other languages and other dialects were largely represented. Next, it seems that the linguistic pressures were still too weak to encourage a uniform French language, outside of official documents and letters. The size of the territory and the scattered population made this improbable. In addition, the high mortality rate, the hostility among social classes, political insecurity, the constant arrival of non-French speakers (Africans, Germans), and the continual movements of the colonists, especially in New Orleans, favored an unsettled linguistic situation.

THE CHURCH UNDER THE SPANISH CROWN

When France ceded Louisiana to Spain in 1762, the Louisiana population weathered the first of many changes of governance which occurred during the next fifty years: a Louisiana person born in 1761 and living to sixty would have been French, Spanish, French again, a territorial inhabitant under US rule, and finally an American. However, this person would also very likely have been a French-speaking Catholic from birth to death. Catholicism, and specifically French Catholicism, was what held the Louisiana identity together. The actual results of the changes were therefore not as profound as if (for example) the British had taken control, for the French and Spanish shared Bourbon rulers and a dedication to Catholicism as well as a multidialectic homeland. And in retrospect, despite some missteps, the Spanish Crown proved in many ways to be better for Louisiana and the French Catholic Church than the French, although no native of the region would likely admit this.

The Spanish Crown naturally put its royal servants at the head of many institutions, and in many important respects the Spanish did well by Louisiana. Soon after Governor Alejandro O'Reilly's arrival, the Spanish Crown promoted liberal trading measures that benefited the interests of the planter class, introduced institutions without mandating the exclusive use of Spanish language and culture, and encouraged immigration of Catholics and nonthreatening, apolitical groups (Acadians from Canada, Isleños from the Canary Islands, Malagán and Catalonian Spaniards) by offering them land and support. A series of new free-trade measures (notably with the English) favored transatlantic commerce and the explosive growth of sugar production in the 1790s, which, in turn, triggered a population boom.[17] Thanks to the Spanish, Louisiana finally had a respectable population. One piece of undeniable evidence is New Orleans's population growth: the city swelled from 6,375 colonists in 1766 to 14,853 inhabitants in 1785.[18] The Louisiana Church adapted to the new domination, with its new Spanish upper level but deep and unchanging French roots.[19] Unfortunately for the Church, the Spanish Crown did not bring it out of poverty, as happened with the commercial side of the colony.

The Spanish made a few administrative changes that had some small effect on language use.[20] Church jurisdiction was transferred to the Diocese of Santiago de Cuba (1771) under Bishop James José de Echeverría, and Spaniards replaced French church officials. To remedy the colony's still deplorable religious conditions, the Diocese of Santiago de Cuba appointed in 1785 Father Cirilo de Barcelona as the auxiliary bishop in residence with Louisiana and the Floridas as his territorial responsibilities. Following his nomination, he chose as the new pastor of St. Louis Church Father Antonio Ildefonso Morenory Arze de Sedella (popularly known even today as Père Antoine), one of the six Capuchins who had come to the colony in 1779. To introduce the population to the Spanish language, the new pastor of St. Louis Church ordered the catechism printed in both French and Spanish.[21] Cuban-based nuns arrived at the Ursuline convent in New Orleans, and the position of superioress was put in the hands of Antonia de Santa Monica Ramos from Havana. Still, the Louisiana Church after 1763 remained essentially francophone with a Spanish overlay.

However, the Spanish inadvertently planted the kernel of the great nineteenth-century language shift just north of New Orleans. Since, as part of the 1763 Treaty of Paris, Britain controlled the area east of the Mississippi River and north of the Isle of Orleans, for a period of sixteen years Catholic missionary work ceased in the area around Baton Rouge. Once Spain gained control of the area in 1779 it resumed, but the problem remained of ministering to an English-speaking population. The Spanish church then found a unique solution and prophetic way of tending to the new English-speaking population: the king of Spain asked the Irish College in Ireland to provide missionary priests, and the first Irish priests, trained in Spain, arrived in the colony in 1788. One of those pioneers of a long line of Irish priests who served the Louisiana Church during the nineteenth century was Father Thomas Hassett, who played a prominent administrative role a decade later and into the American period. In this way the English language quietly entered the Louisiana Church through the offices of the Spanish Catholic Church and the Spanish monarch for the purpose of spreading the Catholic mission to Anglophones.

Father Hassett became the Church's man on the ground in south Louisiana when he was appointed vicar-general to the diocese after Bishop Luis Peñalver y Cárdenas left New Orleans in 1801 to take over the See of Guatemala. Peñalver's move created a void in local ecclesiastical authority that endured for more than a decade,[22] so that from 1803 to 1815 the archbishop of Baltimore supervised the diocese from a distance. Father Hassett's was an ungrateful job, full of tedious details, such as reviewing and investigating the frequent matrimonial dispensation petitions.[23] Besides his clerical tasks, he had to remedy the perpetual lack of priests that was still crippling the diocese and deal with the language problems found in the multilingual communities, often seeking the assistance of Crown officials in unpublished letters. Nevertheless, the local dominance by this Irishman in retrospect seems a clear harbinger of the encroachment of English speakers in New Orleans especially, even though at the time Father Hassett probably seemed like an exotic anomaly to his French colleagues.

SOCIAL TRENDS WITHIN THE CATHOLIC POPULATION DURING THE SPANISH PERIOD

Spain was embroiled in long-term conflicts with France and England at this time, so the Spanish Crown had neither the money nor the energy to drastically change the makeup of Louisiana's population. Instead of giving preference to Spanish-speaking colonists, Spain encouraged and supported immigration of any group of Catholics, regardless of their origin, seeming to favor those who had endured hardship from its rival power, Britain. Two large groups of immigrants entered the territory: the French-speaking Acadians, who were exiled from Nova Scotia, and the Spanish-speaking Canary Islanders.[24] Beginning in 1789, a few French exiles from Saint Domingue started to arrive in New Orleans, the first of many.[25]

The founding population learned Spanish grudgingly, and few Spanish civil officials rushed to learn French. The French language subsided to unofficial functions, but it never lost both its day-to-day utility and covert prestige. Over the forty years of Spanish rule, however, the French and Spanish populations developed ways to interconnect. Knowing Spanish and French was certainly common and necessary among the elite and the business class, and even illiterate Francophones must have learned enough Spanish to deal with soldiers and other ordinary Hispanics. Spanish officials even took local French women as wives.[26] Although the social depth of bilingualism and culture interconnectness is difficult to assess globally over the first Spanish colonial decades, it was robust enough to give way to a new colonial identity—being a Creole—linked to the concept of Latin ancestry, rather than French origin only.

Given that the Church was (at least in theory) the spiritual arm of the Spanish Crown, language interconnectedness was inevitable in the Louisiana Church hierarchy. Because so much archival material from the Church was destroyed in the 1788 New Orleans fire, there is not as much documentary evidence about the diocese's language practices in these early days. What is known is that Spanish was mandatory for new church administrators in New Orleans, at least for the administrative and official documents. Official correspondence was written in Spanish by the 1790s.

St. Louis Cathedral, built after the 1788 city fire, drawing ca. 1810. (Courtesy of the Office of Archives and Records, Archdiocese of New Orleans.)

On the other hand, even the higher-ups in the now-Spanish Church had to deal daily with the affairs of a French culture, especially the parish priests. Indeed, the idea of monolingual Spanish priests at the parish level in colonial Louisiana is absurd and against the Church practice of accommodation to reach the local populace. French priests were therefore needed and retained in the diocese for the transition in the 1760s and later. French and Spanish entries go back and forth in the parish registers. Parishioners' signatures in Spanish in a Spanish register did not mean that a parishioner knew the language any more than he knew Latin when reciting Latin. Most obviously, Spanish priests had to know French in order to serve the native and incoming French Catholics. Colonial missionary work always involved learning the local language, and of course there also is a strong likelihood that many of the assigned Spanish officials and Capuchin priests were already bilinguals, or rather trilinguals (Spanish, French, and Latin).

French remained the language of the home and of most business, for language loss at a societal scale not only takes time but requires mutual interests, a stable sociopolitical environment, and a compelling reason (usually economic) for people to abandon one language for another. But paradoxically, instead of French speakers switching to the language of the overlords, there is striking evidence that educated French speakers, bilinguals or not, actually began using "better" French in the Spanish period than in the earlier French period. In particular, they paid close attention to new standards in the French language being established in France. An attentive reading of historical documents and personal correspondence written during this period shows that the French civil, ecclesiastical, and planter elite was well informed of new pronunciation and grammar changes.[27] By and large, they introduced the new late eighteenth-century variety of Parisian French as the linguistic standard in their correspondence and presumably in time across the social and geographical space of Louisiana. So, instead of perfecting their Spanish, in one sense francophone Louisianans spent the Spanish period becoming more French.

By contrast, the Spanish government, so active in advancing colonial trade, took a rather lackadaisical attitude about forwarding education in Spanish. Only four teachers and three lists of books (wisely including Spanish-language textbooks for learning French) were sent to Louisiana in the early 1770s. By 1788 the introduction of the Spanish language was deemed a failure. Governor Carondelet apparently greeted with derision the Church's proposal to establish a Spanish seminary in New Orleans. About 140 students of all kinds were enrolled in 1794 in Spanish schools. By 1788, in contrast, French teachers had established eight private schools in New Orleans, which were reportedly attended by four hundred students. If one adds to this number the French students studying catechism in parish Catholic schools as well as the Ursuline boarding school, education as a whole in the Spanish period reinforced the learning and use of the French rather than the Spanish language.[28]

THE LINGUISTIC LEGACY OF THE COLONIAL SOCIETY

Although the French language—and variations of it—remained dominant at the time of the Louisiana Purchase in 1803, several colonial social factors heavily influenced later language changes. Education, for example, a function of the Church at that time, was a low priority with nearly everyone outside the elite. With the colony's economy in constant disarray, education was even thought an extravagance. The Crown had also considered Catholic education as a potentially subversive force. What the Crown feared was not the content of Catholic teaching but that it had no control over what was being instilled in the minds of those who would become the elite of Louisiana. Since there was no education other than religious education, the administration never encouraged the establishment of schools. The convent established by the Ursulines was an exception in the eyes of the civil administration for many reasons. The convent did not represent a menace since its mission only concerned women, a key instrument to the expansion of the society but one without power. It also provided to the nonboarder pupils (the majority) only a rudimentary education based on catechism, which limited social promotion. Finally, the civil administration viewed the convent more as a care institution devoted to the sick, orphans, and destitute people than as a real learning institution.[29]

Another development in the eighteenth century was scarcely noticed at the time, namely the introduction of anglophone Irish clergy into Louisiana, although mainly in those parts like Baton Rouge where English was widely spoken already. The Irish far exceeded the French and Spanish in their dislike for English Protestant culture, for Ireland was still an English colony with a subjugated and often brutalized Catholic population. The Irish clergy also came from a land in which Catholicism itself was under threat from the English rulers and even wealthy or aristocratic Catholics had severe social and political disadvantages. Probably because of this subjugation, the immigrant Irish were often much stricter Catholics than their Latin allies, who could take Catholicism for granted.

Finally, even in 1803 the Church continued to be frustrated with the founding population's indifference to religion. Many governors in their letters to French officials in Paris commented on the irreligion of the inhabitants and their consequent refusal to support the Church financially. For their part, the priests placed the blame for such attitudes on the secular administration. Father Raphael, who was the superior of the Capuchins in Louisiana, often mentioned the indifference and hostility of Crown officials toward the priests. To him, the entire weight of keeping morality and order in the colony rested on the clergy. The licentious behavior of Crown officers, post commanders, and military leaders affected the religious morality of the inhabitants, who consequently opposed the construction of new churches.[30] Filling up the pews with people other than the members of the Crown elite was a difficult task. Evangelization was perceived by officials as a mission concerning only slaves and Native Americans. Marriage, burial, and baptism were routinely performed for settlers, but few of them could afford to support the Church's upkeep, even less the annual pew location dues.

Even after the Louisiana Purchase and statehood as part of Protestant America, the Catholic elite, which had generally taken the Church for granted to the point of casually dismissing its very real financial needs, lazily assumed that the Church would treat the maintenance of their own French culture and language as a duty equal to that of saving souls, as it did during the Spanish colonial period. This proved to be a false assumption that unintentionally contributed to the demise of francophone culture in much of south Louisiana.

2

TENDING TO MULTIETHNIC CATHOLIC FLOCKS IN A PROTESTANT NATION, 1812–1861

In the period starting after statehood, the Catholic Church in Louisiana faced familiar challenges held over from the colonial period (the scarcity of priests, poverty, the indifference of much of the indigenous francophone population) and some new ones, especially increased immigration, a rising anglophone and Protestant population, and annexation by the United States—a young, acquisitive nation with very different cultural and linguistic bases. For the first time, the Louisiana Church was wholly severed from the European Catholic monarchies which had supported it for a century, however perfunctorily. Because of revolutionary events in France, Paris had lost its role as the capital of the Propaganda Fide network, or missionary wing of the Roman Curia, in North America. Bilateral relations between the Holy See and the Louisiana Church thus had to be reestablished.[1] Although still a part of a powerful international Catholic organization, politically the Louisiana Church was largely on its own and could expect no support or interest from its new secular masters in Washington, DC. The Louisiana Catholic Church therefore needed a powerful leader, and it eventually found one in Bishop Antoine Blanc, who guided his Church toward religious stability in a politically unstable and socially shifting new state.

Prior to the appointment of Bishop Blanc, though, Louisiana went through a period of unparalleled social and political unrest. The Louisiana

Purchase and the new statehood produced much social tension within the population and within the Catholic Church. Those political events also triggered many political and religious changes not experienced during the colonial period. So although few of the church registers showed language switches before the Civil War, events during the first decades of the nineteenth century shaped the sociopolitical blueprint in ways which set the pattern for later huge linguistic shifts among the religious communities of practice.

LOUISIANA AS A STATE OF REFUGE AND ECONOMIC INEQUALITY

The failure of the French army to defeat the slave rebellion in Saint Domingue (present-day Haiti) between 1801 and 1803 put an end to Napoleon Bonaparte's interest in Louisiana. Deprived of his most prosperous Caribbean colony, he hastily cut his losses and sold the vast Louisiana Territory to the United States in 1803, three years after Spain retroceded it to France, thus ending its direct political connections with Catholic Europe forever. President Thomas Jefferson soon appointed William C. C. Claiborne, from Tennessee, as territorial governor. In retrospect, Claiborne set the pattern for Louisiana's political and linguistic future: he was not Catholic, and he did not speak French. However, he navigated the turbulent waves of social changes adroitly, so that in 1812 he was elected Louisiana's first governor, amazingly defeating French-speaking opponents at a time when Francophones were greatly in the majority. He pushed for bilingualism (French and English) in the legislature and the government. Louisiana's first state constitution in 1812 was published in both languages, though all laws had to be promulgated in "the language in which the constitution of the United States is written."[2]

While one might have reasonably expected considerable resistance by a well-established and proud francophone upper class, several sociopolitical events inadvertently introduced a climate of amiable social adaptation that bound Francophones and Anglophones together.[3] The numerical dominance of the French-speaking elite in the legislature and municipal councils slowly diminished, and over time they found common financial and political interests with their English-speaking counterparts. Almost immediately after the Purchase, American and French-derived planters and merchants universally perceived the authorities' ban on the local slave trade in 1804 as a threat to abolish slavery. In no time, both the recently arrived and the native upper classes united in opposition to the measure until it was lifted two years later. English and French speakers also found a common enemy in Great Britain. The final battle of the War of 1812 against the British army at the Battle of New Orleans in 1815 fostered a new political culture where French and English elites interacted. Although it seems counterintuitive to us today, French-speaking Louisianans developed anti-French sentiments during this period, or more precisely a strong hostility to the French Empire. Their deep resentment of France's sudden sale of their homeland helped to attach white French speakers to the United States. As the New Englander John Windship wrote to his friend while living in New Orleans, "the purchase of this country by the Americans is mortifying to their vanity."[4]

French-speaking Louisianans also found themselves on the losing end of an upheaval in immigration. After an influx of blacks swelled the African-derived population immediately after the Haitian revolt, waves of white immigrants similarly challenged the comparative homogeneity of the native population. The highest influx of immigrants (around sixty-seven thousand people) actually took place during a ten-year period (1810–20) in the "settlements among the banks of the Mississippi above and below New Orleans" and resulted partly from the influx of Anglo-Americans.[5] As in colonial times, the immigrant population was unstable. Cholera and yellow fever again took pandemic proportions and decimated a large number of immigrants. Many immigrants who survived also left Louisiana for various reasons. However, the number of immigrants who stayed was robust enough to have a massive demographic impact. Between 1805 and 1820, the population of New Orleans grew by 246%, from 8,475 to 29,000 inhabitants. Populations of whites and of free people of color increased slightly, from 42% to 48% and from 18% to 22% respectively. By contrast, the slave population decreased from 37% to 25%.[6] For the purposes of this study, though, the most significant change was that by 1860 the Irish represented the largest ethnic population in New Orleans, followed by the Germans; the Francophones by then occupied only third place.[7]

Thus outnumbered in many parts of south Louisiana by the Irish and Germans within three generations after statehood, French speakers nevertheless maintained a powerful French presence in New Orleans, especially until the Civil War. And they did so for much longer in many rural towns. One reason is that the Louisiana French population was reinforced by waves of French-speaking immigrants in the first part of the nineteenth century. In 1809–10, more than ten thousand French-speaking refugees from Saint Domingue settled in Louisiana via Cuba.[8] Because of the considerable economic and political turmoil in France—the Revolution of 1789, the Reign of Terror (1792–94), the First Empire (1804–15), and the Restoration period (1815–30)—a steady stream of French migrants from France arrived in Louisiana (especially between 1810 and 1820) and kept coming until the Civil War. Their number differs according to the sources (one estimate is 8,264 people from France). Some French immigrants were from the lower strata of the socioeconomic scale; others had an aristocratic and noble lineage.[9] Ironically, the very immigrants that the colonial French administration had hoped to attract arrived just as the French influence was beginning to wane and Louisiana was being absorbed into the United States.

Also arriving just after the Louisiana Purchase was the prosperity that had eluded the French colonizers, although its economic sources originated in the Spanish period. The cultivation of cotton and sugarcane jumpstarted the economy. Louisiana was able to maintain its economic vitality despite numerous economic downturns (especially drops in the cotton and sugarcane markets), dubious banking policies, and the disruptions of the War of 1812. The roller coaster of financial disorders led to even sharper inequality within the white population, however. As a result, some planters became wealthier while others lost everything. Overall, though, the planter upper class suddenly found itself in a republic but still with as much if not more clout than it had during colonial times. Wealthy planters became "self-styled Creole aristocrats," and their financial and social interests overrode other considerations, such as religion, language, and ethnicity.[10]

Another sociohistorical development worth noting is the meteoric rise in status in terms of wealth, privileges, responsibilities, and social standing of a minority of Creoles of color engaged in large-scale agriculture. Because of their financial investments in land and real estate (sometimes using money loaned by successful white patriarchs), some Creoles of color acquired a degree of wealth and education parallel to that of the white elite. Their number rose from eighty-two free landowning people of color in 1763 to an astonishing 18,467 by 1860.[11] Not all of these free Creoles of color were wealthy and educated, of course, but their numbers point to an aspect of racial history often overlooked in popular depictions of the antebellum South.

RECONCILING LOCAL PRACTICES WITHIN THE ECCLESIASTICAL AUTHORITY

Louisiana's transformation from a Franco-Spanish colony to an American territory and then state initiated anxiety and confusion about funding, property, rights, and authority within the Roman Catholic Church. The Church now found itself in a nation not only without a state church but one in which Catholicism was regarded with increasing suspicion. The annals of the Society for the Propagation of the Faith are full of letters from Catholic priests indignantly noting satirical plays printed in English-language newspapers describing priests as crass and ignorant, only concerned with increasing the Church's coffers.[12]

The change to US control was announced in writing to the clergy on June 10, 1803, by Father Hassett.[13] Expecting that this political change would lead to the departure of French and Spanish clergy, he made it known that he would like to be informed whether local priests would choose to return to Spain or France or to remain in Louisiana. And indeed, many left over the following years: by 1812 half the parishes were vacant. The Ursuline superior, Mother Ste. Monica Ramos, departed with almost all the Cuban lay sisters.[14] Even the French Ursulines sent a letter to the pope in which they expressed their desire to return to France.[15] Despite the neglect that the colonial church had received from the state, apparently it was nevertheless impossible for many to imagine security in a world in which the Church was severed from a European Catholic monarchy.

The new Ursuline superior, Mother St. Xavier Fargeon, took matters into her own hands while her male counterparts dithered. In 1804, she wrote to Thomas Jefferson directly to express her anxiety about the lands attached to her institution by the preceding governments of Louisiana. Jefferson's letter of reply, which was later published in the *Moniteur de la Louisiane,* the only New Orleans newspaper at the time (1794–1815), was both unequivocal and comforting to the Ursuline superior.[16] He stated that the principles of the US Constitution and the government of the United States were a sure guarantee that the Ursulines' properties were to be considered sacred and inviolable and would benefit from the protection of the government.

Jefferson's diplomatic reply notwithstanding, the Church's insecurities were increased with the death of the able Father Hassett in 1804. Local priests were left stranded without a strong advocate to manage the destiny of the Louisiana Church, especially a strong English-speaking advocate to deal with the American government. Locally, the church administration was divided and in disarray. When Archbishop John Carroll, apostolic vicar for the missions in the United States, appointed in 1812 Father Louis William Valentine DuBourg as the new apostolic administrator in residence with the rights of an ordinary (bishop), his ecclesiastical authority was rapidly contested by the local New Orleans clergy.[17] Bishop DuBourg was so appalled by the local trustees' attempt to obtain a charter to deprive him of his New Orleans cathedral that he took up residency, first, at the Ursuline Convent, and, later on, in the distant city of St. Louis, Missouri, where he established his seminary. Louisiana was considered so inhospitable to Bishop Joseph Rosati, who became Bishop DuBourg's coadjutor (auxiliary bishop) in 1823, that he also chose to administer the province from St. Louis.[18] The New Orleans clergy may have lacked direction, but they knew what they did not want.

Reasons for the frequent mismatch between local clergy and those sent from abroad are many, but Michael Pasquier, in his dissertation on French missionaries in the United States, argues convincingly that foreign-born priests experienced an immense frustration in harmonizing "legal and social customs with their missionary requirements to dispense the sacraments according to canon law."[19] During this period, priests had their minds "fixed on France or Rome," but their "bodies were situated in slave societies a world away from Europe."[20] Reconciling the two worlds was a problem faced by French-speaking Louisiana priests, whose situation was even more frustrating than, say, that of a French-born priest in Maryland. Priests in Louisiana ministered to a Catholic population which had always enjoyed a majority status, with the lamentable effect that the parishioners had the majority's privilege to be lax in their observance. This Old World attitude is reflected in several archival letters from priests. DuBourg was the last bishop who believed that the answer to the Louisiana Church's problems was to make it more French. During the Restoration to France, Bishop DuBourg, then bishop of the Diocese of Louisiana and the Floridas, congratulated his friend Father Simon Brute on his happy return from France.[21] In his letter dated 1825, he wrote about the glory of France and how things there seemed to prosper. He recognized that some people were still afraid in post-Napoleonic France, but he did not share their views: the government appeared solid, the finances prosperous. According to Bishop DuBourg, the entire court was peopled with virtuous individuals committed not only to repair France but to aid the missions abroad. This rosy picture was shared by few people actually residing in France in 1825. Archbishop Carroll had a strikingly different opinion. He was convinced that European irreligion and disbelief forced the Catholic faith to seek solace in American provinces.[22]

Despite his poor reception in New Orleans and retreat to St. Louis, Bishop DuBourg was determined to bring the Louisiana Church into accord with this vision of Gallic virtue. In the mind of church officials like him, only an invasion of well-trained foreign clerics could wage war against Louisiana's scandalous moral laxity, long-standing indifference to religious observation, and postrevolutionary anticlericalism. Therefore, it is no surprise that Bishop DuBourg's most "enduring contribution to the Louisiana Church was the recruitment of the new clergy and religious from France."[23] During his tenure as bishop, he traveled to Bordeaux, France, returning with many priests, subdeacons, and seminarians. He established the Lazarist seminary at Bois Brulé (the Barrens in Missouri) and staffed it with these newly arrived priests, among them Father Joseph Rosati, a Vincentian, and Father Antoine Blanc, who would become bishop of New Orleans. He invited the Brothers of the Christian Doctrine to open a boys' school in Louisiana.

When DuBourg was elevated to bishop of the Diocese of Louisiana and the Floridas in 1815, he requested help from the Sacred Heart congregation, which later established a convent at Grand Coteau, near Opelousas. He made the same demand of the Ursuline Sisters in France, who sent reinforcements to their cohorts in New Orleans; the Sisters of Loretto, who settled in Plattenville (later replaced by the Sisters of Mount Carmel); and the Sisters of Charity, who administered New Orleans's orphan asylum.[24] In an attempt to extend episcopal care to the growing number of Catholics, the Diocese of Louisiana and the Floridas was divided several times from 1825 to 1830. In 1825, Alabama and the Floridas were created a Vicariate Apostolic, later becoming the Diocese of Mobile. In 1826, Upper and Lower Louisiana were split into two dioceses (the Diocese of St. Louis and the Diocese of New Orleans). By 1830, the Diocese of New Orleans corresponded in size to present-day Louisiana and Mississippi. Church politics proved to be too exhausting for Bishop DuBourg, however, and he resigned in 1826. He was replaced by Bishop Leo-Raymond de Neckère, a young Vincentian priest from Belgium, who died seven years later while ministering to the plague-stricken.

EVANGELIZATION AND SPIRITUAL NEEDS AND OBSTACLES

The incursion of French-speaking priests led by Bishop DuBourg undoubtedly reinforced the prestige of the French language. But as a Catholic equivalent of the Protestant "Great Awakening," it was not a success. Bishop

DuBourg, like other church officials before him, had met widespread indifference and was distraught by the population's reluctance to practice the teachings of the Catholic Church. DuBourg's letters provide evidence of Louisiana apathy or even anticlericalism. In an 1825 letter to his confrere Father Simon Brute at St. Mary Seminary, in Emmitsburg, Maryland, he warned his friend that his letters would not have the same vivacity as Father Brute's because he was living among a people who did not believe and this had affected him. Only a few of the people had retained traces of their faith, he lamented. In another, he described New Orleans as "a large city, the population of which is for the most part made up of unbelievers and other enemies of religion."[25] The French priests faced outright lay opposition to Continental Catholic morality; open concubinage and mixed unions were on the rise, for example, and were deemed socially acceptable by the locals. In addition, priests had to sort out Louisiana inhabitants into racial groups using fluid and sometimes inconsistent racial labels in the sacramental registers.[26]

However, it was not just the long-standing moral laxity of New Orleans which frustrated the French priests but something in some ways more dangerous: the Enlightenment. Louisiana society was experiencing tremendous, if belated, intellectual change in the early nineteenth century—a situation which the priests perhaps thought they had left behind in France as a compensation for going to a frontier. In a report sent to the secretary of the Society for the Propagation of the Faith, which purported to be a historical sketch of ecclesiastical affairs in the United States, its author described Louisiana inhabitants as affected by the eighteenth-century philosophy and who lived in a hot-weather country where indolence was usual and slavery the source of corruption. Their spiritual needs were supposed to be met by a sparsely populated clergy, divided by language as well as national habits.[27] As Shannon Dawdy points out, "New Orleans was both a product of, and a participant in, Enlightenment intellectual culture."[28] This philosophy, with its cultural liberalism (especially the libertine aspect), definitively ran counter to ecclesiastical prescriptions, and Bishop DuBourg's priests perhaps felt they had jumped from the frying pan into the fire. This was the Louisiana inherited by Bishop Blanc.

Antoine Blanc, fifth bishop and first archbishop of New Orleans. (Courtesy of the Office of Archives and Records, Archdiocese of New Orleans.)

A native of Sury-le-Comtal, France, Father Antoine Blanc was ordained a priest in 1816; he arrived in Louisiana in 1829, at a time when the "priest ranks were decimated by age, pestilence, and overwork."[29] For a while he served as an apostolic missionary for the Society for the Propagation of the Faith, and as such he wrote many letters to the vicar-general of the Lyon diocese in France. He died in 1860 while still in office. Because of his long-lasting and vigorous influence, first as vicar-general of the diocese under Bishop de Neckère (1831), then as bishop of the Diocese of New Orleans (1835), and, ultimately, as Louisiana's first archbishop (1850), Father Blanc provided much-needed leadership stability to the Church and, by extension, to the Catholic population during a period of sweeping social, demographic, and political changes.

Bishop Blanc's colossal correspondence (1835–60) provides a revelatory slice of Catholic life in mid-nineteenth-century Louisiana and is an invaluable source of information about the Church's changing attitude toward language in south Louisiana while also painting a vibrant picture of him, Godfather-like, deeply involved in both religion and politics.[30] This correspondence is linguistically important in part because the bishop received letters from all types of people in all walks of life. He maintained a steady correspondence with fellow bishops from other American dioceses. They shared their opinions about church regulations, revolutionary France, and American religious phenomena such as the temperance movement. They requested news from clergymen they sent away on missions, described the conditions of their respective dioceses, gave business advice, and planned visits. Bishop Blanc had a powerful influence on priests and sisters who served under him. They continually wrote to him for advice, from places as varied as Guadeloupe, Spain, Italy, France, Canada, and all along the American East Coast. Many letters deal with social grace and church regulations. Finally and most critical for our purposes, clergy and laypeople wrote to him about how to deal with language change in Louisiana.

The most fundamental challenge Bishop Blanc faced was the continued unresponsiveness of the populace to the Church. The Antebellum Correspondence during his tenure offers insights on additional challenges. The first was the continuing difficult financial conditions under which priests had to pursue evangelization, especially in rural areas. These conditions seem more acute during the 1830s, but we also find letters describing dire situations in the 1850s. Father Louis Alaux, a pastor in Avoyelles in 1835, described his situation as such: "To beg from door to door for my existence, to be heaped with insults, threatened with lashes from a whip like the last of the slaves, to be vilified and grossly calumniated, here is the list of what the parishioners of Avoyelles inflicted on the second priest that you sent to them."[31]

In a similar vein, in the early 1850s Father J. E. Blin wrote that Lent was going very badly.[32] His Charenton church was less attended than ever; only four children came to catechism. To pay for church expenses, he had to go from house to house again. His parishioners considered him a good priest, but their inattention to receiving instruction led to their indifference. Thinking that God rejected him for his ministry, Father Blin did not know whether he should accept another church parish or return to France to enter the Jesuit or Trappist communities.

Despite the fact that the lack of money had been felt for a long time in his Nacogdoches parish in Texas, Father Louis Chambodut tried not to lose courage.[33] Nevertheless, he was disheartened to realize that "Texans love money more than God." Bishop Michael Portier of Mobile, Alabama, was horrified by an incident in which Father Etienne Rousselon of New Orleans was almost sent to join "the Fathers" by pistol shots fired in the shadows when his church was plundered and his treasury emptied.[34]

Bishop Blanc also faced significant problems with language use in the state, a challenge caused by the remarkable growth of the foreign-born Catholic population and the scarcity of priests to perform services in non-French languages. Besides the French from the mother country and the Creoles from Saint Domingue, there were three major, non-French European populations. The German colonists recruited as early as the 1720s were slowly assimilated into the French population and posed few problems to the Church.[35] A second wave in the 1820s established two concentrated neighborhoods of German Catholics in New Orleans, while the German Redemptorist priests built two modest churches: St. Mary's Assumption in 1843 and Holy Trinity in 1847. Mass migration of German speakers occurred between 1840 and 1880, so that by the end of 1860 the number of foreign-born Germans in Louisiana had risen from 17,887 to 24,215.[36] Consequently, expectations to receive church services in German were on the rise.

Italian immigrants came to Louisiana in large numbers between 1820 and 1858. During the 1850s, there were close to two thousand foreign-born Italians in New Orleans, and their number steadily increased in the following decades to reach a total of twenty-five thousand in 1890.[37] Having succeeded especially in the tropical fruits trade, as importers and distributors, many first-generation Italians became benefactors of their local church.[38] Originally called Sainte Marie de l'Archevêché, St. Mary's was the leading Italian church of the archdiocese, where Italian and Sicilian immigrants from the lower French Quarter went to hear mass in the Italian language.[39]

The Irish proved to be the most important wave of immigrants, at least to linguistic history. The antebellum Irish population has been divided by historians into three categories.[40] The "Old Irish" were the foreign-born Irish who arrived during colonial times and the early American period, like Father Hassett. The "New Irish" settled in Louisiana between the 1820s and

1830s. The last group, the "Famine Refugees," came to Louisiana between 1845 and 1855. In the period before the Civil War, the Irish population in New Orleans grew exponentially, as did its influence on the Church. Houses of worship were built to serve each district where the Irish settled. The imposing structure of St. Patrick's Church was financially supported by wealthy Irish benefactors and attended by Old and New Irish. In other areas of New Orleans, Sts. Peter and Paul (1847) was established downriver to serve the Irish, while St. Alphonsus (1857) was located just across from the German church, St. Mary's Assumption, in the third district. Established near the flood-prone New Basin Canal, St. John the Baptist Church (1851) provided religious services to the back-of-town Irish neighborhoods.

Bishop Blanc's attitude toward these Irish proved in the long term to be both a critical example of the creative accommodation of the Church and a pivotal moment in the rise of English in the Louisiana Church, for the Irish provided him with an unexpected opportunity which he was not slow to seize. Rather than view the immigrants as polluters of the historically French Catholic Church, Blanc and other church officials and devotees viewed these Catholic immigrants as (literally) a godsend to the Louisiana Church and a bulwark against encroaching Protestantism, which naturally had prospered after statehood. William George Read of Baltimore, Maryland, expresses plainly to Bishop Blanc the immigrants' potential benefit:

> Every emigrant naturalized strengthens our position as Catholics because, although one half of the foreigners who came among us are Protestants, it is an obvious mathematical proportion that equals added to unequals diminish their relative inequality. Now nobody can be held to the direct strides the Methodists, Presbyterians, and others are making towards a covert union of Church & State, through their control over the system of public instruction; and the Catholic policy is so obvious, to increase the Catholic vote by admission of foreigners on the same liberal terms that were adjusted by Washington & confirmed by Jefferson.[41]

The strategy was obvious: welcome the Catholic immigrants and make them feel comfortable in their new churches. The varied languages and religious customs of these newly arrived Catholics led to parishes established along ethnic lines in order to better serve the spiritual needs of the congregation. Each immigrant group organized its own parishes, creating a distinct community of practice to preserve the religious life of the old country. For Blanc and other officials, eyeing with alarm the overwhelming number of Protestants surrounding them, demanding conformity to French church customs would have been counterproductive and was not attempted to any degree.

Like his counterparts in Cincinnati, Boston, Baltimore, and Chicago, Bishop Blanc relied on the increasing numbers of foreign-born Catholics to develop his diocese. He erected new churches, chapels, and infirmaries. To carry out his vision of a strong, centralized Louisiana Church, he sought church leaders from the countries where the immigrants originated. He recruited Redemptorist priests to minister in newly erected German churches where parishioners sought religious services in their native tongue.[42] He welcomed the Dominican fathers, and the Oblates of Mary Immaculate. He increased the number of Vincentians, also known as Lazarists, whose predecessors had come as missionaries under Bishop DuBourg, and staffed seminaries and local Italian churches with priests from the missionary order of St. Charles Borromeo, founded by Bishop Scalabrini of Piacenza.[43] To better serve the Irish, he benefited from the help of the All Hallows Seminary in Ireland, which provided overseas missionaries. In 1860, the number of Irish-born was at its highest; eight out of thirty-two priests in New Orleans had Irish names.[44] Finally, Bishop Blanc's recruitment of teaching sisters from Italian, German, and Irish orders brought Catholic education to the immigrant institutions in their own tongues.

The size of the German, Italian, and Irish populations as well as the locations where they settled (waterfront, back-of-town, or remote rural areas) strengthened the Louisiana Church to a point where the immigrants became the "numerical backbone of the local church."[45] It is true that their number was in constant flux because epidemics regularly devastated their communities: possibly a quarter of immigrants died in New Orleans during the 1853 yellow fever epidemic.[46] German, Italian, and Irish communities had similar immigration challenges, but the Irish, driven from their homeland by a terrible famine, kept coming in larger numbers than the other groups. In short, despite the poverty endemic in many rural areas, rather than surviving at a subsistence level as it had in colonial times, the Church was growing thanks to Catholic immigration.

A natural consequence of the Irish and other English-speaking Catholic immigration was the growing demand for English-speaking priests. DuBourg's French priests were not appealing to the growing number of English-speaking Catholics, who initially experienced many frustrations in their search for English-speaking priests and a place to worship in English.[47] A parishioner in St. Francisville wrote in 1835 that the town would be content with a very humble edifice and a clergyman at least three times a year, one who knew English since French and German Catholics knew the language well. Priests who ministered at the Irish St. Patrick's Church repeatedly and quite naturally begged for many more priests who were able to hear confessions in English. In 1840, parishioners from Bayou Goula and New Iberia requested a bilingual priest. In 1837, Catholics of Texas deplored the fact that they had no priest who could speak English. Finding one was a necessity, they argued, since even Protestants would send their children to English catechism to receive religious instruction. Likewise, Bayou Teche parishioners protested against the parish trustee's rule to endorse only French-speaking priests, arguing that English-speaking priests were needed and that people of other faiths gathered to hear English mass. On the other hand, a military man complained in 1846 that Catholics enrolled in the army in Texas had to go to a Protestant minister although they represented, according to his estimation, two-thirds of the army regiments.

Thus, very early on, French priests notified Bishop Blanc that English-speaking priests and teachers were needed throughout Louisiana, even in the most remote francophone areas. Requests like the ones just cited started as early as the 1830s and kept coming until his death in 1860.[48] A schoolteacher in Baton Rouge took the liberty in 1836 to ask Bishop Blanc for another experienced schoolteacher who knew both languages and a little Latin. His request was repeated two years later. In 1847, Father

Louis Dufour mentioned to Bishop Blanc that both Pont Breaux (Breaux Bridge) and Lafayette needed an English teacher in their parochial school. Five years later, he wrote that Plaquemine would soon need a priest who could use English as well as French. Father Abbadie reported preaching in 1840 in three languages (English, French, and Spanish) *pro opportunite, et necessitate.* While visiting settlements in Houma and Thibodaux, Father Jouanneault wrote that he was asked to preach in English, which he did to attract parishioners. Because one had to know English well to convert and to preach in his Charenton parish, Father J. E. Blin considered himself an obstacle to good evangelization. He requested repeatedly to be replaced by an English priest with a "modest character and good judgment." Once transferred to St. Peter's in New Iberia, he emphasized the need of an English-speaking priest to attract Protestants. Father A. Lavadiere indicated in his letter that a priest without knowledge of English was useless at St. Michael's. Sister Thérèse Chevrel, from the Carmelite order, warned Vicar-General Etienne Rousselon in 1848 that the lack of English teachers would do great harm to their young establishment. Sister Emily from the Sisters of Charity in Baton Rouge wanted the new church's pastor, Father Hyppolyte Gache, a Jesuit, to learn English (Father Gache would eventually become the Jesuit chaplain of the Tenth Louisiana in 1861).[49]

Blanc also faced a more threatening challenge than finding English-speaking priests, namely the rapid establishment of diverse Protestant institutions in Louisiana. The francophone Catholics' influence was diminishing in proportion to the increasing power of anglophone Protestants in state and local governments. Although French was still the vernacular language of a majority, Bishop Blanc understood that Louisiana's Catholic politicians would need to speak and understand English, the dominant language of the rulers, if they were to succeed in their political aims. He also recognized that without church services in English, in particular sermons and confessions, newly arrived English-speaking Catholics would be tempted to leave or ultimately would convert to Protestantism. Conversely, as the letters quoted above show, Catholic services and education in English would be attractive to Protestants who might not have adequate Protestant churches and schools locally. When he was apostolic missionary in Baton Rouge, Blanc experienced first-hand the ideological struggle between the two faiths. In a letter dated in 1830, he wrote: "You would not believe how threatening our weekly Catholic newsletters [*Sentinelle Catholique* and *Presses Catholiques,* published in Boston but disseminated in all dioceses] and the incoming provincial council are for the Protestant sects. They have raised alarm bells in their own numerous newsletters. Their clarion call was 'Popery will invade the country if we are not careful.' To prevent them from hurting us or the Church, we need to preach the Gospel where there is no missionaries [*sic*]."[50]

Many parishioners and priests wrote about the threat posed by other denominations that preached primarily in English, especially the Methodists and Presbyterians. Recruitment of church members was intensely competitive. Anti-Catholic sentiment, a political and social problem especially in the North, was found even in Louisiana, so that priests who could not speak English fluently were ironically accused by Louisiana Catholics themselves of aiding and abetting the enemy by giving them fodder for their "calumnious falsehoods." Anglophone Catholics such as Maria B. Williams of Rapides Parish, in north Louisiana, wanted priests who could speak their native language and advance their faith. In her letter to Bishop Blanc, she argued that "the advancement of our holy faith is, of course, the first object to be considered, and an elegant clergyman [. . .] would doubtless be the means of drawing so early the whole parish within the pale of the Catholic Church."[51] She complained that her parish priest, Father Chartier, drove worshipers away and he "owed his extreme unpopularity to the difficulty he found in expressing himself well in English." Finally, she warned Bishop Blanc that "the Episcopalians with I understand a renegade priest at their head are making the most strenuous attempts to utter the most calumnious falsehoods against Catholicity from the pulpit. They or rather their renegade head seem determined with a deadly hatred to establish their church only upon the ruins of ours."

With such forceful complaints from their own parishioners, no wonder francophone priests hastily volunteered to be transferred to safely francophone parishes where sermons in English were not yet necessary. For example, in 1835, Father Beauprez announced to Bishop Blanc that he would prefer to exchange place with Father Brassac, who could preach in both French and English.[52] In his opinion, there seemed to be an unhealthy move in his parish toward Methodists, who had built a two-story meetinghouse. He believed that Father Brassac could better compete with the Methodist minister than he could.

ACCOMMODATION STRATEGIES TOWARD BILINGUALISM

From a language perspective, what most characterizes Louisiana society during Blanc's tenure was the emergence of a "collective bilingualism." During the time of Bishop Blanc's various administrative duties, which extended from 1835 to 1860, the social frontiers between the anglophone and francophone populations gradually began to blur. In matters of religion, the Irish were naturally allied to the Francophones, but by way of their language, they also became the natural interlocutors of the Anglophones. Arrivals who did not speak either English or French eventually chose one or the other, or even learned both, according to the linguistic composition of the population with which they came into contact. Most Italians and Germans realized after a generation that there was no viable future for their language in Louisiana. Marriages between Anglophones and Francophones of all social classes multiplied in urban centers. They were the most frequent among the elite and between the children of large plantation owners. These upper-class unions easily justified themselves: the francophone elite, whatever their origin, brought prestige of birth and European ancestry, while the anglophone elite opened the door to state political circles and national business opportunities. This state of linguistic affairs is called "collective bilingualism," a condition in which two languages are socially equal and the socially adept are at ease in both.[53] There were limits to where bilingualism was acceptable, notably in church services and in state government, but in the world of the Church as in the world of business, one truly needed to be bilingual to survive and thrive.

Collective bilingualism emerged not only in large cities among the wealthiest populations and the business classes; it also appeared in the coastal and agricultural regions and in more modest communities. Economic and political reasons explained why English was already sufficiently present there and why the need to speak it was a necessary commodity—Louisiana was part of the anglophone United States and the Louisiana economy was part of the American system. The English- and French-speaking populations had a vested interest in learning the language of the other, some seriously, others in a purely functional and basic way. Linguists have repeatedly demonstrated that people have a pragmatic approach to second-language learning; that is, they do not learn another language for the pleasure of doing so. Since the French and English cultures and economic entities were juxtaposed, sometimes intertwined, there was a mutual interest in knowing the language of the other and a benefit from the integration that this learning provided. Because of these benefits to preserving both languages, the children of mixed-language unions were often naturally bilingual.

Louisiana bilingualism was, by and large, not enforced or supported by formal education, and certainly not a product of it. While the upper class's access to private education was facilitated by the newly established schools in and around New Orleans, outside the urban centers (white) children from the middle and lower classes—that is, the great majority of Louisiana children—had little or no formal education.[54] Consequently, the learning of English during this period cannot have taken place at school. For some, it was achieved through work relations in the fields and mills, while for others it came from more or less sustained contact with local anglophone merchants and administrators. This learning process, surely very approximate in the beginning, made possible the stream of marriages between Francophones and Anglophones that was to follow. Marriage registers of church parishes provide ample evidence that intermarriage was frequent, surely a sign that many people "spoke the same language." Paul F. Lachance has demonstrated that Anglophones who married Francophones were often absorbed into the French population.[55] Romance aside, in the Antebellum Correspondence we also find numerous examples of bilingual behavior among priests and parishioners. According to the circumstances and the interlocutors, people used both French and English.

Here is a rare case in historical linguistics where a single individual can be seen as critical to language change, or at least as someone with the power to solidify trends already underway. One point is plain: Bishop Blanc was the main architect of this bilingual behavior within the Church. He saw that this collective bilingualism allowed the Church to reach out to anglophone Catholics, compete with Methodist and other Protestant institutions, and adapt to the new bilingual behavior of the middle class and elite. Since collective bilingualism had a positive social and economic value, it was not considered irrelevant by lower-class populations (as it was during the Spanish period), and Blanc understood that the Church had to use bilingualism to win souls up and down the social ladder. Therefore, it should come as no surprise that it also had a compelling interest for Bishop Blanc, dealing from his first day in office (and likely before) with the proverbial laxity of Louisiana Catholics. Over time, he oversaw the change of the Louisiana Church from an aggregate of French-speaking church parishes into a mix of bilingual, French-speaking, and English-speaking parishes.

His correspondence shows clearly that to retain and recruit English-speaking parishioners, Bishop Blanc expended much energy and time finding priests who could minister in English, as suggested by the letters quoted above. Unlike DuBourg, who brought Blanc and other French-speaking priests to America to shore up the Church, Blanc turned instead to Ireland; or more precisely his immediate strategy was to request more Irish priests and new recruits from American dioceses and archdioceses. Table 2.1 lists the names of bishops and archbishops with whom Bishop Blanc discussed in writing the issue of English-speaking priests, where they ministered, and the language in which they wrote to Bishop Blanc.

Not surprisingly, the choice of language in the letters was usually linked to ethnicity. American bishops wrote letters in English, whereas French bishops wrote in French. But topics also determined their epistolary behavior. American-born Bishop Chance, who was of French origin on his mother's side, and French-born Bishop Flaget corresponded in both French and English. The only exception is Bishop Loras, a descendant of a French noble family, who always wrote to Bishop Blanc in English.

TABLE 2.1. List of Bishop Blanc's correspondents, where they ministered, and the language in which they wrote

Bp. Auguste Marie Martin	Natchitoches, LA	French
Bp. Michael Portier	Mobile, AL	French
Bp. Célestine de la Hailandière	Vincennes, IN	French
Bp. Jean Baptiste David	Bardstown, KY	French
Bp. Benedict Flaget	Bardstown, KY	French & English
Bp. John Chance	Natchez, MS	French & English
Bp. Mathias Loras	Dubuque, IA	English
Archbp. Francis Kensick	Baltimore, MD	English
Archbp. John Joseph Hughes	New York, NY	English
Bp. John Baptist Purcell	Cincinnati, OH	English
Bp. John Oliver Van de Velde	Chicago, IL	English
Bp. Ignatius Reynolds	Charleston, SC	English

As a result of Bishop Blanc's calls for help, pastors from congregations as far away as New York offered him their services. Most of these priests noted emphatically that they were bilingual or trilingual, which indicates that Bishop Blanc had made it plain to the applicants that he considered bilingualism rather than monolingualism in English a more valuable and suitable asset for Louisiana. He even gave positive responses to offers from French priests from France, Haiti, and all of Europe, but only if they were young enough to learn English *in situ.*

While Bishop Blanc's need for bilingual priests might seem to represent a unique problem because of Louisiana's history, the correspondence reveals that other American bishops faced similar situations because of the growth of immigrant Catholics. New towns, packed with new arrivals, demanded new churches, and bishops could not supply them with their needs.[56] Bishops such as John Chance of Natchez, Mississippi, August Martin of Natchitoches, Louisiana, and Benedict Flaget of Louisville, Kentucky, were also in pursuit of English-speaking priests. These bishops had to deal with congregations where the number of French-speaking people was dwindling. One of their solutions was to swap priests. Monolingual French priests from American congregations were sent to preach in Louisiana francophone parishes, and Louisiana priests who spoke only French were dispatched to American congregations where they could learn English while assisting at Catholic colleges.

Another of Bishop Blanc's tactics to promote bilingualism among local priests was to send them for a few months, or sometimes an entire year, to seminaries and retreats held in English in other states, such as Bardstown, Kentucky, and the Barrens, Missouri. As an alternative, he would appoint French priests to northeast American church parishes, where they would further their progress in the English language by helping local pastors and by living among the anglophone Catholic families approved and recommended by his fellow bishops. In this, he was a pioneer in the "immersion" process, with often good but overall decidedly mixed results. Fortunately for our research, during their stay many priests kept Bishop Blanc informed of their progress through letters. Chaplain to the Ursuline convent and vicar-general of his diocese, Father Etienne Rousselon was one of those priests sent away to learn English in 1840. While in Vicksburg, Mississippi, he wrote in both English and French to Bishop Blanc.

> Monseigneur,
>
> My first words in French have been to my dearest mother now my first letter in Anglish will be for my Father in America and I think that as she was so kind for excuse my mistakes in speaking as you will be so good one to forgive my omissions in writing.
>
> I am gone, on the Smithland, Wednesday at none, and I arrived to Vickburg Saturday at four o'clok afternone. The travel has been long, but happy, without misfurtunes. My fellows was butafinall number, and every one of them was of the Kentucky, I endeavoured to speake with them, but neither they nor I we did not understand ourself. I have forgotten the french language, but I am far from having learned the Anglish. Revd Mr Oreily received me in a very kind manner, he resides upon his churche, and he has a wom forme.

We board at the neighbouring family, trice a day we go there, they are American but of a good and fashionable manner.

Mr Oreily has not yet mows to tell you about his churche, but next wek he will write to you. He looks very anxious on that affair.

En voilà bien je crois assez, pour la première fois. Je suis déjà en peine de savoir comment vous aller et ce cher Mr Jeanjean continue-t-il à aller mieux [. . .] [Our translation: There it is, I think that is enough for the first try. It goes without saying that I want to know how you are doing and whether Father Jeanjean's health is getting better.][57]

Three weeks later, Father Rousselon wrote again about his lack of progress in learning English and his room-and-board American family's way of life. He started in English and switched to French afterward.

Monseigneur,

Definitively if you cannot obtain forme, from the holy Ghost, the gift of the Understanding I believe that never I could learn English. From more that fornight I hear nothing but that and I cannot yet attend a conversation. Believe not, nevertheless I may be discouraged for it, not at all, I hope, so help me God.

Mr O'Reily is very good for me, We speak, as often as he is not hinderd by his employment, he is much obliging for suffer my mistakes, and for reprouve me kindely. All the day long I spend my time in reading, speaking or writing english. If I have no succel in it, certainely, it will not be for want of means or willingne n.

It is very hard to acustom myself to the american manners of life. No bread, no wine, but som beef, hog, pig, ham, and so forth, all thins accumlated, and mixted upon my plate with some mustard, butter, pickles, cornbread, and above all, tea or coffee. That turns my stomach and I cannot eat. I have sufferd a great deal in biginning, now it is so so. Perhaps You will think we are boarding with any poor Irishman. No Monseigneur, we are in a good American family, well bred in their manners. We are serve on the table, with china-plates and ever plentifully.

Such is composed the family. 1. Mr Creecy American of north carolina, sinc some years established and married to Vicksburg he must be very near forty five years old, he speaks french, un petit [*a little*] he professes not any

> religion, but he never objects any thing against us. 2. Mrs Creecy. She cannot be more than thirty, is born in Maryland, her Father was Catholic and she was baptised and educated in this religion but now she had forsaked it and she observes none. 3. Mrs Crumps he sister, good Catholic, very assiduous to the exercises of the congregation, keeping religiously fasting and fish days. 4. Mr Crumps her husband very good living American, non baptised, substantial and enraged Whig. He has an advantageous employment, he is inspector of the Railroad, from Vicksburg to Jakson. 5. Mr Willson brother of the two sisters, was baptised and educated in the Catholic Religion, but now he is nothing and an insignificant man. 6. a boy of twelve and more son of Mr Creecy in first marriage. At last Mr Oreily and your humblest servant.
>
> Before mal Revd Oreily loudly and religiously says Blessus o Lord etc. All this certainely are very indifferent for you Monseigneur, but it is an occasion for me to become skilfull be practice and to exhibit to You my improvements, if they are any. Because You know better than anybody for what and for Whom I am working, and wishing to progrebe.
>
> Je vous ai écrit, Monseigneur, la première semaine de mon arrivée ici. [Our translation: I wrote to you, dear Grace, the first week upon my arrival here.][58]

Some priests reported to Bishop Blanc astonishing progress in learning English, no doubt eager to please him and perhaps to get back to Louisiana sooner. Father Pitrat claimed, after no more than twenty days of studying, that he understood English and was understood by local Catholics and Protestants while preaching every Sunday in Milliken Bend, Louisiana.[59] But these highly talented priests were an exception; priests usually experienced learning difficulties such as those of the unfortunate Father Rousselon. Another example is Father Lafranc, who was sent to the Barrens in Missouri in 1840.[60] He reported attending daily classes in grammar, reading, and public speaking. Considering his efforts, he was profoundly disappointed by his mediocre improvement. Refusing to give up hope, he promised that his next letter to Bishop Blanc would be written entirely in English, which he did with great difficulty a year later. Another example is Father Mathias Loras, thirty-seven years old in 1844, who was mortified because he provoked laughter from his Iowa parishioners when he spoke English.[61]

While letters directly from priests with such personal comments about their English-learning experience are not common in the Antebellum Correspondence, Bishop Blanc was normally kept up-to-date on the priests' linguistic efforts by fellow bishops, priests, and nuns ministering to American congregations.[62] In 1845, for example, Bishop Benedict Flaget praised Father Napoleon Perche's talent in the pulpit. His progress in English was such that Bishop Flaget predicted that in a few years he would be able to speak English as eloquently as he did French. Father August Martin reported on Father Chambost's arduous effort at preaching in English in Baton Rouge in 1849. Another example is a letter from Father John Mary Odin in Galveston, Texas, who wrote in 1853 about his six seminarians' great improvement in English. He specified that English was always spoken in the evening and that seminarians also practiced preaching.[63]

Priests were not the only clergy learning English, for sisters ministered to the same shifting group of the faithful.[64] Sister Mary Hall in Emmitsburg reported to Bishop Blanc on the sisters' progress in English. Both Sisters St. Arsène and St. Stanislas in Galveston, Texas, promised in 1847 to learn English soon and to write their next letter to Bishop Blanc in English. Letters reporting Irish and German priests' progress in French give other proof of bilingualism as a necessary criterion for Louisiana priesthood.[65]

As should be plain by this point, the archival correspondence addressed to Bishop Blanc shows—in practice—the requirement of local priests and nuns to practice English writing and speaking as much as was possible. As early as 1839, priests and nuns mentioned in their letters the newly established custom of students speaking English among themselves.[66] Father Armengol in Assumption Parish wrote in French in 1841: "Your Grace would be particularly pleased to hear that everybody at the seminary strives to speak in English since I have made it a commandment after your departure from here."[67] This comment also shows how Bishop Blanc did not just govern at a distance through letters, but toured the parishes personally and made his will known. In this case it would not be too fanciful to imagine Blanc stepping into classrooms and listening to examples of spoken English. Some French priests serving in other dioceses (e.g., Kentucky) but traveling in Louisiana even used the services of local bilingual priests to write to Bishop Blanc in English. Instructed by Father Stephane Theodore, Father Julian Priour wrote in 1844 that "the cath. Popul in these West. Parts of yr Dioc. Is fully equal to that of all Ky, where we have as many priest as are employed in yr Dioc. and we want more."[68] In a personal letter written in English, William Lowndes, a French Creole and Bishop Blanc's godson, anglicized his name by calling him "Bishop White," perhaps affectionately joking with his godfather about Blanc's commitment to bilingualism.[69] Blanc's efforts to lead his priests into bilingualism even extended to correcting English letters he received from French priests.[70] To show off their burgeoning aptitude in English writing, priests and nuns sprinkled their French letters to him with the occasional English word and phrase. Mother Julie Bazire's letter of 1835 is a good example: "*Je craindrois, Monseigneur, en entrant dans de plus longs details* to encroach too much on your precious time: *au reste il nous est bon quelque fois d'être calominiée."* [I would have worried, dear Grace, by going further into detail to encroach too much on your precious time: besides, it is good to be maligned.][71]

Balancing the needs of incoming American and European settlers with the expectations of the native French population in some parishes was hard to achieve even beyond the language differences. They did not always have the same religious customs or heroes; they did not want sermons preached in a language they did not understand; they wanted to confess their sins in their native language. The outstanding case is again that of the Irish, who practiced a more fervent and puritanical brand of Catholicism than did the Louisiana French and had a somewhat different pantheon of saints, notably St. Patrick. Some had the courage to voice their discontent in writing. Parishioners from Carrollton (now a part of New Orleans) wrote in 1859 that "on the last Sundays, there was no other sermon but English. It made ill will with the French and Germans as [the other] priests are both competent in all three languages."[72] Some priests, such as Father Hyacinthe Tumoine in Lafayette, argued that speaking English was pointless in his parish, despite earlier accounts to the contrary.[73]

Several of the examples above point to one of the main limits of collective bilingualism: although bilingualism in most affairs of life was the norm in Louisiana, Catholics usually drew the line at religious services.

People who cheerfully and easily switched languages dozens of times in their daily business affairs suddenly were highly proprietary about the language of their weekly sermon and/or confession. Satisfying the divergent requests of a multiethnic and multilingual community practicing within a single church parish was therefore an often impossible task, and conflict between ethnic groups about church services was frequent, with the result that "the products of this ethno-religious interaction were as unpredictable as the weather."[74] Sometimes ethnic groups simply set up new churches for themselves. In the Lafayette area of New Orleans (today part of Uptown), three national churches were erected: St. Mary's Assumption (German) and St. Alphonsus (Irish) were (and are) across a narrow street from one another, and Notre Dame de Bon Secours (French) was just down the block. The trio of churches was ministered by the Redemptorist priests, and the house chronicles attest to conflicts between the attendant priests. In 1854, Father Rulland wrote to his superior that the German Catholics were demanding that pews not to be rented to the French. "They complained of the French . . . having service in their church and occupying their pews. Hearing this I told them: I could not change the state of things."[75] The annals also document the number of children who made their first communion, separating the statistics by nationality: French, German, or English. The German and English numbers consistently outweigh the French. Thus bilingualism has its limits. Sunday morning became, to borrow a modern phrase meant for another context, "the most segregated hour of the week." Unfortunately for Bishop Blanc and his fellow clergymen, this was the hour with which they were most concerned.

The languages in which the Antebellum Correspondence documents are written provide a good picture of the extent of bilingualism in the Church from the later colonial era to Bishop Blanc's death in 1860. Since the documents which survived to tell the tale of the French colonial period are mostly deeds and receipts written in French, our language analysis must focus on the subsequent time periods. During the Spanish colonial period, that is from 1762 up to two years after the Louisiana Purchase in 1803, 90% of the letters are written in Spanish by bishops and Crown officials. This is predictable and says little about what languages were actually being used in churches by priests and laymen (Latin excepted). Few letters from local priests are found. By 1806, the language of the Church had returned to French at 77%, with Latin at 10% and English at 11%. Only four letters written in Spanish appear in the correspondence for that year, suggesting that Spanish as an official church language disappeared as soon as Spanish rule ended and the Hispanic clergymen were transferred. French as the dominant epistolary language then lasted until 1859, with slight fluctuations over the years.

From 1835 to 1854 the data show two trends. The first is the expected gradual rise in letters written in English by English-speaking writers. The second trend is predictably the spectacular increase of English-language letters written by Francophones. In 1830, 18% of all letters written by French priests and laypeople are in English; this percentage goes up to 47% thirty years later. This is clear evidence that the lay and priest populations began to learn English and experimented with writing in English rather than exclusively in French during this period, and that Bishop Blanc's efforts were successful and not restricted to the examples we have included above. This shift also reflects the plain fact that Louisiana was by then part of an anglophone nation of which south Louisiana was a very small part. By 1860, French letters are only slightly more numerous than English ones (52% versus 46% respectively). There also are nine letters sent in a mix of French and English—a large number compared to 1840 and prior years, when there were none. It is unfortunately difficult to measure the diocesan letters written after 1860. First of all, their number grew exponentially, and important gaps exist for some years because correspondence was not being received regularly after the Civil War broke out. Another reason is that personal letters from outside the South were censored, a fact that contributed to the letter disparities. However, it is relatively certain that English letters outnumbered French letters in the archdiocesan correspondence in the decades following the Civil War.

During the first decades of the 1800s, the Louisiana Church took strong steps toward becoming a more unified institution despite being severed from its secular European sponsors. Bishop Blanc inherited and relied on a repertoire of formal management and language practices used throughout the course of the Church's long existence, but he also followed the Church's ancient practice of adapting to local conditions in less important cases (such as language) to achieve a greater good for the Church's mission. It is during his tenure that the first language changes in sacramental registers started to appear and English became a practice in the Church's codified procedures. When reading his correspondence, one can sense that there was a real negotiation of resources, challenges, and constraints, not only between diocesan officials and local priests but among them all, to reach the appropriate balance in the use of both the French and English languages (and other languages such as Italian and German). Therefore, Catholic prelates and priests should not be viewed as stoical representatives of a static church, but thought of as contributors to a common Catholic culture with varying degrees of cultural capital.[76] The Church under Bishop Blanc became a real joint enterprise with members mutually engaged toward the propagation of faith to local parishioners in English as well as in French. Despite their different nationalities, religious and secular priests shared the same faith; they held the same basic theological assumptions, despite differences in practices mostly inherited from Europe. At the end of this period, we can see the Louisiana Church's transformation from a small, highly centralized nucleus of beleaguered francophone clergy to a spiritual joint enterprise driven by a mutually engaged, ethnically diversified, and bilingual membership. Faced with such unprecedented social and demographic changes, the Louisiana Church chose the winning of souls over the maintenance of the francophone culture with which it had always been so closely identified. Blanc knew that languages were important sources of identity and could be used to win souls. He probably also thought that modern languages were otherwise relatively unimportant, ephemeral things, whereas the Church and its Latin were immortal.

3

THE REGISTERS SPEAK

The Rise and Fall of Louisiana Bilingualism and the Luck of the Irish

Although claims and myths about the switch from French to English in Louisiana are many, unpublished data from the official records of the Louisiana Catholic Church may be used to verify, disprove, or augment at least some of them. Most importantly, scholars describing the nineteenth-century language situation in Louisiana have tied the shift to English to the post–Civil War period since statewide measures were adopted in 1862, 1864, and 1868 that restricted (temporarily) the use of French in public settings. Using such laws as evidence, it has been claimed or implied that French-speaking people stopped writing French and switched to English as quickly as possible,[1] as part of the forced "Americanization" of Louisiana and the state's sudden entry into membership of "the South," especially regarding race relations. The Church's sacramental registers can give a more nuanced pattern of actual language change.

The registers record three sacramental services: baptisms, marriages, and burials of individual members within the church parish. In total, sacramental registers of more than 241 parishes were examined, for an average of one hundred years of records for each parish. From this data, a database was created to document the languages used in the sacramental registers. Then, the date of the language shift from French to English was codified, as

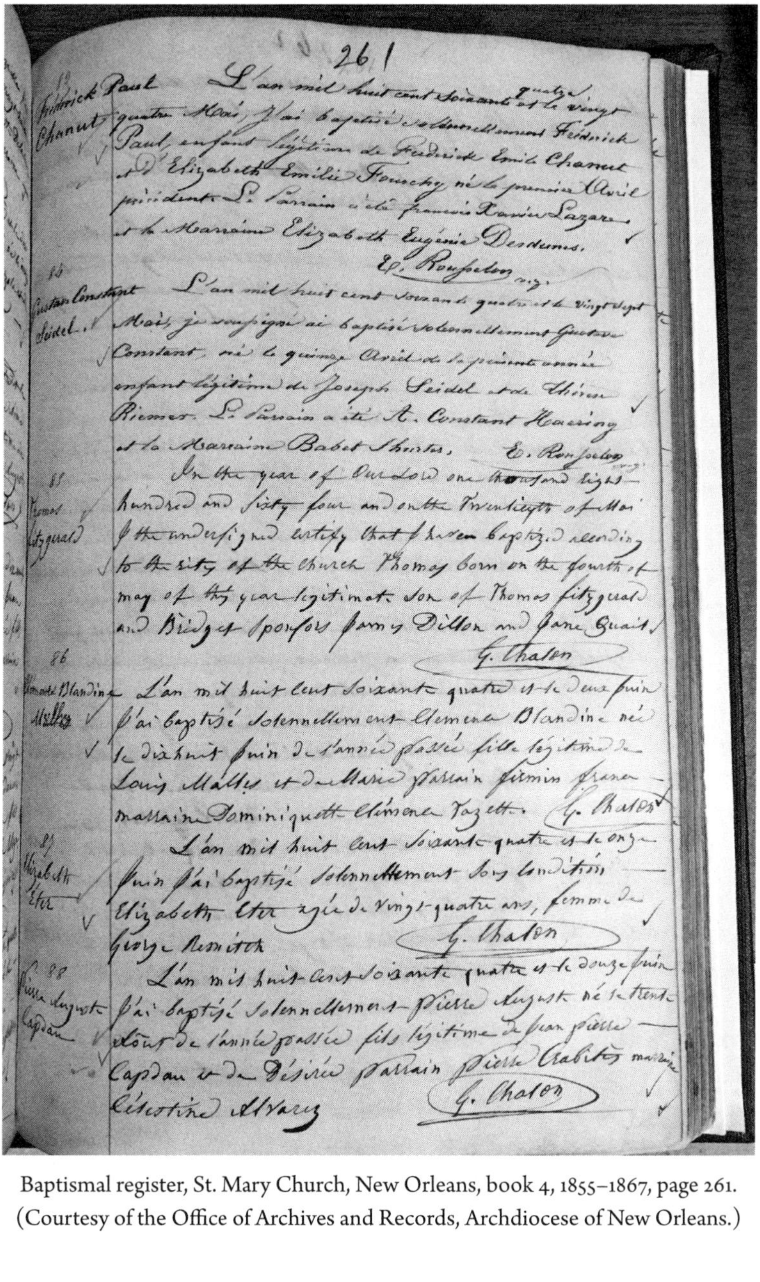

Baptismal register, St. Mary Church, New Orleans, book 4, 1855–1867, page 261. (Courtesy of the Office of Archives and Records, Archdiocese of New Orleans.)

well as verifiable internal or external factors—such as a change of priests, a new register book, and so forth—that seem to contribute to the switch.[2] Using the 1853 boundaries of the Archdiocese of New Orleans, 241 church parishes were identified as established before 1950.[3] Attention is focused here on the eighty-six churches in Louisiana where registers switched from French to English.

In addition, the register changes of each church parish are placed into a broader framework of language chronology, one that takes into consideration churches where records originated in English as well as those that switched from French. This wider examination shows that the language switch did not take place until well after the antebellum and Reconstruction periods, contrary to the frequent view that French died out rather quickly after the Civil War except in rural and/or remote areas. Admittedly, this study deals with only a specific category of written church records, but these are family-related records that are close to ordinary Louisiana Catholics and assuredly reflect linguistic preferences of a large part of the parish population. Church administrators from Archbishop Blanc onward were highly sensitive to the linguistic preferences of parishioners. The data from the sacramental registers show both the surprisingly strong resilience of French for many years after the Civil War and, conversely, the pivotal roles of the Irish churches in New Orleans in fostering the change to English in the outlying parishes.

THE SACRAMENTAL RECORDS OF THE LOUISIANA CHURCH

Sacramental records preserve some of the most important moments in Catholic life. According to church teaching, the seven sacraments of the Roman Catholic Church are visible signs of God's love, the foundations of Christian life, and instituted by God but entrusted to the Church: baptism (the first and basic sacrament), confirmation, the Eucharist, penance, the anointing of the sick, marriage, and Holy Orders.[4] Canon law prescribes the safekeeping of parochial registers for baptisms, marriages, and deaths.[5] These so-called "sacramental registers" include information about families (parents, godparents, aunts, uncles, siblings, etc.), communities (witnesses at a marriage), and events. They tell a story far beyond that of one individual or couple. If maintained properly over time, they reflect much of the entire social experience of all Catholic communities of practice. Because sacramental registers detail the life history of the local community over time, they have always been recognized by church officials as having unique value. They are permanent, historical records, and "the legal property of the local parish and presiding bishop and the information they contain—often of a confidential nature, e.g. legitimacy, adoption—is rightly protected by law."[6] Although today's registers are produced in preprinted formats which allow priests to enter only dates and personal names, register entries in the eighteenth and nineteenth centuries were "a reflection of the personality of the priest who made the record. Some priests had fine, legible handwriting and obviously took some pride in writing out neat, sometimes beautiful records about even the humblest of persons. Others had abominable penmanship and wrote in what gives every appearance of being haste, if not annoyance."[7]

Sacramental registers of the Louisiana Catholic Church are exceptionally informative about Louisiana social practices in the eighteenth and nineteenth centuries. Besides the basic entries which record the administration of sacraments, they contain information about religious life (those becoming priests, brothers, or nuns) as well as persons often ignored or slighted in other records—African Americans (including slaves and free people of color), Native Americans, and immigrants. They also contain anecdotal annotations that have nothing to do with the individual reception of a sacrament but concern the social, political, and ecological history of the communities of practice. These annotations appear "some in the margin, some on the face of a page and some pasted onto a page."[8] In this way they are a continuation of the Church's tradition extending back to the early Middle Ages, when priests and monks recorded remarkable events as marginalia in their official records. The Louisiana annotations can be about historic visits, epidemics, wars, hurricanes, floods and fires, as the following examples from the St. Louis Cathedral registers attest. All of the following marginalia have some bearing on linguistic history and, perhaps more significantly, illustrate the importance the priests put on these registers as permanent records of Catholic life in Louisiana (our translations):

> In the month of April 1799, there passed through this city the French princes, the Duke of Orleans, the Duke of Montpensier, and the Comte de Beaujolais.
>
> (AANO-ABR, St. Louis Cathedral baptisms, vol. 3 [1796–1802], part 1, page 85 bis.)
>
> . . . .
>
> In the year 1809 there came to this city the French immigrant families from Santo Domingo and from the Isle of Cuba which is annotated here to serve for the ages and posterity.
>
> (AANO-ABR, St. Louis Cathedral marriages, vol. 3 [1806–1821], part 1, loose note between pages 40–41)
>
> . . . .
>
> In the summer of the year 1783 there arrived on this Mississippi River such a large quantity of snow that it caused a major blockage so that the ships leaving could not cross the river due to the chaos of mountains of snow which covered the whole surface of the said river, annotated here to serve for the ages and posterity.
>
> (AANO-ABR, St. Louis Cathedral marriages, vol. 1 [1777–1784], part 1, page 152 bis.)
>
> . . . .
>
> On the 23 of December, 1814, the English entered the plantation of Mr. Villere, 2 leagues from this capital.
>
> (AANO-ABR, St. Louis Cathedral marriages, vol. 3 [1806–1821], part 2, page 150 bis.)
>
> . . . .
>
> Today, the 21 day of March of the year 1788, Good Friday, there occurred in this city the first fire which consumed almost everything, the church having been destroyed.
>
> (AANO-ABR, St. Louis Cathedral marriages, vol. 2 [1784–1795], part 1, loose note between pages 56–57)

. . . .

From the 19th to the 20th of August, this city and its jurisdiction experienced a terrible hurricane in which many people died, drowned and many buildings were destroyed with the exception of the Church which God preserved intact.

(AANO-ABR, St. Louis Cathedral baptisms, vol. 7 [1811–1815], part 1, page 41)

. . . .

On the 8th day of January of 1815, a grand battle between the American [*sic*] and the English wherein the latter had four thousand men who died, were wounded or taken prisoner, as a result of which they were obliged to raise the siege.

(AANO-ABR, St. Louis Cathedral marriages, vol. 3 [1806–1821], part 1, page 151)

. . . .

The 6th day of this month of May at 2 o'clock in the night this river burst on this side and from the upper section at about 2 leagues from this capital on the plantation of Mr. Macarty y Lanusse, and its damage was so extensive that it flooded not only the outer neighborhoods of this city but also Burgundy and Dauphine streets to such an extent that pirogues were entering houses.

(AANO-ABR, St. Louis Cathedral marriages, vol. 3 [1806–1821], part 3, page 172 bis.)

. . . .

During the whole summer of the year 1817 there occurred in this city and all its jurisdiction, the first epidemic of "vomito prieto" known here by the name of yellow fever.

(AANO-ABR, St. Louis Cathedral marriages, vol. 3 [1806–1821], part 3, loose note between 193–194)

Despite the variability of penmanship and written formulas and frequent nonstandard spelling, the sacramental registers are the best preserved and most norm-enforced linguistic written practice within the broad span of the Archdiocese of New Orleans. Making entries was a necessary priestly activity to be performed every time a death, a birth, or a marriage of a parishioner occurred. Preserving records—and also devising ways to preserve them in the volatile Louisiana climate—was the (literally) sacred duty of each local priest. The devastating New Orleans fire of 1788, which led to a significant loss of church records, caused Père Antoine to risk his life while hurling as many records as he could out of the St. Louis church windows. In reaction to this fire, in 1790 the auxiliary bishop of Cuba, Cirilo de Barcelona, put policies in place for all communities of practice so that sacramental records would be better safeguarded in the future. He sent a letter to New Orleans parish priests informing them that "as the fire of March 21, 1788 destroyed baptismal records which would have been saved had they been in a closet in the sacristy, in the future the baptismal records are to be kept in such a closet and are not to be removed from the sacristy without express permission of the bishop."[9]

Given the vagaries and violence of the Louisiana climate and history, Bishop Cirilo's orders have been remarkably successful. Following this new regulation, the books of marriages, deaths, and baptisms dated from 1720 to 1790 that survived the fire were placed in a closet and locked with a key in the sacristy of the parish church of St. Louis. Today the historic sacramental registers from all of the early churches currently in the Archdiocese of New Orleans are carefully preserved in the Archdiocesan Archives. These registers, totaling more than 1,500 volumes, were evacuated to Baton Rouge after Hurricane Katrina in 2005 and returned to New Orleans eighteen months later. Other registers from early churches formerly a part of the Archdiocese of New Orleans are preserved and cared for in their respective dioceses. These form the basis of our data, and we hereby give our thanks to Bishop Cirilo and his successors.

LANGUAGE SWITCH OVER TIME IN DIOCESES AND PARISHES

A 110-year range from the first register switch to the last demarks the breadth span of change, with the center of change at the turn of the twentieth century: at St. Theresa of Avila Church in New Orleans, the registers switch to English in 1844, just four years after its establishment as an Irish parish; the last church parish to switch from French to English was Our Lady of Prompt Succor in Golden Meadow, which switched in 1954.

The dates when registers began in French and switched to English have a mean year of 1907 as a switch date and a median of 1910. Of churches founded after the colonial period, 70.68% of all initial parish registers began in French. After 1900, this percentage dropped dramatically, with only four parishes beginning their registers in French. These figures are consistent with the mean switch date of 1907, and even if parishes continued the practice of recording sacramental entries in French, almost all of the newly established parishes (97%) began in English after 1900.

In table 3.1, the mean of language switch is shown over time in the registers according to the present-day diocese and civil parish boundaries. What is striking is that most of the language changes in the registers happened around the turn of the twentieth century. Churches in the New Orleans area which belong today to the Archdiocese of New Orleans switched on average a decade earlier (1891) than the ones from the Diocese of Baton Rouge (1906). Churches within the dioceses of Houma-Thibodaux and Lafayette maintained French records until 1916 and 1917 respectively, approximately thirty-six years after the New Orleans registers switched.

One revealing way to illustrate the switch is to correlate it with time periods that naturally emerge by breaks in the data. Figure 3.1 displays the shift in language of the sacramental registers from 1803 to 1954. It clearly defines the bulk of the shift between 1888 and 1935 with sixty-seven of the eighty-six parishes switching during those periods, representing 77.91% of the registers. The most important time period is from 1901 to 1917, when twenty-nine registers switch.

Perhaps the most important observation to be made here is that the average switch in Louisiana (1907) happened much later than would be expected from reading most linguistic histories of south Louisiana, especially those linking the change to the laws enacted during the Civil War prohibiting the use of French in public. The evidence here suggests something more gradual and qualified. No one will deny that important social changes in the wake of the Civil War conditioned the language choices local priests made. But even if Reconstruction is regarded as the catalyst to English monolingualism, the switch to English as the language practiced by a majority of local priests took until the turn of the twentieth century and, in some parishes, until World War II or even after.

TABLE 3.1. Switch mean from French to English in sacramental registers in Louisiana, by dioceses and parishes

Geographical Scale	Switch Mean
Louisiana (86)*	1907
Archdiocese New Orleans (23)	1891
Diocese Baton Rouge (25)	1906
Diocese Lafayette (26)	1917
Diocese Houma-Thibodaux (12)	1916

Civil Parishes	Switch Mean	Civil Parishes	Switch Mean
East Baton Rouge (1)	1854	St. John the Baptist (3)	1910
Orleans (9)	1880	Terrebonne (4)	1910
Jefferson (2)	1885	St. Landry (4)	1911
Iberville (5)	1887	Lafayette (3)	1915
Ascension (2)	1887	Acadia (5)	1916
Pointe Coupée (3)	1890	Assumption (6)	1919
St. Tammany (3)	1893	Vermilion (5)	1921
St. Charles (1)	1898	Iberia (3)	1923
St. Bernard (1)	1899	St. Martin (3)	1924
Plaquemines (4)	1900	Lafourche (7)	1926
West Baton Rouge (2)	1901	St. James (5)	1930
St. Mary (4)	1906	Livingston (1)	1934

*Numbers in parentheses represent the number of churches investigated. The switch mean is based on all churches with registers that changed from French to English, starting with the first switch in 1844 to the last one in 1954. For parishes with only one church, the date given corresponds to the switch date.

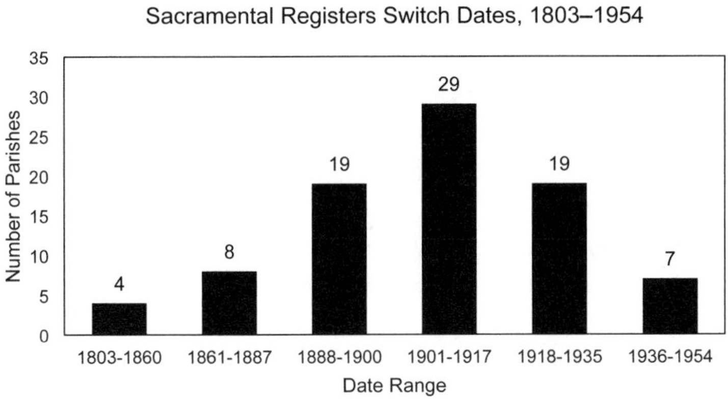

Figure 3.1. Switch dates of sacramental registers, 1803–1954

SPATIAL DIFFUSION OF LANGUAGE CHANGE FROM FRENCH TO ENGLISH

Language shift does not only happen across time; it also takes place across space. The origin and spatial spread of language change cannot be accounted for without factoring in the 155 churches where records began in English, and the data here include all church parishes where records begin in French and those starting in English. It is worth remembering, though, that the year of the first register entry does not always coincide with the year the parish was established. Often Catholic communities began as missions and were served by a visiting priest. Communities built churches or chapels where sacraments were administered, and these were recorded in the sacramental register. Some churches remained missions for years before a resident pastor was assigned and/or the mission received parish status.

Of the seven pioneer churches established in Louisiana during the French colonial decades, 1699–1760, records were found for two churches.[10] Established in 1720, St. Louis is the first parish in New Orleans. Its first permanent church was completed in 1727. Destroyed by fire in 1788, St. Louis took six years to rebuild, at which point (1794) it was raised to the level of cathedral. The second church is St. Francis of Pointe Coupée, where records began in 1727. Under Spanish rule, nine churches were established; all of them used French as the primary language of record.[11] The years of first register entry for these nine churches are:

St. Martin de Tours in St. Martin Parish, 1765
St. James in St. James Parish, 1772
Ascension of Our Lord in Ascension Parish, 1772
St. Gabriel in Iberville Parish, 1773
St. Landry in St. Landry Parish, 1776
St. Bernard in St. Bernard Parish, 1787
St. John the Baptist in St. John the Baptist Parish, 1792
Assumption in Assumption Parish, 1793
St. Joseph in East Baton Rouge Parish, 1793

One critical fact emerges from the data: writing sacramental registers in English was an innovation introduced by recently established Irish churches in New Orleans in the second third of the nineteenth century. The first Catholic church parish with English records was St. Patrick's, established in New Orleans in 1833. The second and third Irish churches are St. Vincent Chapel (1836) and St. Joseph (1845) in New Orleans. During the antebellum decades, eight more churches with all their registers written in English were established (Sts. Peter and Paul in Orleans Parish, 1848; St. Joseph in St. Mary Parish, 1848; Our Lady of Mount Carmel in West Feliciana Parish, 1849; Immaculate Conception in Orleans Parish, 1850; St. John the Baptist in Orleans Parish, 1851; St. Alphonsus in Orleans Parish, 1853; St. Ann in Pointe Coupée Parish, 1856; and Our Lady of Perpetual Help in West Feliciana Parish, 1858). This wave of new churches conforms closely to the new demographic importance of the Irish population in Louisiana. By sheer weight of numbers, the Irish became the first challengers to the French domination of Catholicism in Louisiana. The number of English registers was subsequently increased by new English-language churches in the new towns in the northern and western parts of south Louisiana. Their establishment, more pronounced after the Civil War, tends to follow the railroad track which linked new towns with English settlers in southwestern Louisiana.

What is equally striking is the low number of register changes from French to English despite the increase of churches starting with English records from 1817 to 1880. From the Louisiana Purchase until the Civil War, only four register changes can be found in French churches established prior to this period. The first church to change its records from French to English was an Irish church in New Orleans, St. Theresa of Avila, where the switch occurred four years after its establishment (1844). St. Joseph in Baton Rouge was the second church parish to switch its sacramental registers to English, in 1854,[12] and the decline of French in this church parish actually began earlier due to pressure from the parishioners.[13] Two churches in New Orleans switched in 1856: St. Vincent de Paul eighteen years after the first register entry and St. Anthony of Padua fifteen years after its first French register began.

Although the number of new churches with English records was on the rise before the Civil War, mainly in the northern part of south Louisiana, French language use steadfastly continued. Four new churches were established around the time of Louisiana statehood (St. Michael the Archangel in St. James Parish, 1809; St. Joseph in Lafourche Parish, 1817; Sacred Heart in St. Landry Parish, 1819; and St. John the Evangelist in Lafayette, 1821), but there is a remarkable number of thirty-two new churches that kept their French sacramental registers well into the Reconstruction period. The robust presence of French is particularly striking; it suggests again that an extensive period of bilingualism existed and was maintained even after mass English migration was over.

During this period, the Louisiana Church can be seen as truly bilingual. This result also implies that the loss of French as a prestige language or everyday language was by no means a foregone conclusion; the "triumph of English" was thus by no means a given but rather the result—at least in part—of sociolinguistic events which happened in the next decades. The "language tip" did not actually take place until about fifty years after Reconstruction began.

After the Reconstruction period and until the beginning of the twentieth century (or from 1881 to 1901), the language switch in the sacramental registers was at its full swing, when twenty-two church registers shifted to English. Two spatial observations are necessary: more churches in New Orleans and in the surrounding parishes adopted English in this period; and a movement of English registers from the northern parishes to the southern ones is discernible. Still, there is also an almost equal number of newly established churches with registers in French (twelve) and English (eleven). During this time, English churches were established in predominantly French areas; these were, however, mostly started by Josephite priests, a Catholic anglophone order invited by Archbishop Francis Janssens in 1888 specifically to serve the African American communities in the Deep South. Two such examples are St. Augustine Church, established in New Roads (Pointe Coupée Parish), and St. Benedict the Moor, established in Bertrandville (Assumption Parish).

From 1902 to 1919, the diffusion is even more accentuated. The shift around New Orleans was now complete, and English registers were more numerous in the southern parishes along the Mississippi as well in the western area. In thirty-two church parishes, registers switched from French to English, and thirty-three new church parishes were established with registers in English. Three new church parishes were established with registers in French, but two of the three switched to English nine years after their foundation.

During the next period, 1920–35, fifteen church parishes switched to English, leaving only six parishes with registers in French. The final period, 1936–48, marked the demise of French as a Church language practice as the six last churches clinging to French registers at the beginning of the period relinquished what was probably still the preferred language of many of their parishioners. Of these churches, two switched before World War II (St. Joseph in Cecilia, St. James in St. James Parish), one switched during the war (St. John in Henry), and three switched after the war (St. Philip in Vacherie, Sacred Heart in Cut Off, and Our Lady of Prompt Succor in Golden Meadow).

These findings demonstrate conclusively two important points. The first point concerns the era of the new Louisiana bilingualism, most clearly found before Reconstruction, during which no register changes came about until the pastor of St. Joseph Church in Baton Rouge decided to keep records in English in 1854. These findings were unanticipated for many reasons. Following the Louisiana Purchase in 1803 and especially statehood in 1812, it would be reasonable to expect more robust language changes in sacramental registers, at least in New Orleans. Even more register changes would be expected during the antebellum period when English, as the language of the ruling power, increasingly dominated the political and economic landscape.

The second point is that a majority of register switches occurred between 1870 and 1940.[14] The Civil War, in itself, did not have a significant influence on the Church's linguistic practices as far as the registers are concerned. Apparently the most powerful forces behind the switches were a combination of the linguistic "liberation" of the Church by the Irish and the social forces, especially "Americanization," resulting from the economic devastation of the war.

IRISH CATHOLICS IN NEW ORLEANS: THE FIRST SOURCE OF LANGUAGE CHANGE

Two important historical factors support the hypothesis that the Irish were the primary source of language change: the growth of Irish influence within the Church in New Orleans and their concomitant energy in asserting themselves in the political process.

Despite their ongoing troubled history with the English language, the Irish very quickly and firmly established English as a language of power in New Orleans.[15] Before the establishment of the first wholly ethnic Irish church, "the Irish Catholics attended Mass either at St. Louis Cathedral or at one of the three chapels" in New Orleans where the priests preached in French, a language which probably only a few understood upon landing in Louisiana.[16] While many Irish would of necessity have learned French, the prestige language and the language of business in early nineteenth-century New Orleans, as devout Catholics they would surely have been unhappy listening to sermons in French. In 1833, therefore, a group of Irish businessmen obtained from the Roman Catholic Church and the state legislature the authorization to build St. Patrick's (construction was completed in 1851), as well as a school, an orphan asylum, and a cemetery. Bishop Leo de Neckere appointed an Irish native, Father James Ignatius Mullon, as pastor of St. Patrick's in 1835. For the next thirty-two years, Father Mullon was instrumental in creating a powerful anglophone component in the Louisiana Church.

Father Mullon was, in fact, a classic Irish-American success story of the nineteenth century. His parents immigrated to America when he was young, and he served in the US Navy during the 1812–15 war between England and the United States. He was thoroughly familiar with the Catholic Church in America, which he joined as a young man. Ordained in Maryland, he served as missionary priest in Cincinnati, Ohio. As pastor, Father Mullon maintained a firm hold on St. Patrick's and objected to anything that would undermine his local authority. He was also quick to discipline fellow priests, of any national origin. When de Neckère's successor, Bishop Blanc, proposed Father Simon Paris as assistant priest at St. Patrick's, Father Mullon wrote that Father Paris was "in no good repute" and therefore Bishop Blanc would do better for his Church not to send him.[17] Indeed, he was never afraid to stand up to the powerful Bishop Blanc. For example, Father Mullon wrote to the bishop indignantly in 1856 that he would rather resign the pastorship of St. Patrick's, dear as it was to him, than to consent to have Father Hector Figari as an assistant.[18] When Father Mullon learned that Father William Ivers would resume his duties at St. Patrick's, he slyly suggested to Bishop Blanc to ask Father Ivers whether he knew a certain Mrs. Flowers, the sister of the lady who kept a boardinghouse on Diamond's Row, suspecting that Father Ivers might have taken this woman in his room. In 1839 Father Walsh wrote to Vicar-General Rousselon to ask why he had received from Father Mullon the bishop's mandate to take away his permission to celebrate mass at St. Patrick's. Father Rousselon wrote back that he knew nothing about such a mandate, and seven days later, Bishop Blanc replied that he had given no instructions to Father Mullon with regard to Father Walsh, whose authority was renewed—but in another New Orleans church.[19]

Thanks to increasing waves of Irish settlers scattered all over New Orleans and its surrounding areas, the Irish community—and hence Father Mullon's influence—quickly expanded. The demographic impact of the Irish cannot be underestimated. Although the Irish settled in cities up and down the East Coast, "the absolute number of Irish in New Orleans ranked fourth after New York, Philadelphia, and Boston."[20] Under Father Mullon's thirty-two-year leadership, parochial institutions such as new churches, rectories, schools (some charging tuition), and orphanages multiplied. Father Mullon also promoted temperance crusades (a social movement which would have shocked or amused eighteenth-century French colonists), which received intensive newspaper coverage, organized fund-raising drives to finance the construction of new churches, and was one of the promoters of the establishment of the Catholic Institute of New Orleans, which sponsored cultural and intellectual lectures in English, a library, and an English newspaper.[21] In 1844, Bishop Blanc appointed Father Mullon to edit the *Catholic Sentinel,* "the first English-language Catholic newspaper ever to appear in New Orleans."[22]

Another factor in the success of the Irish, both within the Church and in politics, is that they came to New Orleans with a crucial legacy which none of the previous immigrant groups possessed, including the French: a tradition of political activism. Irish people landed in New Orleans with a history of about seven hundred years of open and covert struggle against the English. The Irish were denied their Catholic Church and political rights for three hundred years, but they maintained a checkered but real tradition of at least the forms of self-government, including their own parliament starting as long ago as 1297. Thus when they settled in Louisiana, their political tradition was intact, their brand of Catholicism suddenly became not only tolerated but preferred by church authorities, and—at last combining religion and politics openly and freely—they quickly yearned for their own church where "God spoke in English."[23]

The Irish Catholics thus had the aptitude, the will, and the numbers to begin affecting the Louisiana Church community of practice. French Catholicism was a soft target in Louisiana since its adherents came from cultures in which Catholicism was assumed and never seriously challenged (or not to the same extent as in Ireland). Notoriously, Louisiana French Catholics displayed religious indifference; men considered religion as "the duty of women and children and usually appeared in church only for weddings and funerals."[24] Although there were anticlerical ideologies afoot, they were mostly limited to certain members of the elite influenced by the Enlightenment and the French Revolution. Most of the French Catholic immigrants came from rural church traditions (Nova Scotia and Saint Domingue) that were far removed from the intellectual debates within French Catholicism. As a result, French Catholics in Louisiana had no real religious challenges against them during the colonial and early American periods. It is true that Protestantism was increasing because of the "Americans" who migrated from the North after the Louisiana Purchase, but until the massive migration of the Irish, the Louisiana Church maintained its French character and nobody challenged the idea of homilies being delivered in French and sacramental registers being written in French (or Latin). In contrast, the Irish had the zeal born of a new social freedom, something like that of the eastern European Jews who migrated to western Europe and the United States after the middle of the nineteenth century.

The effect of the Irish on the Louisiana Catholic Church has at least two significant aspects. First, they changed the community of practice from within, with struggles that seem quite minor in hindsight. No battle for the soul of the Church was fought between the Irish and the French. As Michael Doorley points out, the Irish "found not just one host culture but two competing societies as they tried to assimilate."[25] The French native population and the Anglo-Americans had their respective territories, language, and religion (a majority of Anglo-Americans being Protestants). Doorley is right to say that the Irish settlers did not take over the local Catholic Church as they did in other American states. The Irish spoke the language of the new rulers but could not ally themselves with a religious institution other than the Roman Catholic Church, the open enemy of England for the better part of three hundred years. (Catholic emancipation in the United Kingdom, including representation in the English parliament, came only in 1829.)

The Irish aspiration was not to Americanize the Louisiana Church, which was still firmly in the hands of local French priests and French or French-dominant clerics. Rather, they wanted to create a separate community of practice composed of fervent Irish Catholics within the Louisiana Church, a community with its own set of ethnic but still Catholic practices: strict religious observance, unquestioned faith, temperance, devotion to family values, and utter respect for church authorities. By developing an English-speaking Irish community of practice, whose faithfulness was endorsed and even preferred by the French church authorities, the Irish also created bilingualism as an emergent language practice within the Church. English did not replace French; English was added to French in the Church's repertoire of language practices.

Another significant aspect is that religious purity trumped ethnic affiliation. The Irish created their own community of practice because they saw themselves as being truer to the Catholic faith than their slack French counterparts and—surprisingly—the French church higher-ups agreed and took their side on important issues. The Irish introduced and sustained real but ultimately not seriously divisive tension with the French Catholics. Irish church officials and priests (as well as lay Irish) regularly portrayed French Catholics as religiously apathetic and afflicted with low moral standards compared to their own, just as the French officials and priests had been saying for over a century.

One revealing example of the way the Irish were able to manipulate events to their own advantage with the French Catholic hierarchy is the "war of marguilliers" (also known as trustees or churchwardens). Because of architectural problems encountered during the construction of St. Patrick's and fund-raising difficulties, the Irish church parish owed $54,000 in 1844, and the financial fiasco was blamed on the trustees who managed the parish finances. In his letter dated January 11, 1844, Bishop John Purcell of Cincinnati, Ohio, warned Bishop Blanc not to allow the cathedral to fall into their "heretical hands."[26] Bishop Blanc ended up buying back St. Patrick's at a sheriff's auction in 1845. During the same period, the trustees asked to review episcopal appointments of priests originally approved by the bishop. Outraged by this lack of confidence in Bishop Blanc, the

Temperance Society of St. Patrick publicly denounced "his persecution by the marguilliers and other evil minded persons styling themselves Catholics," professed their abiding loyalty to Bishop Blanc, and, as a result, had their action officially commended in Catholic papers throughout the United States.[27] In response to these accusations, French Catholics "attacked the Church for being too reactionary and obedient to Rome" while they accused the Irish of being "bound with the iron shackles of an odious spiritual tyranny."[28] Another source of tension between the two groups was the connection that the French Catholics had with Masonic organizations such as the Know-Nothing party (specifically anti-Irish anti-immigration), which was denounced loudly by the Irish political machine.[29]

Despite these squabbles, Irish and French Catholics were forced in the end to accommodate one another to fight Protestantism, the "true enemy." One of their priorities was to fight such intrusive Protestant practices as door-to-door recruitment and the introduction of the reading of Scripture from the King James Bible in public schools. Bishop Blanc strongly encouraged the Irish leadership, which in turn defended his authority, and he also supported the rights of Irish and American immigrant populations because he believed that these anglophone populations were and would become "the chief support for authority" for the Church. In the eyes of Bishop Blanc, the Irish Catholics had attained economic, social, and political power over the French Catholics in New Orleans. It is therefore no surprise that the Louisiana Church did not object to the Irish tradition of preserving their sacramental registers in English. Its use in sacramental registers became a reification of that language practice in the Archdiocese of New Orleans.

THE "ETHNIC PERIOD": SOCIOECONOMIC CHANGES BETWEEN 1870 AND 1940

Life for the residents of Louisiana changed profoundly from the Reconstruction period through the Great Depression and World War II, with equally profound effects on language usage and the attitudes of most

Louisianans about language, especially French. When the federal government took control of the Confederate states at the end of the Civil War, the economy of Louisiana was wrecked. Fields and plantations were abandoned or undercultivated, and numerous white landowners who were financially ruined sold their plantations and left Louisiana. White planters were not alone, for the post–Civil War period saw a large migration of blacks from a society which, rather than offering hope of freedom to people of color, suddenly became extremely hostile to all black people. The Reconstruction period had led to a brief moment when, for example, a number of black men became members of the Louisiana legislature, the African American Oscar Dunn was elected lieutenant governor, and the politician P. B. S. Pinchback became a real political force in the state. Despite the prevailing stereotypes, there were real attempts at conciliation.

Nevertheless, these ultimately failed in the atmosphere of violence following the dislocation and vast destruction of the war, while the creation and multiplication of racist groups, especially the Knights of the White Camellia, radicalized racial separation. Because of the extent of their financial assets, elite free people of color became the target of both white Francophones and Anglophones, who used all means to diminish their social influence. They successfully modified the three-tier society that was Louisiana (whites, blacks, and people of color of different status) by substituting a stark black-and-white racial system opposing whites (regardless of their self-identification) and the rest of the population, blacks and people of color alike.[30] The violent resentment that many Louisiana whites exhibited, no matter their language and ethnicity, caused a large portion of liberated blacks and free people of color to flee to the northern United States.[31] For the first time in Louisiana since the earlier eighteenth century, the white population became the majority, and so it remains today.

The history of the francophone population during this period is particularly complex. Before the economic and sociocultural chaos generated by the war, south Louisiana was bilingual. French- and English-speaking populations each realized the benefits of learning the other's language. There was no profit in being monolingual. The turbulent time following the war disturbed this language equilibrium and rendered bilingualism clearly less desirable and even suspect. The disastrous effects of the economic situation directly touched all Louisianans, whatever their language of origin, but even more so the Francophones.[32] The entire farming population—landowners and tenant farmers, laborers and seasonal workers—was financially dependent on the big landowners and merchants, and by the 1870s the big landowners were Anglophones and for the most part monolingual.[33] English became the language of communication between them and their French-speaking employees, and also the language in which all business was conducted. There were therefore few economic advantages for monolingual landowners to learn French except to communicate in basic terms with employees, much like Spanish in the construction industry today. On the other hand, monolingual Francophones saw the benefits of learning English as a second language, and quickly.

White Francophones who self-identified as Creoles also found themselves risking identification with the large portion of the French-speaking population composed of people of color and freed blacks who also claimed to be Creole.[34] These white Francophones, particularly the elite, worked hard to bring themselves closer to the Anglophones and had everything to gain politically from this assimilation. They needed to become "southern," and did. Eventually, many even stopped self-identifying as Creoles.

The elite people of color in New Orleans, used to being considered superior to other blacks and enjoying economic advantages, opposed by all means possible the legal sanctions that were suddenly imposed upon them.[35] Realizing that English now was replacing French in critical social and economic areas, they considered the learning of English and education in English as a strategic means to achieve their political goals. In order to give themselves socioeconomic advantages, affluent people of color enrolled their children in English schools well before instruction in English became compulsory. The rest of the black population, largely former slaves, lived in extreme poverty, often in difficult, inaccessible rural regions. They spoke little English. Generally they did not see themselves as ever attaining the liberties that the New Orleans black elite struggled to defend, much less attaining the social position of the former "free people of color," both of which seemed part of another world. Consequently, they ignored the struggle and usually continued speaking French as before.

Besides the rise of a stark and simple black/white divide in Louisiana, a nationalist discourse would profoundly change the attitudes of the francophone elite of the white race. In Louisiana, this discourse was above all directed by the Irish community. A part of this discourse advocated the cultural unity of the nation, which was profoundly socially and economically divided following the Civil War, and "English only" was seen as a key in rebuilding a nation.[36] This linguistic nationalism had two principles: (1) that the exclusive use of English drives Americanization and, by consequence, creates a more homogenous nation; and (2) that exclusive use of English implies a degree of superior intelligence.[37]

Another part of the nationalist discourse had immediate negative effects on bilingualism throughout the United States, principally in the domain of education. The State of Louisiana, which until this point had tolerated the use of French in school, would now formally prohibit its use. Despite this linguistic policy, bilingualism at least had a chance to survive within the family. However, the use of evaluative measures in the domain of education, like the Stanford Binet or IQ Test, which claims to measure the link between level of intelligence and scholarly success, would have a devastating impact on bilingualism, even in the family context. Certain researchers arrived at the bizarre conclusion that bilingualism actually inhibits intelligence. Educators themselves thus concluded that bilingualism is more a weakness than an advantage, and that this weakness can only retard the acculturation of bilingual children. Parents were therefore strongly discouraged from raising their children in any language other than English since only the exclusive use of English could guarantee scholarly and consequently financial success.[38]

Events of a demographic and economic nature therefore reduced the use of French to merely symbolic capital, and that only among the elite, where the ability to speak French fluently—in a limited number of social circumstances—still had a cultural cachet. The sociopolitical climate isolated the poorer French-speaking population in order to better subordinate it. The Louisiana francophone population was now considered an "ethnic" group since its members displayed values as well as specific social and linguistic attributes that differed considerably from those of the majority of the population of Louisiana, the South, and the American nation. The institutionalized racism of Louisiana society also fractured the francophone population. There were not one but two (black and white) francophone cultural enclaves.

How did bilingualism deteriorate into monolingualism within the remaining French-speaking population, which was largely rural or found in small communities across south Louisiana? With so many small French-speaking communities geographically and socially isolated from each other, a number of scenarios have been imagined. However, most frequent collective scenarios during this period can be represented in the form of three dominant tendencies.[39]

The first tendency is the decline of bilingualism within the population of white French speakers. After the profound transformation of Louisiana society after Reconstruction, social reality changed for them. Their bilingualism, which had been until this point an advantage and symbolic of veritable capital, now became a handicap, not only for them but above all for their children. Afraid of seeming unpatriotic, non-American, and antisocial, the majority of them would reject their francophone heritage for that of the Anglophones. They gradually erased the most evident trace of their cultural bilingualism: the use of French in public. White Louisianans who knew English and French from childhood would continue to use the two languages, but they adopted a totally different linguistic behavior with regard to their children. Acting on the recommendations of teachers, they would from now on raise their children in English alone.

Another tendency concerns the decline of bilingualism within the population of black Francophones. Economic changes had crushed the economic capital of the Creoles of color, and they had also been excluded from the political and social system of Louisiana society. They therefore suddenly shared with the descendants of the slaves the lowest echelon of the socioeconomic system that forbade all social mobility. Those that did not flee Louisiana during this period mixed with a free black community who had arrived in Louisiana as slaves between 1830 and 1860, all of whom were Protestants and spoke only English. (Creoles of color were mainly city dwellers, and had little or no contact with those blacks in remote communities who, like the whites, continued speaking French well into the twentieth century.)

Given the numeric, political, social, and legal status of English, this black English-speaking population did not see a lot of advantages in learning a language being abandoned by the white classes. By contrast, the black French-speaking population had every interest in acquiring English. Evidently, the same sociopolitical events that taught white Francophones to raise their children solely in English also had an influence on them. However, the black French-speaking population had to submit to an additional pressure: biases from other blacks. The black English speakers considered the French origin of the black French speakers as a constant reminder of their former condition and their participation, however involuntary, in a system of submission instituted by others, that is to say, whites.[40] The black French-speaking population suffered thereby from a double discrimination: their race alone kept them at the lowest rung of the social ladder, while their French language marginalized them even within the black community. Consequently, whatever advancement a black person could make began with a command of English.

The retention of French among the rural population represents the final tendency. As is well known, an indeterminate number of white and black French speakers continued to use French at home and at work. They even educated their children in French. But many of those who had children before World War II especially raised them using both languages, even if their children usually responded to them in English.[41] These black and white Francophones held several common characteristics. They were poor and earned their meager living as fishermen or hired farmers, or even as seasonal workers. Their life was hard, since before 1950 agricultural work in Louisiana was primarily done manually or using horses and mules. They lived well outside of urban centers, in small locales on the coast or in rural zones. They benefited from religious instruction dispensed by the parish church, but the youth, above all the boys, could not go to public school because they were needed to work on the farms or in the home. They were part of a very closed-off network, maintaining profound family relations and proud to help each other in times of crisis.

These white and black populations lived in separate, segregated villages but were situated within proximity of each other. Sometimes they shared the same location. A present-day case in point is the town of Parks, which since the end of the nineteenth century has always been inhabited by an equal number of whites and blacks keeping their relationship, for the most part, distant but harmonious. These disparate populations have developed individual variations in their francophone culture. To cite common stereotypes, the blacks have zydeco as their music, eat red beans and rice, and play Pittypat for recreation, whereas the whites prefer traditional folk music, are avid about jambalaya, and play Bourré. These are of course ideological representations but indicative of a real cultural difference. One thing is certain: these black and white French speakers intentionally have differentiated themselves as members of their racial group.

The division between these Francophones and the Louisiana Anglophones was not only physical and linguistic but also in social attitudes toward one another. Louisiana Anglophones considered Francophones to be near-illiterates who were not only without a worthwhile culture, but also lazy and simple-minded. Francophones of the generation born before World War II still often mention the contemptuous way in which they were treated at work and at school. These francophone populations did not yet identify themselves as Creole or Cajun; they also did not identify their language as Creole or Cajun. They considered themselves to be "Frenchmen speaking French." The English term "Cajun" was even an ethnic insult used by "Amaricains" or Louisianans living outside of these little French-speaking communities—at least until being "Cajun" became fashionable after the 1960s and 1970s. Now even exclusive New Orleans restaurants advertise formerly despised "Cajun" dishes for tourists.[42]

But a century before "Cajun" restaurants popped up even in the spiceless United Kingdom, the Louisiana church records show how the French language was declining at home. To judge from these records, the bulk of the language shift happened between 1888 and 1935, with 78% of parish registers shifting to English during this period, the tip occurring from 1901 to 1917, when twenty-nine registers switched. Notably, these register changes took place under the direction of three solidly European archbishops who "moved increasingly into the mainstream of American Catholicism and away from [the Louisiana Church's] French distinctiveness."[43]

4

LANGUAGE PRACTICES OF THE ARCHDIOCESAN ADMINISTRATION, 1861–1917

As Bishop Blanc's life drew to a close, a cataclysmic event, the American Civil War, was rapidly approaching. Archival letters from the dramatic year before the Union fell apart reveal that no one in the Church seemed to be making strategic plans to deal with the inevitable. This war created a new and, in some ways, narrower Louisiana society. The Civil War and its aftermath devastated Louisiana's economy as well as its population and brought marked changes in Louisiana society. Blanc's immediate successors, all European-born, had to deal with an increasingly "Americanized" Louisiana that was less tolerant of ethnic and language differences.

THE ARCHDIOCESE AND ITS STRUCTURAL CHANGES

Though today each Catholic archdiocese has a clear hierarchical structure of power, and regulations from above govern an archbishop's authority, in early nineteenth-century Louisiana, the ecclesiastical structure of power and its exercise was amorphous. The local management of the Church was capricious and internal conflicts abounded. The Roman Catholic Church has always struggled with centralization, and the Louisiana Church, and indeed the American Catholic Church as a whole, did not prove an exception. To address the governing of the Roman Catholic Church in the

United States, the archbishop of Baltimore, as the apostolic delegate to the United States, called periodically throughout the 1800s a plenary or national council (1852, 1866, and 1884). No such council could be called without the authority of the Holy See, and decrees were submitted to Rome for recognition and revision. All archbishops and bishops of the nation were obliged to appear and vote on important matters.

One significant management change—the appointment of a council in each diocese—was recommended at the Second Plenary Council in 1866 and later decreed at the Third Plenary Council (1884).[1] The diocesan council was to advise the bishop in pastoral governance, including the appointment of priests/pastors to parishes, the establishment of parish boundaries, the creation of new parishes, and property management.[2] The Third Plenary Council also recommended that those studying for the priesthood needed preparatory seminaries where they should be taught, among other things, English and at least one other language "according to the necessities of the diocese." Seminarians were also to learn to speak and write Latin and be taught Greek. Following the Third Plenary Council's decree, the small group of clergy that aided the archbishop in his decision making at the Archdiocese of New Orleans was reorganized as the Archiepiscopal Council. This consultative body can be considered, then and now, as a community of practice with its own rules and membership.

THE ARCHBISHOPS, THE ARCHDIOCESE, AND THEIR ATTITUDE TOWARD LANGUAGE CHANGE

The Third Plenary Council's position on instructing immigrants in their native language by priests of their own language did not address the use of well-established languages in areas of the country where English was not the native language of the resident population. In other words, French speakers in Louisiana were not considered an immigrant population, but English and German speakers were. To meet the decree of the council on Catholic immigrants' instruction, the Archdiocese of New Orleans established German and Italian parishes, the English population already having their own parishes. It may be assumed that the intention was that if the congregation spoke a language other than French, then a priest who was fluent in that language should be assigned. Thus there would continue to be French-speaking priests assigned where French was dominant, and English-speaking priests for those who spoke English.

The archbishops who managed the Louisiana Church before and after Archbishop Blanc's death in 1860, when most linguistic changes occurred in sacramental registers, are listed in table 4.1. To situate these archbishops over time, we indicate the years of tenure and the country of origin of each of the bishops/archbishops who have presided over New Orleans.

TABLE 4.1. Bishops and archbishops of New Orleans, 1793 to present

Year	*Name of Bishop/Archbishop*	*Country of Origin*
1793–1801	Luis Peñalver y Cárdenas	Cuba
1801–03	Francesco Porró y Reinado	Spain
1815–26	Louis William Valentine DuBourg	Saint Domingue
1830–33	Leo-Raymond de Neckère	Belgium
1835–60	Antoine Blanc	France
1861–70	Jean Marie Odin	France
1870–83	Napoléon Joseph Perché	France
1883–87	Francis Xavier Leray	France
1888–97	Francis Janssens	Holland
1897–1905	Placide-Louis Chapelle	France
1906–17	James Hubert Blenk	Germany
1918–34	John William Shaw	Alabama, US
1935–64	Joseph Francis Rummel	Germany
1964–65	John Patrick Cody	Missouri, US
1965–89	Philip Matthew Hannan	Washington, DC, US
1989–2001	Francis Bible Schulte	Pennsylvania, US
2002–9	Alfred Clifton Hughes	Massachusetts, US
2009–	Gregory Michael Aymond	Louisiana, US

Among Blanc's successors, two groups can be distinguished. The first group is composed of the native French archbishops who presided over the Archdiocese of New Orleans between 1861 and 1887. Three archbishops—Jean Marie Odin, Napoléon Joseph Perché, and Francis Xavier Leray—ruled during the wrenching Civil War and Reconstruction periods. Although some registers switched from French to English during this twenty-six-year period, there were no significant changes in language practices during their tenure. Bilingual register entries, a practice introduced during Blanc's tenure, were still common in some church parishes. French registers sometimes shifted to English, then back to French, then again to English. Despite this lack of change, the transformation of the activities of the Church from primarily missionary to functioning as a fully established church changed sharply the agenda of those at the helm of the archdiocese. These officials made recommendations to the pope about who should succeed as archbishop, having an indirect but strong influence on the selection of New Orleans archbishops. Sociopolitical events, combined with the archbishops' policies, set the scene for the language negotiations that took place in the following decades. Moreover, their tenures coincide with a period of language transition in Louisiana society at large.

A second group of archbishops—Francis Janssens, Placide-Louis Chapelle, and James Hubert Blenk—administered the archdiocese at the time when most of the switches in the sacramental registers occurred (1880–1920). Analysis of the contributions of each of these archbishops and the composition of their Archiepiscopal Council provided evidence of a switch from French to English within the archdiocesan administration as well.

Four sources of materials were tapped: (1) the annually published Catholic directories, which listed diocesan officials; (2) the Archiepiscopal Council minutes from 1858 to 1921, which provide the languages used by the administration; (3) the pastoral letters written by the archbishops to the clergy and laity from 1844 to 1934; and (4) the correspondence from the archbishop to the clergy and laity, which will, once again, shed light on the diminishing power of the once-dominant French-born administration.

MANDEMENT

DE

MGR L'ARCHEVEQUE DE LA NLLE. ORLEANS

POUR LE CAREME DE L'ANNÉE 1853.

ANTOINE BLANC, PAR LA GRACE DE DIEU ET L'AUTORITÉ DU SAINT-SIEGE APOSTOLIQUE, ARCHEVEQUE DE LA NLLE.-ORLEANS, ET ADMINISTRATEUR APOSTOLIQUE DE NATCHEZ PENDANT LA VACANCE DU SIEGE,

Au Clergé et aux Fidèles des deux diocèses, salut et bénédiction en N.-S. J.-C.

Faites pénitence, parce que le royaume de Dieu est proche. (1)

Au moment où nous allons commencer la Sainte Quarantaine, Nos Très Chers Frères, nous ne pouvons mieux vous exhorter à entrer dans l'esprit de l'Eglise, qu'en vous rappélant les paroles que le saint Précurseur adressait à la multitude pour la préparer à la prédication du Sauveur, et que Notre-Seigneur Jésus-Christ lui-même

(1) St-Matth. c. 3. v. 2.

Pastoral letter of Archbishop Blanc, 1853. (Courtesy of the Office of Archives and Records, Archdiocese of New Orleans.)

Despite the interest shown in language use both by the highest church authorities and by Archbishop Blanc and others in Louisiana, no top-down language policy was ever issued by the Louisiana archdiocesan administration. Even though switching the most critical records of the Louisiana Church from French to English clearly reflected an important social change in Louisiana, there is no evidence from any archival sources that a decree, ruling, or even guideline about language preference ever came from the local ordinary before or after the Civil War. The switch from French to English in the Louisiana Church appears to be a bottom-up rather than a top-down change, or perhaps it is more accurate to say that the diocesan authorities trusted the decisions of the priests who were in daily contact with their parishioners. Even Bishop Blanc worked on a case-by-case basis. So if there was no language policy coming from the higher-ups, how did the ecclesiastical administration in its structure, decisions, or statements influence or affect the course of language change from French to English in the Church?

THE FRENCH ECCLESIASTICAL POWER DURING A TIME OF WAR, DEBTS, AND PRIVATION

The period from the death of Archbishop Blanc in 1860 to the arrival of Archbishop Janssens in 1888 was a time of extreme financial exigency in the Louisiana Church, as indeed in the South as a whole. The Church not surprisingly chose three French-born priests as archbishops during this period, and not surprisingly French retained its importance in the Church. However, at the end of the period at least one important churchman saw clearly the end of French dominance and urged yet more accommodation with the anglophone world which controlled Louisiana and which, given the passions and racist practices unleashed by the war and Reconstruction, was becoming more aggressively anglophone.

Archbishop Blanc's successor, Father Jean Marie Odin, native of Ambierle, France, arrived in New Orleans at the beginning of the Civil War in 1861, after the Federal troops captured and occupied New Orleans.

What he found was a church in the midst of armed violence, privation, and financial difficulties. "Like other Southern bishops and the great majority of his clergy," writes Charles Nolan, "[Archbishop Odin] supported the Confederation cause, worked to alleviate the suffering caused by the war, and spoke out continually of the need for peace."[3] However, clerics were advised by Archbishop John Purcell of Cincinnati to stay away from politics and avoid making political statements, verbally or in writing, which could only bring harm to the Church.

Archbishop Odin issued new financial regulations to prevent the Church from declaring bankruptcy. Many churches, convents, and schools throughout the archdiocese were requisitioned by Federal troops; some were damaged or entirely destroyed.[4] Pews could not be rented. The publication of the archdiocesan newspaper, *Le Propagateur Catholique,* was suspended during the war, and its editor, Father Napoléon Joseph Perché, placed under house arrest. In 1864, Archbishop Odin described his health as feeble and his duties as above his strength.[5] When he passed away in 1870, Louisiana was still occupied by Federal troops, but the archdiocese was free from debt and the number of churches had nearly doubled.[6] This was quite an astonishing achievement.

The French archbishops who followed Archbishop Odin were less successful and less accepted. The editor Father Perché first succeeded Archbishop Odin. Born in 1805 in Angers, Father Perché, recruited by Archbishop Blanc, came to New Orleans in 1841. Considered a talented scholar but lacking administrative ability, Archbishop Perché held a tenure (1870–1883) marred by extreme financial difficulties.[7] Louisiana was in turmoil as well. Father Ferreol Girardey in New Orleans describes a society in extreme anxiety and financial torment in February 1879.

> The people are making a slow recovery from bad government and the late epidemic. This recovery would be better if the city and state were not so near to bankruptcy. Since the war millions of dollars have been spent without benefit to anyone except the unscrupulous men who are filling their purses from public money. The laws are so nicely framed that, while the perpetrators of these swindling schemes cannot be brought to justice by a fair trial, innocent men are seized by apparently legal processes and brought from

> far distances to appear in sham court trials before judges and juries packed for the sole purpose of condemning them. While these men wait for weeks until this farcical trial takes place, their families are reduced to want and starvation and the most fertile parts of the state remain uncultivated. The best business men aim merely at meeting current expenses scarcely able to realize any profit. Those who have money idle fear to invest it and lose it all. Twenty per cent of the people are unemployed now.[8]

Many priests criticized Archbishop Perché's financial decisions and the management of his vicar-general, Father Gilbert Raymond.[9] In August 1879, the officials and councillors of the Corporation of the Diocese of New Orleans wrote a letter in French to Cardinal John Simeoni in Rome to expose the financial situation. To prevent an increase of the debt and improve the management of the archdiocese's affairs, Rome resolved the conflict by the appointment of a coadjutor and administrator to Archbishop Perché.

By the 1870s, anglophone priests were growing restive with the French-dominated clergy, and suggestions for potential non-French candidates to the New Orleans coadjutorship are found in many letters. The common opinion of the Irish priests in New Orleans was that an energetic English-speaking bishop was needed since the English-speaking Catholics were the more zealous. In their opinion, Archbishop Perché's replacement by another French bishop would produce great dissatisfaction. Bishop William Henry of Natchez, Mississippi, argued in his 1876 letter to Archbishop Perché that his coadjutor should be one who spoke and wrote fluently in both languages.[10]

Rome's preferred choice in 1879, however, was something of a compromise. He was yet another Frenchman, Father Francis Xavier Leray, but an experienced apostolic administrator/bishop at the diocese of Natchitoches who had been in the United States for over thirty-five years. Father Leray, a native of Brittany, arrived first in Louisiana in 1843. After completing his theological studies at the Sulpician seminary in Baltimore and following his ordination to the priesthood in 1852, he was appointed to the see of Natchitoches in 1877. His long years in America and his experience as a Confederate priest would have mollified many anglophone New Orleans Catholics. When Coadjutor Leray advanced to the position of archbishop of New Orleans after Perché's death (December 27, 1883), the pope urged him to repair the archdiocese's financial state as soon as possible and he did. During his tenure from 1883 to 1887, he managed to reduce by half the archdiocesan debt.[11]

Given his background, it is not surprising that Leray was acutely aware of language issues and willing to make changes. As bishop of Natchitoches, Leray mandated the use of English in the diocese. All religious instruction, including prayers, sermons, and educational training, had to be given in English. Up to this time, French was the language used by the clergy and religious in the diocese of Natchitoches, whereas most of the native population spoke only English.[12] Leray thus extended Blanc's policy of making sure parishioners heard sermons in a language they could understand. (That such a counterproductive language policy could be in place in mostly anglophone north Louisiana into the late 1870s shows that not all archbishops were as sensitive to the importance of language as Blanc.)

At the end of his tenure, Archbishop Leray, nearly the last of New Orleans's French archbishops, left revealing correspondence about the language situation. Before his death in 1887, he requested a coadjutor, insisting that it be French-born Father Placide-Louis Chapelle, a pastor well-known among diplomats and statesmen who ministered at St. Matthew Church in Washington, DC. Archbishop Leray explained his choice of a French-born bishop by the fact that in the New Orleans countryside, "the immense majority of Catholics . . . at least 100,000, were descended from French and Spanish settlers and especially from Acadians: who all spoke only French, *plus ou moins corrompue* (more or less corrupt)."[13]

To illustrate his point, he provided valuable linguistic information based on language use in the civil parishes of south Louisiana. He stated that French was used on Bayou Lafourche, Bayou Teche, in Attakapas, Opelousas, and the parishes along the Mississippi River. Because of trade, English was used in the city of New Orleans, but there were still twelve churches where only French was used and five where sermons were delivered in French and English. There was one church using French and Italian and four where only German was spoken. Eight churches used English only. Of the archdiocesan clergy, only seven secular priests did not know French—three of German origin and four of Irish origin. Most of the religious communities were bilingual or French-speaking. Archbishop Leray's description makes clear why he did not mandate an English-only language policy in the Archdiocese of New Orleans.

Archbishop Leray died before receiving a coadjutor, and the archdiocesan see remained vacant for almost a year with Father G. A. Rouxel administering its affairs as auxiliary bishop. Two candidates arose for the position: Archbishop Leray's choice, Father Chapelle; and Francis Janssens, bishop of Natchez, Mississippi, and member of the province of New Orleans.[14]

Many of the priests of the archdiocese wanted a French-born bishop. Like the late Archbishop Leray, they felt that New Orleans was inherently French and therefore a French-born bishop was in order. One priest, however, Father Jean Baptiste Bogaerts, a Belgian-born priest and former secretary of the Corporation of the Diocese of New Orleans, wrote three remarkably prophetic letters expressing the need for the Louisiana Church to become part of the mainstream of American life—in other words, to appoint a non-French-born bishop. In his opinion, over the next ten years, English would be the dominant language even in rural areas. English was already used by 75% of those 250,000 living in New Orleans. He stated that English was the official language of the state, and it was the only one taught in the public schools. Bogaerts also warned that immigration from the northwestern part of the United States would rapidly speed the need for English-speaking priests. If the Catholic Church tried to force these immigrants into the French Catholic culture, he argued, they would seek refuge with the Protestants, who were proud of being a part of American culture, and thus give Catholics the mark of being foreign.[15]

Archbishop Leray and Father Bogaerts present starkly conflicting views on religious identity in Louisiana, although more nuanced than it might first appear. Although Archbishop Leray pointed out the large number of French-speaking Catholics, this argument alone does not explain his inclination. After all, 100,000 French Catholics represented a minority when compared to Louisiana's overall population of 939,000 in 1887.[16] What he wished for was the preservation of the Church's bilingual identity, an identity more in sync with the multilingual character of the nineteenth-century Louisiana population. His preference for a French-born priest with considerable political connections also served the purpose of fighting off upward Protestant influence in two ways: by maintaining the long-standing tradition of French ecclesiastical power and by improving relations with the Washington executive and legislative branches of power during a period of anti-Catholicism. As his entire career had shown, he was arguing not for a francophone church, but for maintaining the unique identity of the nineteenth-century Louisiana church.

By contrast, Father Bogaerts promoted cultural assimilation and a shift to English. In his opinion, preserving the Louisiana ecclesiastical tradition could only be done at the expense of learning English. With the Irish now being the largest immigrant population of Catholics in southern Louisiana, he argued that French could no longer be considered as a marker of Catholic identity. Holding on to this attribute would only turn immigrants away from the Louisiana Church. In his letters, Father Bogaerts suggested that devoted faith rather than language should be the determining marker of Louisiana Catholicism. Since no identity could exist in a vacuum, the Church's identity should be expressed in a language that benefited from the higher social and political advantages in Louisiana (English) and was represented by a significant group which epitomized devotion to the Catholic faith (the Irish). Although, in hindsight, his letters appear prophetic, in a real sense Father Bogaerts's opinion mirrored that of the Church for nearly two thousand years.

DIOCESAN GROWTH UNDER A NEW ECCLESIASTICAL REGIME

At last, on August 7, 1888, the Dutch priest Francis Janssens was appointed archbishop of New Orleans. A revealing journal entry from the Provincial Redemptorist Archives describes the ceremony and the reception while giving an indication of the Church's tolerance of the languages of its members.[17] Arriving in a "cortege," Janssens processed to the St. Louis

Cathedral, where he was greeted by a large crowd. He was addressed by Administrator Monsignor Rouxel "in French of course." He answered and gave his blessing. Janssens "listened to five minute speeches in Italian—French—German—& English. Having made some good remarks the Archbishop gave his blessing again."

Francis Janssens, born in Tilburg, the Netherlands, studied for the priesthood at the American College in Louvain (Belgium). He spoke many languages, including Dutch, Latin, French, and English. During his tenure in New Orleans, Archbishop Janssens decreased the archdiocesan debt, founded fifteen new church parishes, and recruited many Dutch priests to labor in Louisiana. Realizing the need for a native-born clergy, he established a local seminary north of Lake Pontchartrain. To minister to Sicilian immigrants, he invited Scalabrini priests to work at St. Mary's Church in the French Quarter. Unlike his predecessors, Janssens understood that African Americans needed an African American clergy to better relate the teachings of the Church. To serve black Catholics, he invited the Josephites (Society of Saint Joseph of the Sacred Heart) to work in the black communities of rural Louisiana. After nearly a decade of progressive work, on June 10, 1897, Archbishop Janssens died aboard the steamer *Créole.* The vessel was still on the Mississippi River, having left New Orleans the day before.

In 1896, Cardinal Francesco Satolli, the first apostolic delegate to the United States, toured the country. His secretary, French-born Alexis Orban, kept an account in French of his trip to New Orleans at the very end of Janssens' tenure. Among his final observations, he wrote with great acuity his observation that sums up the Church during this next period:

> We were now leaving this city whose people were still so French after almost a century of separation from their mother country, so Catholic in their traditions and their religious institutions. Now as they are a part of the Union, the English element penetrates little by little, and a new clergy accordingly replaces the old. The transition has already begun, and as a rule Belgians and Swiss [i.e., from multilingual counties] are being used. The present Archbishop, who is worthy of his office, marks the end of the old regime and the beginning of the new. The French clergy is going to

> disappear gradually, and the Irish will move as quickly as possible into the parishes which yield a sufficient income. Let us hope that the Church and souls not only will not lose but even gain by the change.[18]

The first choice of the New Orleans French clergy to replace Janssens was, again, Father Chapelle (by then archbishop at the Archdiocese of Santa Fe). The Holy See finally granted their wish. Placide-Louis Chapelle, born in Runes Lozère, France, studied in France, Belgium, and at St. Mary's Seminary in Baltimore, where he received a doctorate in philosophy and theology. Fluent in French, Spanish, and English, Chapelle was known in Washington, DC, for his linguistic and diplomatic skills. His appointment to New Orleans (1897–1905) coincided with the start of the Spanish-American War. The Holy See appointed him apostolic delegate to Cuba and Puerto Rico and envoy extraordinary to the Philippine Islands.[19] These duties took him away from the archdiocese for long periods, and during his absences the vicar-general was in charge of the archdiocese.

Continuing the tradition of Archbishop Blanc, Chapelle was more concerned about keeping the faithful in the fold than with maintaining French Catholic culture. During his tenure, Chapelle recognized that the French and German churches were losing the younger generations to neighboring English churches.[20] He also recognized the need for an official Catholic newspaper published in English.[21] He established seven new parishes. In 1904, he had the pleasure of announcing that the archdiocesan debt was eliminated. Finally free from overseas travels, Chapelle returned from Havana, wishing to visit all the parishes in the archdiocese. He died selflessly tending to his flock: while visiting Lake Charles in 1905, the archbishop was notified of a yellow fever epidemic in New Orleans. He quickly returned to the city to be with his people. Sadly, on August 9, 1905, Chapelle fell victim to the fever himself and died.

The next archbishop had a very different background from his predecessors. James Hubert Blenk was born in Neustadt, Bavaria, but moved to New Orleans at a very young age and converted from Protestantism to Catholicism at age thirteen. Educated at Jefferson College in Convent, Louisiana, he later went to Lyon, France, for his philosophical studies and

Dublin, Ireland, to study science and higher mathematics. After becoming a priest, he returned to Jefferson College and was elevated to its presidency.

Recognizing his abilities, both Archbishop Janssens and Archbishop Chapelle appointed him to their board of consultors. Archbishop Chapelle asked Blenk to accompany him to Cuba and Puerto Rico as auditor of the Apostolic Delegation. After Chapelle submitted Blenk's name to Rome, the latter became the first American bishop of Puerto Rico in 1899.[22] When Chapelle died, Blenk was recalled to New Orleans, becoming archbishop on July 1, 1906, and served until 1917. Archbishop Blenk was dedicated to educational reforms, creating the first archdiocesan school board. He established twenty-one new parishes, five of which were separate parishes for African Americans. What Janssens had begun as an experiment, Blenk put into policy.[23] Blenk realized that the Archdiocese of New Orleans was too large an area to govern and recommended that a new diocese to the southwest be established. Archbishop Blenk died before seeing the Diocese of Lafayette created.

With Blenk's death on April 20, 1917, the unbroken line of foreign-born bishops and archbishops ended, and the Archdiocese of New Orleans received its first American-born archbishop, John W. Shaw. Louisiana Catholics had to wait another ninety years to see a New Orleans native serve as archbishop, Father Gregory Michael Aymond (2009 to the present).

THE ARCHIEPISCOPAL COUNCIL, THE COUNCIL MINUTES, THE PASTORAL LETTERS, AND LANGUAGE SHIFT

Although the archbishops from the Civil War to 1917 were foreign-born and usually French, they supported a bilingual Church and were not afraid to use English to confront the threat of Protestantism, with its close attachment to American culture. The records of the Archiepiscopal Council reveal much about language practices in the upper reaches of the Louisiana church administration when it met in formal sessions. An analysis shows a persistent but fading prevalence of French, even when members expressed openness to the use of English in churches.

The Archiepiscopal Council of the Archdiocese of New Orleans in the late nineteenth century consisted of the archbishop, vicar-general, chancellor, and the consultors. The Archiepiscopal Council administration was the epicenter of the network of church parishes. The church parishes, each comprised of a priest and his parishioners, existed as their own communities of practice but were connected to the Archiepiscopal Council, creating an interrelated constellation of communities.

Since the council records are the reports of oral meetings, they tell us much about the actual linguistic practices among the higher clergy. The annually published *Official Catholic* Directories from 1889 to 1917 were used to create an Archiepiscopal Council administration database to determine the country of origin of the priests who held administrative office during the tenures of Archbishops Janssens, Chapelle, and Blenk. Besides the country of origin, the database includes yearly information such as the number of religious order/secular priests, the number of churches and chapels or stations, the names of the administrators, and the positions held.

Figure 4.1 shows the composition of the Archiepiscopal Council from 1889 to 1917. The first observable trend is that the administration was heavily represented by French-born priests under the tenures of Janssens and Chapelle. From 1890 to 1902, with the exception of 1893, there were seven council members. During those twelve years, five members were French-born and one member was Belgian-born, representing a top-heavy administration of French-language officials. Then, in 1903, the council was expanded to nine members, with the additions of Italian-born, Dutch-born, Belgian-born, and Irish-born members, but five French-born members remained. Thus the council's composition began changing in 1903, with a notable shift occurring in 1910, when the number of non-French-born finally outweighed the number of French-born, four to two. The council had decreased its size during those years, and when it expanded again to nine members in 1914, its composition was representative of a multi-ethnic, multilinguistic, diverse membership. This change directly correlates with the arrival of German-born Archbishop Blenk in 1906.

The Archiepiscopal Council minutes book, 1858–1921, is a 141-page ledger-style register which documents the discussions, actions, and deci-

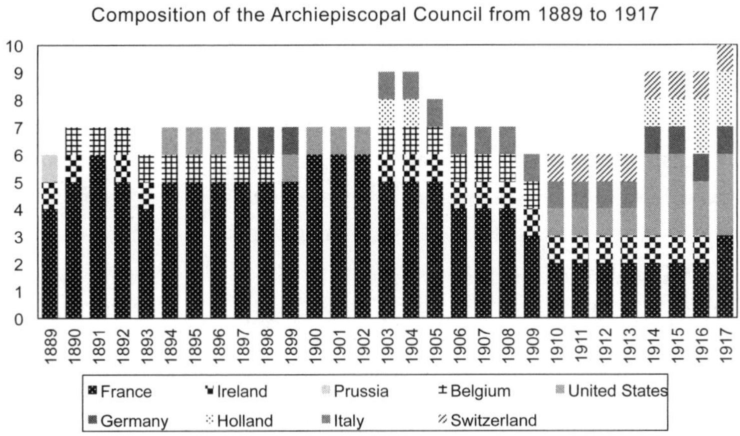

Figure 4.1. Composition of the Archiepiscopal Council, 1889–1917

sions of the council. Minutes are recorded in longhand and signed by the secretary. The first minutes, recorded in English, are dated March 9, 1858 (Archbishop Blanc's administration). The same year, the council called for the translation of prayers into three languages: French, English, and German. The second set of minutes are recorded in French and dated May 31, 1861 (Archbishop Odin's administration). In 1887, the council decided that the meeting would be held in French rather than English due to the composition of the council—a decision which shows that a high number of French-born officials had the effect of preserving French as an administrative language. There are a few occasions when English quotations from letters or legal documents are inserted within the French minutes, but administrative issues are discussed entirely in French. As an example, concern for the French and German parishes where boundaries were not well defined was raised in French in 1898. Membership at these churches was in sharp decline, due largely to the younger generation going to neighboring English-speaking churches. In 1899, the need for an official English Catholic newspaper was discussed in French.

The minutes remain in French until November 13, 1913 (Archbishop Blenk's administration), after which they appear mainly in English. There was a short period of bilingualism from 1903 to 1913 during which an Italian-born and multilingual administrator, Father Peter Scotti, officiated as chancellor. He recorded and signed the minutes "Pierre Scotti, chancelier" most of the time. In one particular entry in 1908, he switched from French to English midway through the minutes and then signed "Peter Scotti, secretary." His last recorded minutes in 1913 are signed "P. Scotti, secretaire." In 1913, Father Vincent, a Louisiana-born priest, was appointed secretary and from that time forward, minutes were recorded in English.

A final matter of interest relating to language use in the upper church administration is its most formal communication to its clergy and laity, the archbishop's pastoral letters, containing praise, admonition, and/or instructions for the conduct of Catholics. These letters were published in only two languages, French and English, and were written by the archbishop or the administrator in his absence. Table 4.2 illustrates the different editing styles of the pastoral letters to the clergy and laity over the years. In table 4.3, style and format are cross-tabulated with two other criteria: the year in which these letters were written and the archbishop or administrator who wrote them.

Reviewing the editing choices the archbishops made from 1844 to 1934, we can see that two separate editions of the pastoral letters were published, one in French and one in English, from 1844 to 1883. These two editions correspond to the most prominent language communities in Louisiana: the French Catholics, and the Irish and English-speaking Americans. With overlapping years from 1879 to 1888, Archbishop Leray (first as coadjutor) and his administrator, Father G. A. Rouxel, used the side-by-side layout of French on the left-hand side of the page and English on the right-hand side. As is described earlier, Archbishop Leray did everything he could to eliminate the archdiocesan debt, and shifting from two separate editions to one bilingual layout was a money-saving strategy rather than the result of a new linguistic policy. The proof is that Archbishop Janssens reverted to the two separate editions, one in French and one in English, in 1889.

Archbishop Chapelle moved to a unique layout. His letters were published side by side, but now English rather than French appeared on the left side. During Archbishop Chapelle's appointment to the Philippine Islands,

TABLE 4.2. Style and language of pastoral letters

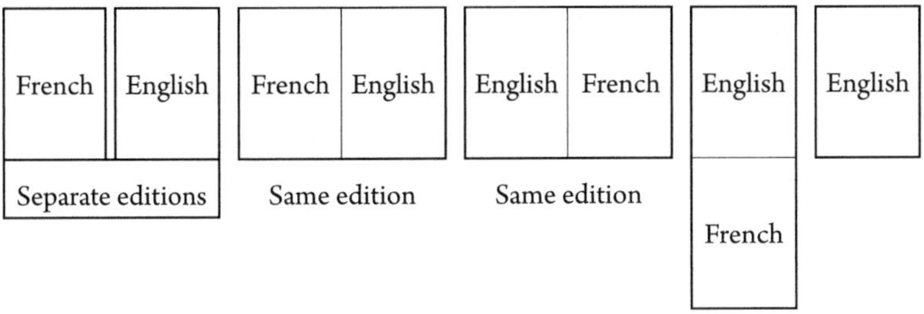

TABLE 4.3. Pastoral letters to clergy and laity analyzed by style, language, year, and archbishop/administrator

		PASTORAL LETTER			
Year(s)	*Archbishop/administrator*	*Separate editions*	*Side by side F/E**	*Side by side E/F*	*One edition—entire letter E/F***
1844–60	Blanc	x			
1861–69	Odin	x			
1870–83	Perché	x			
1879–86	Leray		x		
1879–88	Rouxel (administrator)		x		
1889–95	Janssens	x			
1899–1906	Chapelle			x	
1900	Rouxel (administrator)				x
1904	Laval (vicar-general)				x
1906–12	Blenk				x
1913	Blenk	x			
1914–18	Blenk				x
1919	Shaw	x			
1920–34	Shaw	English only			

*F = French; E = English

**There was no edition with the entire letter F/E.

his administrators (Rouxel and Laval) began using a different format where the entire English letter appeared first and the French letter followed. No longer were the texts side by side. Archbishop Blenk continued with this format. With only two exceptions, in 1913 and 1919, each archbishop was consistent in format. Archbishop Shaw wrote only one letter that was published in French and English in separate editions. This was the first year that he was archbishop. From 1920 forward, the pastoral letters were published in English only.

To summarize, for the predominantly French administration that managed the Church from 1861 to 1887, bilingualism was the *modus operandi.* The Archiepiscopal Council minutes were in French, archdiocesan newspapers were published in French, and pastoral letters were written in French and English to reach out to francophone and anglophone communities. Still, many sacramental registers switched from French to English during this administration. The decline of French registers was somewhat compensated for by the creation of new churches in French-speaking areas. If Archbishop Blanc's tenure, during which English was introduced within the Church, is taken together with the tenures of Archbishops Odin, Perché, and Leray, one can say that French and English cohabited in the Louisiana Church during a period of more than seventy-five years. This being said, the Archiepiscopal Council minutes and the metalinguistic comments demonstrate increasing concern at the turn of the century for those Catholics who spoke English and who no longer attended services where French and German were spoken. While French archdiocesan administrations endured political and social disruptions as well as financial disarray, bilingualism was fading out from Louisiana legislative and judicial civil branches and being replaced by English only.

By 1888, one could no longer be certain that archbishops in the Archdiocese of New Orleans would be French. In the archbishops' administration, there is written evidence, other than the archbishops' nationality, that a switch from French to English occurred. Recruitment of English-speaking clergy, both native- and foreign-born, considerably augmented the staff of the Archiepiscopal Council. Administrative discussions entirely in English were more frequent and minutes began to be transcribed in

English by 1913. A few years after the sacramental registers at the St. Louis Cathedral, the heart of the archdiocesan administration, switched from French to English (1911), the publication of a new Catholic newspaper in English was approved by the Archiepiscopal Council and pastoral letters were only published in English (1920). The archdiocesan administration's location also influenced its practices. Being situated in New Orleans, where the shift from French to English was almost completed within the general population, local language factors (education, church parishes, French-speaking communities) no longer existed or were not robust enough to slow the path of language change within the last French institution in Louisiana.

5

PARISH PRIESTS AS AGENTS OF LINGUISTIC CHANGE

Analyzing the Data

As both rural and urban communities develop, places of worship are usually among the first structures built in them. In south Louisiana, that first structure was usually a Catholic church which inevitably formed the heart of the community. Prior to building a church, Catholics often gathered in someone's home and attended mass celebrated by a visiting priest. Once the community grew large enough, the Catholics would build a church and petition the bishop to assign a permanent priest, thus establishing the church parish and becoming what would fit Wenger's definition of a community of practice. The church brought together the community, and the church's documents —the sacramental registers, parish visitation reports, correspondence to the archbishop, and the historical documents of the parish—recorded the life of the parish in a way state or civil parish records never could. These documents were the responsibility of the parish priest, either to write or to respond to. He was the church official who most intimately dealt with language issues.

As in all Catholic parishes for the last millennium and a half or more, the priest (pastor) was in charge of the church parish administration, its school, councils, committees, finances, building maintenance, and so forth; his ecclesiastical duties included celebrating Mass, baptizing babies (and adults), hearing confessions, performing marriages, burying the dead, and counseling the faithful. He was the visible head of the local Catholic community, and direction of the parishioners came from him. However, he did not leave the parishioners without a voice, sometimes a powerful one. In the end, the church parish was only as strong as its parishioners wished and the money that supported it. In antebellum times, Louisiana congregations were not always interested in having a dominating priest in the area. At several churches, including St. Louis Cathedral in New Orleans, Ascension of Our Lord in Donaldsonville, and St. John the Baptist in Brusly, the friction between the church wardens and the priest escalated to the point of temporarily closing the church until the control issues were resolved. The Antebellum Correspondence is peppered with complaints about parish priests who delivered bad sermons, mismanaged finances, were hot-tempered, etcetera. As noted previously, among the metalinguistic comments were complaints concerning the inability of priests to provide sermons in English and/or the inability of the parishioners to understand a priest with heavily accented English.

Accordingly, the archbishop was often called upon to settle disagreements between the priest and his parishioners. This often resulted in a face-to-face meeting with the dean, who relayed the information to the archbishop, and if necessary, the priest was summoned to New Orleans to meet with the archbishop to discuss the complaints. Directives to the priest and his parishioners were ultimately conveyed through the top-down structure of the institutional Church. But as in all organizational structures, conflict often resulted in local agreement and accommodation without decisions from above. Even with parishioner against parishioner and priest against priest, the local pastors and the laity often collectively negotiated the church's community life and their local relationships in order to make peace with each other and, not coincidentally, to avoid a decision from the archdiocese that possibly would satisfy no one.

Although known for conservatism, the upper rank of the archdiocese nevertheless understood that parish priests, both foreign-born and native-born, were more in touch with the local parishioners than the archdiocesan administration. Language choice in the sacramental registers as well as

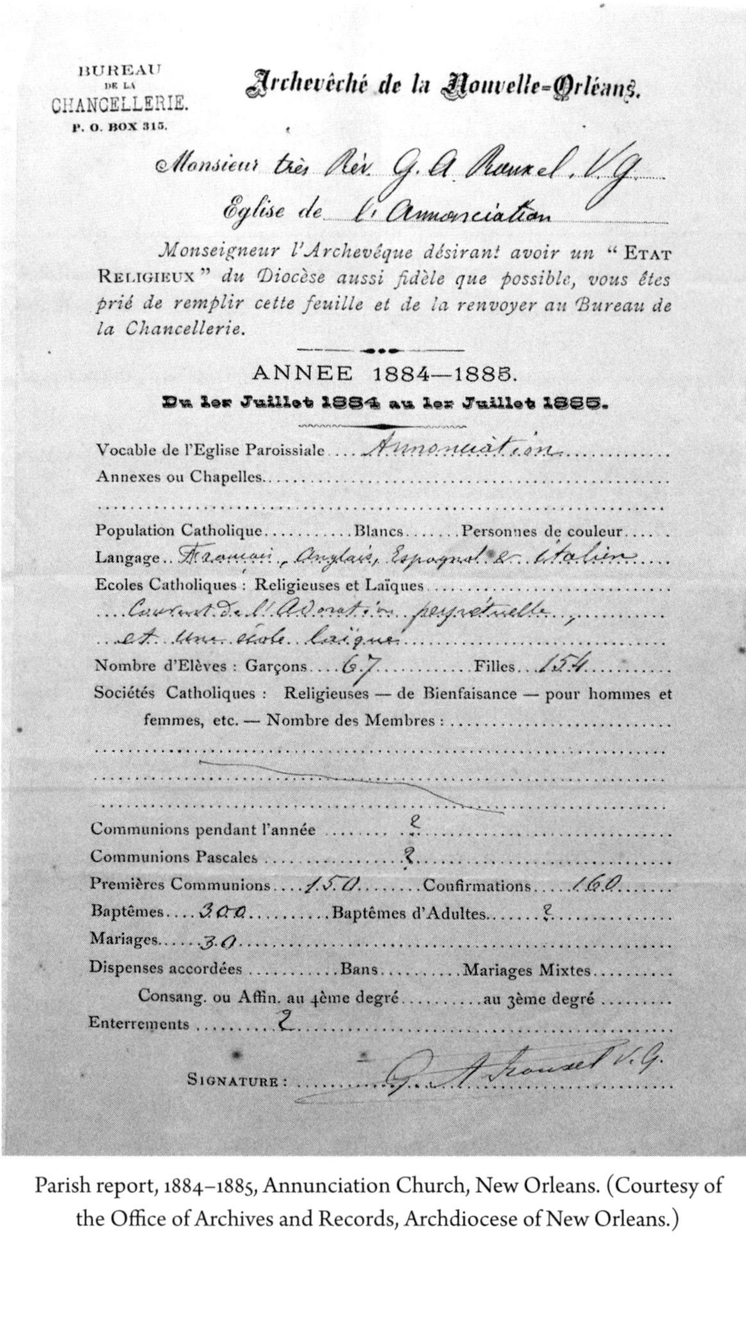

BUREAU DE LA CHANCELLERIE.
P. O. BOX 315.

Archevêché de la Nouvelle-Orléans.

Monsieur très Rév G. A. Rouxel, V.G.
Eglise de l'Annonciation

Monseigneur l'Archevêque désirant avoir un "ETAT RELIGIEUX" du Diocèse aussi fidèle que possible, vous êtes prié de remplir cette feuille et de la renvoyer au Bureau de la Chancellerie.

ANNEE 1884—1885.

Du 1er Juillet 1884 au 1er Juillet 1885.

Vocable de l'Eglise Paroissiale ... Annonciation ...
Annexes ou Chapelles ...
...
Population Catholique ... Blancs ... Personnes de couleur ...
Langage .. Français, Anglais, Espagnol & Italien ...
Ecoles Catholiques : Religieuses et Laïques ...
... Couvent de l'Adoration perpétuelle, ...
... et une école laïque ...
Nombre d'Elèves : Garçons ... 67 ... Filles ... 154 ...
Sociétés Catholiques : Religieuses — de Bienfaisance — pour hommes et femmes, etc. — Nombre des Membres : ...
...
Communions pendant l'année ... ? ...
Communions Pascales ... ? ...
Premières Communions ... 150 ... Confirmations ... 160 ...
Baptêmes ... 300 ... Baptêmes d'Adultes ... ? ...
Mariages ... 30 ...
Dispenses accordées ... Bans ... Mariages Mixtes ...
Consang. ou Affin. au 4ème degré ... au 3ème degré ...
Enterrements ... 2 ...

SIGNATURE : G. A. Rouxel V.G.

Parish report, 1884–1885, Annunciation Church, New Orleans. (Courtesy of the Office of Archives and Records, Archdiocese of New Orleans.)

sermons was a matter left in the hands of the local pastors, who literally had to speak the language of the people. Therefore, parish priests acted as agents of linguistic change within the Church and by extension their community. By switching registers from French to English, they gave a tangible sign of the church's agreement to language change within their parish. But more importantly, these record switches reflect the linguistic attitudes of the priest and his language beliefs, or perhaps his beliefs in what was best for his parish. Given the amount of autonomy granted to parish priests in language matters, the local priests therefore determined the diffusion of language change throughout the Louisiana Church and are key figures in determining the cause and rate of diffusion. While it is impossible to tell the personal motives of any of these priests toward language, the evidence uncovered can help make inferences.

DATABASE CONSTRUCTION

With the expectation that the Archdiocese of New Orleans Antebellum Correspondence would reveal the internal and external constraints upon language switch in the sacramental registers, approximately 1,450 letters that contained metalinguistic comments about the south Louisiana language situation were analyzed. From those comments, databases were created that organized the information so as to allow comparison with material from the sacramental registers. The databases help clarify three aspects about what led parish priests to switch their language practice from French to English.

1. *The role of the parish priest.* Did the arrival of new priests cause or influence the register switch—the "new broom" explanation? The assumption is that the arriving priests started writing sacramental entries in English because of their lack of language skills in French, their belief that English was the language of the future, or their determination that the congregation would prefer English records. Answering this question requires determining first how many register switches clearly correlate with a change of parish priest. Then, to evaluate whether the register switches converge with the changing population of priests (that is, with the addition

of more American-born priests), it is necessary to ascertain the origins of new parish priests serving in the Archdiocese of New Orleans from 1860 to 1920. Several sources can be used to collect data on the priests during this time period: the archdiocesan *Official Catholic Directory* collection, the United States Census, and Archbishop Janssens' diary.[1] Combining these three sources gives a detailed if not perfect data about the nationality of south Louisiana priests over an extended period.

2. *The diffusion of English registers throughout the Louisiana Church.* Conversely, did population and geographic factors, especially population density and distance from the administrative see, influence parish priests in their language practice and lead to a measurable geographic pattern of spread? For example, was New Orleans a diffusion center that first affected language practices in neighboring cities or parishes and afterward those at a greater distance? Was language change related to urbanization, so that language change moved outward from New Orleans to other cities and only later to towns and villages? Would priests preaching in remote parishes be more inclined to maintain registers longer in French? Did priests assigned to parishes with a high-density population bring about language change sooner than those performing duties in less populated parishes? To understand the spatial trajectory of the English registers in the archdiocese, the effectiveness of three social geographical models (the wave model, the hierarchical model, and the gravity model) were tested.

3. *The effect that the spread of rival Protestant congregations had on language change.* Was the parish priests' overriding motivation for language change rooted in important religious changes taking place in their locality? In other words, did social and perceptual constraints not accounted for in purely geographical models affect language change within local parishes? Was the spread of rival Protestant congregations one of these constraints?

THE ROLE OF THE PARISH PRIEST

Within the sacramental registers from 173 selected church parishes, the switch to English in the registers was seldom accompanied by an explanatory comment, direct or indirect. In the records analyzed there was only one such case: a priest's annotation on the margins of a register from St. Peter Church in Reserve in St. John the Baptist Parish, where Father Bandearin wrote on December 6, 1914: "From the First Sunday of Advent of the year 1914, these records will be written in English, this doing away with the necessity of translation when copies are made from them."[2] This interesting statement indicates that there was a nominal economic motivation for language change, but also that the major demand was for English-language copies. Translation could be an additional expense and was apparently not one of Father Bandearin's skills. Writing in English could save the parish money and time as well as possibly inaccurate copies. But mainly the statement suggests strongly that by 1914 Father Bandearin and other priests were still keeping French records that could not be read accurately by their parishioners or others who needed official copies. In another revealing instance of an obvious reason for change, two switches, St. Mary in Charenton in 1921 and St. Anne in Youngsville in 1924, were clearly related to the bishop's visit. After he inspected the records for accuracy (formula, up-to-dateness, no irregularities, etc.), he signed them. In both cases, all entries prior to the bishop's signature were in French; those following his signature were and continued in English. It would be highly revealing to know what the bishop said to the priests about the language of their registers, but, this being lost to history, only an educated guess based on the results of this conversation can be made.

For most churches, however, no such obvious clues whatsoever from the registers shed light on the priests' motives for the change. Nevertheless, a wider examination of evidence shows that individual priests had an important impact on the language shift in record keeping. Most notably, half of the register switches coincide with a priest change. At the height of the shift period, was the incoming population of priests different in terms of language use than the one already in place? To answer this question, a priest database was created which includes their social attributes (year of birth, name, secular/religious order) as well as their country of origin and church parish (city, civil parish, and present-day diocese). Country of origin was established for 99% of all parish priests collected for this study.[3] In total, the database includes 1,043 new priests during a period of six decades, ranging from 1860 to 1920.

Results from the quantitative analysis indicate one strong tendency: the body of priests who ministered in the Archdiocese of New Orleans from 1860 to 1920 changed from a heavily dominated French-born clergy to a more multi-ethnic clergy. Figure 5.1 is a bar graph depicting the priests from the six countries with the highest percentages of priests. Trend lines were added to display the decline of French-born priests in comparison to the rise in American-born priests. In 1860, of the sixty-two priests serving in parishes, thirty-nine were from France, nine from Ireland and seven from Italy. These numbers and their proportions in themselves reveal the attention of Archbishop Blanc's administration to patterns of immigration to the state. None were from Louisiana or other US states. From 1860 to 1890, more than 60% of the priests who served in the archdiocese were born in France. However, between 1900 and 1920 this percentage diminished by half (31%), in direct contrast with the number of American-born priests, which more than doubled (25%). The number of Netherlands-born and German-born priests went from 0% to 10% and 8% respectively.

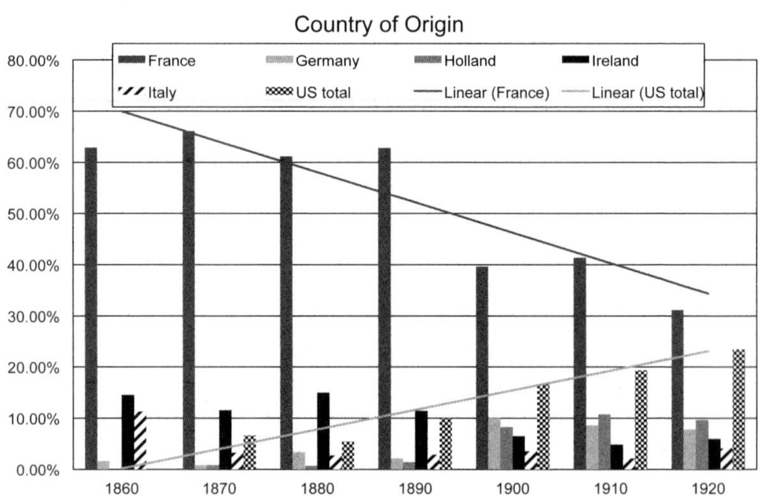

Figure 5.1. Countries of origin of priests

What figure 5.1 does not reveal, however, is that over half the American-born priests in 1920 were also Louisiana-born. This indicates that, during the preceding decades, the archdiocese began to recruit men from Louisiana to enter the priesthood and started to appoint native-born Louisiana seminarians. The change first happened around 1885 when Archbishop Janssens invited German Benedictines to establish a minor seminary (St. Joseph Seminary in Gessen)[4] to educate Louisiana-born men. Later, Archbishop Chapelle opened a short-lived major seminary (St. Louis Seminary in New Orleans). These facilities had an impact on the number of Louisiana-born and American-born priests who served in Louisiana. In 1870, there were four Louisiana-born priests and four American-born priests; by 1910, their respective number doubled and it tripled ten years later.

Let us recall what led to this institutional change. Foreign-born priests were no longer available to work in south Louisiana for a number of socio-political reasons, all of which were raised exponentially by the First World War. Recruitment from within the United States was therefore critical to meet the need of the archdiocese. In 1915, Archbishop Blenk addressed the issue of the shortage of priests in his pastoral letter of March 22:

> It is high time that our people realize their responsibilities toward the Church in Louisiana. The war now raging in Europe has only emphasized and aggravated a problem which is daily becoming more serious in this diocese. If the old faith is to be preserved and handed down to future generations; if the Church is not to be checked or retarded in her onward march, a sufficient number of priests is necessary to carry on her blessed work. We can no longer count upon Europe to come to our assistance in our need. She was more than generous in the past in sending to us the choicest of her sons who willingly and cheerfully left home and country to give the best that was in them to the service of the Church in Louisiana. But to-day [*sic*], conditions at home forbid her to continue to make such sacrifices. A large number of her seminaries are closed and the students dispersed. Some sixty-five thousand of her consecrated sons have answered their countries' call and are now serving under their respective flags. When the war-cloud will have cleared away, the ranks of the Clergy will have been so thinned and decimated that there will be no priests to spare for the mission fields afar.[5]

Data results point to some explanations for the preservation of French-language records in many parishes. First, the priestly population was rapidly changing from French-dominant to bilingual-dominant at the end of the nineteenth century. Second, many of these new priests were local seminarians. As such, they could write in both French and English and switching registers could not have originated from a lack of knowledge in the French language. Since the archdiocese was conscious that appointing priests who could not speak French would antagonize its French-speaking base, this new membership contributed to the preservation of French records until the twentieth century and well after the prohibition of French in Louisiana schools.

One might, however, suppose that the minority of newly arrived English-speaking priests would immediately initiate a change, all other things being equal, but the actual situation was more nuanced. Although in a few cases a new monolingual English-speaking priest would indeed arrive and switch all registers to English, bilingual priests of both French and English origins initiated most of the language changes to English. In several instances, French-born priests actually started using English in the sacramental registers that were previously kept in French by English-speaking priests.

However, when there was more than one priest ministering at a church, the arrival of a new priest would often lead to an extensive period of bidialectal recording, each priest writing in a different language. This was the case at St. Elizabeth in Paincourtville, which had twenty-seven years of bilingual registers, after which the registers were kept only in English. The most interesting extreme bilingualism case is St. Mary in New Orleans, a one-priest church with register entries switching back and forth between French and English for sixty years due to a long succession of new priests.[6] Father Ceuppens introduced English, but Father Vallée who succeeded him five years later reinstated French. Following Father Vallée's death, Father Bichlmayer started writing in Latin and English but this practice ended with the arrival of Father Fusilier, who switched back to French. Ten years later, he suddenly began writing all his entries in English and from then on French vanished. The extensive bilingual behavior of most of the priests and the bilingual nature of several registers due to a succession of officiating priests at one church are particularly striking and represent another argument against the idea that language change in Louisiana happened suddenly. However, the number of francophone priests such as Father Fuselier who made an obviously reluctant but nevertheless decisive and permanent switch to English suggests the considerable social pressure to make the change.

Sometimes bilingual priests waited for an auspicious moment or an important change in the way registers were published. Upon their arrival, new priests might either introduce English or make their first entries in French (perhaps out of respect for the tradition or the former priest) but then change to English with the convenient arrival of a new register, a new year, or even a new month. These types of switching strategies account for a third of changes by priests. More importantly, of all transition-time switches we recorded, many coincided with a change of the register book format, that is, the replacement of hand-written registers by standardized preprinted forms in French, Latin, and English which became available chiefly during the first two decades of the twentieth century. Local priests were suddenly given the option of ordering registers formatted in the preferred language (French, Latin, or English). After investigating this issue, we noticed that preprinted forms often paved the way to language change in the registers of the churches from the diocese of Lafayette, as compared to the Archdiocese of New Orleans and the Diocese of Baton Rouge, where a higher number of priest changes are found. Before the introduction of preprinted registers in English, all handwritten entries in registers from several churches in Abbeville, Arnaudville, Breaux Bridge, New Iberia, St. Martinville, and Ville Platte were written in French. For a very short period the priests completed English forms in French and soon after they shifted to English one after another.

Evidence of the priests' daily moving easily from one language to another is found in the entries themselves in the form of capitalization of French months (*Mai* instead of *mai*), calques (buried the *corps* rather than the *body*), gallicisms (*legitimate girl of* rather than *daughter*). The presence of both languages within a single entry, however, is more an indication of the priest's bilingualism, although sometimes it is not clear which language the priest is more comfortable in. At St. Paul in Bayou Goula, one burial entry reads,

> *Dans le cimetière de St. Paul le dixseptieme jour de Mai 1889 a ete inhumé le corps de Marie Louirou* daughter of Jean Louiriou and Lucia Vandevegna aged three years who died of aphesia.[7]

These mixed entries were not an exception. Another from St. Raphael on the same date reads,

> *Dans le cimetière de St. Raphael a ete inhumé Dina Bernard* daughter of Taylor Bernard and of Cécile Bernard aged about thirteen years old who died in West Baton Rouge.[8]

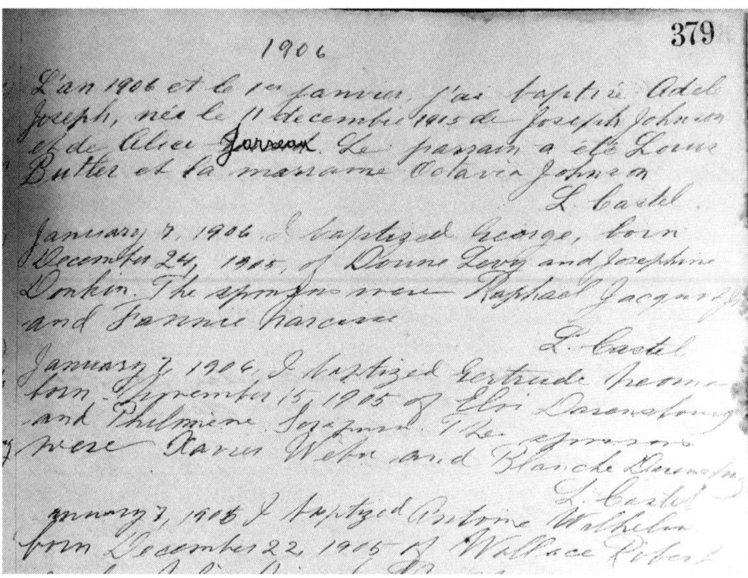
379
1906
L'an 1906 et le 1er janvier, j'ai baptisé Adele Joseph, née le 11 décembre 1905 de Joseph Johnson et de Alice Jarreau. Le parrain a été Louis Butler et la marraine Octavia Johnson
L. Castel
January 7, 1906 I baptized George, born December 24, 1905, of Donne Levy and Josephine Dorkin. The sponsors were Raphael Jacquet and Fannie Narcisse
L. Castel
January 7, 1906, I baptized Gertrude [illegible] born September 15, 1905 of Eloi [illegible] and Philomene [illegible]. The sponsors were [illegible] Weber and Blanche [illegible]
L. Castel
January 7, 1906 I baptized Antoine Wilhelm born December 22, 1905 of Wallace Robert

Baptismal register, St. John the Baptist Church, Edgard, Louisiana, book 12, 1886–1906, page 379. (Courtesy of the Office of Archives and Records, Archdiocese of New Orleans.)

This entry is also the last one in (partial) French; from this date forward, all records are in English. These examples suggest the tug of one language against another by priests who used both daily and dropped easily from one to the other.

THE SUCCESSIVE DIFFUSION OF ENGLISH ACROSS THE SOUTH LOUISIANA SPACE

In his article in the *Handbook of Language Variation and Change*,[9] David Britain argues convincingly that sociolinguists should pay more attention to the concept of geographical space to better understand change and status within communities and differentiation among language features and innovations.[10] In order to apply spatial geographical models to the current data, New Orleans, the cathedral city and administrative center for much of the period, was selected as a central area, leaving seventy-six local churches situated outside of Orleans civil parish for investigation.

The first spatial model examined is the wave model, "whereby innovations, over time, radiate from a central local area, reaching physically nearby locations before those at even greater distances" as explained in detail by Britain.[11] The prediction based on this model would be that New Orleans as a diffusion center initially affected language practices in neighboring cities or parishes and afterward those at a greater distance. After calculating the distance for all places, the scores were divided into five categories ranging from very close (8–28 miles), close (38–57), medium (65–78), far (83–116), and very distant (130–58) localities from New Orleans.

The second explanatory spatial model is the hierarchical model, "with innovations descending down an urban hierarchy of large city to city, to large town, to town, village, and country."[12] To calculate the effect of population density, the year 1895 was selected because most switches from French to English in the sacramental registers happened during this period and especially because accurate population numbers from the Louisiana 1895 census for all cities, including small villages, were available. The underlying assumption is that French would be supplanted by English first in churches located in urban centers such as Donaldsonville (pop. 3,121), Plaquemine (3,222), and Gretna (3,332), followed by smaller towns such as Napoleonville (723), New Roads (525), and Bayou Goula (769), and finally in villages such as Vacherie (100) and French Settlement (76). This hierarchical model is composed of four categories: urban centers (10,000–3,000 inhabitants), cities (2,000–1,000), towns (750–300), and villages (100–50).[13]

Finally, the gravity model is a combination model of "distance and population [which] interacted in the likely influence two places would have on each other, and that they could be used to predict the routes of change an innovation can take."[14] This model predicts that places with high gravity index should adopt innovations earlier and smaller centers less so. Juan Hernández-Campoy has shown the explanatory potential of the gravity model by calculating a formula index called the "interaction potential index."[15] This gravity index was adapted here by multiplying the 1895 population of each city (where a church is located) with New Orleans as a diffusion center, and then "dividing that total by the square of the distance between the two places." This calculation provided a continuous index ranging from 31 to 0.007, which was subsequently divided into five gravity categories: very high, high, medium, low, and very low. This gravity index anticipates that the new practice of English registers in New Orleans will be disseminated in a hierarchical way, starting with cities with a very high index and in the end reaching cities with a very low index.[16]

Table 5.1 shows the mean results (categorical variable) and probabilities (continuous variable) for the three geographical models. In general, the results from these models were not encouraging in their explanatory power for this case. The explanatory potential of the wave model is weak, since it shows that very close cities switch earlier but those situated farther away from New Orleans do not shift according to distance. The gravity index for Baton Rouge as a diffusion center was also calculated, excluding cities near New Orleans. The assumption was that this urban center could have influenced cities located in southwestern Louisiana, where many Acadians lived (e.g., Opelousas, Lafayette, Breaux Bridge). None of the

TABLE 5.1. Correlation between three models of geographical diffusion and the switch date in registers used as a categorical (mean) and continuous variable (probability). New Orleans as the diffusion center (population: 242, 039 in 1895).

	Number of Cities	*Switch Mean*
WAVE MODEL		
Very close	5	1893
Close	16	1915
Medium	18	1910
Far	14	1886
Very distant	23	1917
	76	**Prob. > 0.24**
HIERARCHICAL MODEL		
Urban centers	13	1888
Cities	16	1909
Towns	17	1911
Villages	30	1918
	76	**Prob. > 0.0001**
GRAVITY MODEL		
Very high	5	1867
High	11	1900
Medium	7	1903
Low	30	1913
Very low	23	1921
	76	**Prob. > 0.04**

geographical models had a significant effect. Thibodaux and Opelousas as diffusion centers were also calculated in their own geographical locations. No correlation was found.

Of the three models, the hierarchical model is the best explanatory model for the data, with urban centers introducing English registers first,

Figure 5.2. Analysis of variance between the date of switch from French to English in church registers and each population density category.

followed by cities, towns, and villages last. However, the distribution of all data values per category is extremely broad. Some of the earliest village switches happen before the last switch in both cities and towns, and the latest city switches occur later than those in some towns. Since population density is calculated within the gravity index, its effect is low but perceptible, with English replacing French hierarchically from very high to very low, but the mean values for the three median categories are extremely close and, again, the extensive range for all switches per category remains a problem.[17]

Figure 5.2 shows the results of a more elaborate analysis of variance between the date of switch from French to English and the population density categories. The mean switch for all cities is shown as a horizontal line across the plot. The rectangular boxes represent the ANOVA mean for each population category with a line drawn at the average switch. The upper and lower points of each box span a 95% confident interval computed from all switches for each population category, whereas the height of each box spans the distance on the horizontal axis proportional to the category size, which shows the numerical importance of villages compared to urban centers and cities, including the extreme values from the center of the data. What is observed from this graph is that the mean of the urban centers is much lower; that is, the shift occurs much earlier, but the mean scores of the other population categories appear to be nearly the same. There is tremendous variation within each category. For urban centers, the mean switch is 1888, but the earliest switch happened in 1854 (Baton Rouge) and the latest in 1925 (St. Martinville)—that is, after a majority of churches located in cities and towns changed their records. The range of variation is even larger for villages where switches happened before the switch mean of cities and towns.

Figure 5.3 is a graph that confirms the restricted effect of population density (calculated here as a continuous variable) on the database. The first regression line (top graph) shows that population categories significantly condition the switch from French to English records ($p < 0.001$). However, when a new regression analysis is done with urban centers alone (bottom graph), this factor loses its significance ($p < 0.05$). In other words, only the distinction from urban centers to other less populated cities is significant; the effect of the hierarchical model cannot explain the spatial spread of English records in cities with less than two thousand inhabitants.

Satisfactory spatial causes and motivations so far using regular statistical methodologies alone to determine the language practice of the archdiocese are few. There appear to be no physical constraints for its diffusion. Although the establishment of Catholic churches follows the Mississippi River and the western railroad track from north to south, these physical landmarks did not shape the shift. The same can be said about population density as well as spatial distance between the cities and New Orleans, where the new practice was introduced. The only significant motivation is that highly populated cities (thirteen urban centers with more than two thousand inhabitants) all switched earlier. The underlying hypothesis is that parish priests first started recording in sacramental registers in English in high-density localities to accommodate the ever-growing number of English speakers as well as the French families of successful planters who became bilingual and even monolingual in English. However, no spatial models explain the diffusion of English for the majority of churches located in sparsely populated cities, towns, and villages, several of them situated in undesirable or undeveloped farming areas.

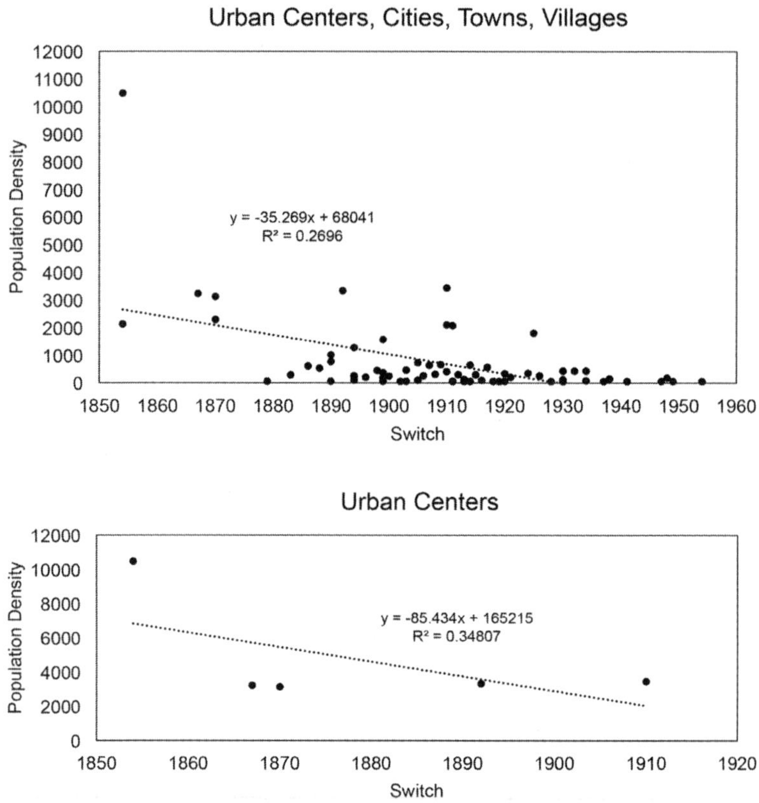

Figure 5.3. Regression analyses of the date of the language switch and population density. The first graph shows all communities (urban centers, cities, towns, villages); the second, urban centers.

One important aspect of the language situation in Louisiana cannot be extracted from the registers and is often overlooked by researchers, linguists, and humanities scholars alike: when French-speaking Louisianans started to learn English in the earlier nineteenth century, *English speakers were already found at all levels of society, from the top to the bottom of the social pyramid.*[18] Before the Civil War, English was observably important in all parishes in Louisiana and English speakers quickly became the majority in urban areas such as New Orleans (Smith 1936, Scott 1992, Walton 1994, Lambert 1995, Cheramie 1999, Fontenot 2003, Emmitte 2013).[19] What is less commonly known is that they also were in the majority in several rural areas. Both French-speaking and English-speaking sugarcane and cotton plantations of different sizes were established throughout rural Louisiana. Most slaves in the rural regions, including St. Landry and St. Martin civil parishes, were Protestant and English-speaking. In other words, the entire local population—the French-speaking elite and planters, French-speaking landowning farmers, field hands, laborers, and slaves—came into contact with English-speaking groups simultaneously during periods of massive immigration and began to learn English concurrently.[20] (Of course, language contact did not happen under the same conditions for each social class in each locality.)

These facts call for an exploration of a locally based spatial approach that could better reveal the social constraints of language change. One authority puts this aspect succinctly: "Linguistic change is slow to the extent that the relevant populations are well established and bound by strong ties, whereas it is rapid to the extent that weak ties exist in populations."[21] In this present study, several constraints could have led to place-specific effects. The established register of the churches in each civil parish was first examined. The prediction then would be that early established churches would have had decades to develop a solid congregation of French-speaking wardens and parishioners and, therefore, would be more resistant to change. Churches established early on would inhibit language change not because there were fewer English-speaking parishioners in these regions but because the bilingual or French-dominant local priests and church wardens chose to maintain bilingualism rather than outright change as the accommodating strategy to language contact, that is, the ever-increasing English speakers who came to their localities. However, again the prediction was not supported by the data. After analysis, the date of the earliest registers proved to have no overall particular effect on language change. Conversely, churches with late registers did not switch sooner or later than churches with early ones, even when registers are analyzed separately according to their current diocese. Further explanation must be sought.

THE ESTABLISHMENT OF PROTESTANT INSTITUTIONS WITHIN CATHOLIC PARISHES

At the turn of the twentieth century, when most of the switches occurred, the archdiocese was particularly concerned with the increasing number of Protestant institutions setting up across south Louisiana. It also feared their influence over state affairs and was concerned about the increased number of English-speaking local parishioners who might feel more affinity with anglophone Protestants. Several letters mentioned the political threat posed by other faiths, indirectly highlighting the importance of preaching in English to prevent people seeking out other religious avenues.

In the preface of the 1830 *Annales* of the Society for the Propagation of the Faith, the author reported on the progression of Protestant denominations in the United States.

> We must now form an idea of the appalling intellectual confusion in which the Americans have fallen; they hear in turn the ministers of varying beliefs, who strive to attract them to their side; but more often, their disconcerted reason by the perpetual shocks between the varying and conflicting dogmas that we submit for their approval, not daring to speak of it. This singularly promotes the enterprises of these protestant preachers; it is the pleasure that the American have at hearing the preaching; they go to the sermon as we go to a show; the long speeches don't disgust them, they are tormented by the need to occupy themselves with religion.[22]

With suggestions like this from the data, another hypothesis was posed: the increasing number of Protestant institutions in parishes once dominated by the archdiocese triggered the language change at a local level. The assumption is thus that a higher proportion of Protestant organizations in one location would have compelled local parish priests to shift from French to English early on, not only to lure more parishioners to the Catholic faith but also to avoid losing the ever-increasing number of English-speaking Catholics of French origin. The priests' overriding motivation for language change would therefore be rooted in their perception of the spread of Protestant institutions in their locality.

To verify the effect that the Protestant congregation had on language change within parishes, data was collected from the 1850 and 1890 US Census statistical reports on religious organizations, which list the number of churches and the value of church property for each denomination per Louisiana civil parish. The 1850 report is of lesser value because the number of Protestant churches during this period was very low in several Louisiana southern civil parishes, the majority having not a single Methodist, Episcopalian, or Baptist church. Once again, New Orleans prefigured future trends. The 1850 census shows there was an almost equal number of Protestant (11) and Catholic (13) churches in New Orleans with the value of Protestant property significantly higher ($2,385,000) compared to that of Catholics ($722,000). Moreover, a comparison between the 1850 and 1890 reports shows that the number of Protestant organizations exploded everywhere in Louisiana, with the founding of sixty new churches in New Orleans alone. Pointe Coupée Parish held the Protestant growth record with no churches in 1850 but thirty-nine in 1890. By that time, there were approximately four times more Protestant churches than Catholic churches in all parishes studied with the exception of Plaquemines (4/4).

Using the 1890 statistical report, the proportion of Methodist, Southern Baptist, "Colored Baptist," and Evangelical churches to the number of Catholic churches in each civil parish was calculated. Since by 1890 Protestant churches were more numerous and smaller than Catholic churches, the number of Protestant churches was normalized by adding 4 and multiplying the obtained value by the number of Catholic churches in each parish. A similar calculation was done for the value of church property because the value of Protestant property was in average 0.6 times lower than Catholic property. This proportion was then correlated to the switch date for each parish.[23]

Using this method, we arrived at one of our most critical findings. Figure 5.4 shows that the only significant correlation is between the proportional number of Protestant churches and the switch date from French to English, meaning that the higher the proportion of Protestant churches, the earlier the parish switch. Conversely, bilingual practices in the archdiocese were preserved until World War II in several parishes where the

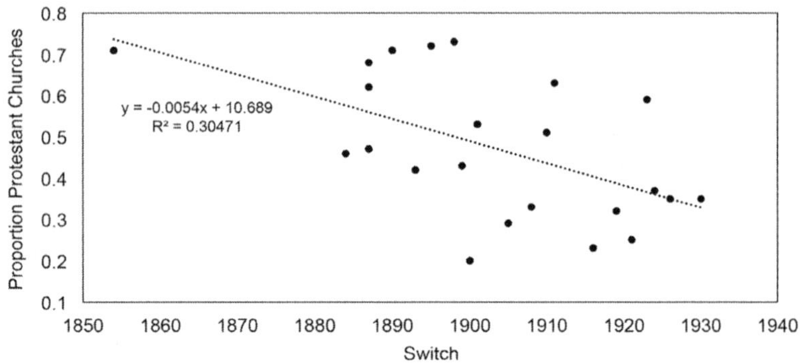

Figure 5.4. The proportion of Protestant churches versus Catholic churches in each parish in correlation with the switch mean of sacramental registers.

number of Protestant churches and the consequent level of competition were low.

Since, as we have seen, parishioner recruitment was intensely competitive and anti-Catholic sentiment was high, priests who could not speak English or conduct church business in English were aiding and abetting the enemy by giving them fodder for their "calumnious falsehoods."[24] These attitudes generated political tension between French Catholic and English Catholic priests, as between the old French-dominant and the bilingual young priests who were favored by archbishops for their ability to learn English quickly. The archdiocese was not going to hold on to French where its preservation lowered their chances to maintain the spiritual welfare of its practitioners and even convert new members.

A preliminary study conducted in 2005 by Louisiana State University graduate student Robert Connor shows the same direction.[25] Connor used the date of establishment of Protestant Episcopal churches in Louisiana from 1844 to 1900 (an aggregate number from the date of incorporation and the reported number of communicants from churches which preserved membership rolls). His reasoning was that the Protestant Episcopal Church was the most natural competition for the Catholic Church compared to other Protestant denominations which involve learning different practices and significant changes in beliefs. Episcopalians—members of the "reformed" Catholic church—and Catholics shared many practices and rituals but differed in language. Both churches were historically related and continued to worship, speak, and believe similarly. And they both also sought to expand to meet the religious needs of the communities from 1850 to 1920. To some extent the Protestant Episcopal Church even conducted sporadic missionary work in French in Louisiana. From 1835 to 1840, a French Protestant Episcopal church existed in New Orleans, providing bilingual worship services and Sunday School to fifty pupils in English, French, and Spanish. It was resurrected in 1847, grew to fifty-four communicants in 1851, but finally closed in 1874.[26]

Connor found a highly significant correlation between the switch date in sacramental registers and the date of the establishment of Protestant Episcopal churches in fourteen towns outside New Orleans ($p > 0.001$). When he included the ten churches in New Orleans (for a total of twenty-four churches), the probability that this establishment influenced the switch from French to English in registers grew stronger ($p > 0.0001$). The same happened when he removed the four small towns from his sample (Thibodaux, Pointe-à-la-Hache, Theriot, and Bayou Goula), a result which supports the geographical trend (urban centers shifted earlier than small towns) presented earlier. Connor also found a correlation between ten key towns of ten influential civil parishes where Protestant Episcopal and the Catholic churches were in competition ($p < 0.0001$). The establishment of a Protestant Episcopal church regularly predated the register switch from French to English by no more than ten years on average, except for small towns where the Episcopal membership was extremely low. Catholic churches located in cities with Protestant institutions (twenty-four) also switched earlier (1894) than those situated in cities (fifty-nine) without a strong Protestant presence (1914).

In other words, decisions by individual bilingual priests, most following their local knowledge of what was best for the Church, had an important impact on the language shift in record keeping. It is at the parish level that the decision to switch the language of record was made.

The fate of widespread bilingualism in the Louisiana Catholic Church was sealed by sociogeographical forces at their zenith at the turn of the twentieth century. Constraints such as population growth in urban centers, decreasing number of French speakers requesting church services in their language, and the spatial establishment of Protestant organizations throughout south Louisiana pressured the Church from outside. The hierarchical model, which measures population density, shows that the spread of written English as a new language practice first occurred in the few urban centers. Since the archbishop and his administration were located in New Orleans, the pressure to switch to English was greatest there, and it therefore occurred earlier. There were more Irish Catholics but also more Protestants in the urban areas, especially in New Orleans, which explains the early shift in the registers where these populations were located.

However, this model fails to explain the spread of written English throughout the majority of less populated church parishes. The Antebellum Correspondence proved invaluable in revealing social attitudes not found in the matter-of-fact entries in the registers and led us to test the correlation between the register switches and the establishment of Protestant churches, which inevitably appeared within each parish as immigrants poured into Louisiana and dispersed. To come to a valid conclusion using spatial data, then, it is necessary to use a variety of data, some of it possibly nonquantitative.

Nevertheless, some priests, even new ones, proved resistant to incoming change and kept writing registers in French. The way registers changed from one language to another and then back again as the officiating priests changed is particularly striking, suggesting that bilingualism and linguistic toleration were the norm.

6

LANGUAGE PRACTICES OF PRIESTS AND PARISHIONERS

Case Studies, 1885–1954

The priests were naturally in interaction with the language preferences of their parishioners from sunup to sundown, but many questions about the priests' role with respect to language change are unclear. What actual role did they play in the language shift, and in what parishes, and when? They were, after all, the speakers of the languages the Church had to accommodate. As early as 1832, parishioners in some parts of south Louisiana begged for English-speaking priests. But was this a collective call which reflected a strong linguistic shift in a parish? Or was it a demand emanating from a vocal language minority? What, indeed, were the language practices in individual church parishes? These very large questions are too complex to be answered solely from our evidence from church sources, if indeed they can be answered adequately from any of the surviving sources. But sufficient church documents can be analyzed to answer related questions: What did the local priests report about parishioners' bilingual competence? Is there evidence to indicate the priest's need to preach and/or conduct additional services in English or his ability to conduct these services in French? Answers to these questions will provide a more nuanced picture of the Church's role than the data about register changes, for additional church documents actually show the Church itself investigating some of the same questions.

Assessing the linguistic behavior of people living in a nineteenth-century community of practice is an elusive task which goes only as far as the volume of historical materials available about them and especially those written by them. Very little written material from ordinary citizens has been preserved until well into the twentieth century, for example, and that material is usually of little help. Extracting data from private correspondence might be one option but, even though large amounts of Louisiana family or personal documents have been preserved, the genre of private correspondence restricts any extrapolation or projection to the entire community of Catholic Church parishioners. The linguistic practices of the Church could easily have been discussed in private correspondence (high-ranking church officials did), but the Archdiocese of New Orleans's Antebellum Correspondence suggests they were not. Even if some letters are found that touch on the issue, they are still the reflections of an individual, and an individual who was likely to write a letter to a church official was in a distinct minority in the rural parishes at the time.

Yet fortuitously for researchers, the Church *itself* showed an interest in discovering and recording the language preferences in individual parishes. The Church's numerous codified procedures imbedded in its administrative documents and correspondence can provide wide, varied, numerically significant, but still largely standardized information on the direction of change in different church parishes. Analyzing the large amount of such church documentation can make a significant—although not decisive— contribution to understanding the changing language situation in many parishes.

Much valuable data may be found in varied documents which might be regarded as the Church's own linguistic study of its people—documents which suggest the language practices displayed both by the priests assigned to local church parishes and by the people who occupied the pews and attended Sunday services. A major archival source studied here is the "parish visitation reports," which attempted to indicate the ability and/or inability of the faithful to understand spoken English. Other sources include parish annual reports, correspondence files, historical boundaries, and financial reports. Taken together, they form a substantial if often fragmentary data collection of local church language practices.

Much language documentation was also reported by the Church to the US government, which collected data on religious organizations from 1906 to 1936, completing four surveys on religious membership. The 1906 US Census of Religious Bodies is especially important as it reveals the priests' language behavior at church services at the beginning of the twentieth century. The Archdiocese of New Orleans kept duplicates of the original census cards sent to the US government in 1906, and they are available for analysis. (No cards exist at the archdiocese for the subsequent census years.)

Questions on the census cards include the year of establishment, amount of debt on church property, number and value of church parsonages, language in which services were conducted, salaries paid to ministers, sex of communicants or members, and the number and membership of Sunday schools conducted by church organizations. Information pertaining to the "language in which services are conducted" was gathered from 160 cards that ranged from church parishes to small mission churches.

The vast amount of archival material, the large number of church parishes, their varied size, and the availability of comparable archival documents made it both more practical and revelatory to use case studies than to make one vast survey of all parishes of the Louisiana Catholic Church. This methodological choice allows a more refined look at the local conditions and sociolinguistic realities of representative church parishes. Thus, our analysis concentrates on six civil parishes, each composed of five or more church parishes with registers that began in French: Orleans civil parish (9 church parishes); Lafourche civil parish (7); Assumption civil parish (6); Iberville civil parish (5); St. James civil parish (5); and Vermilion civil parish (5), for a total of 37 church parishes. Grouping by civil parish geographical boundaries provides an easy visual demarcation and helps define the geographical area under study. Since many civil parishes were settled by immigrant populations, legal civil boundaries allow us to describe each network of church parishes with a supplemental cohesiveness and regional identity.

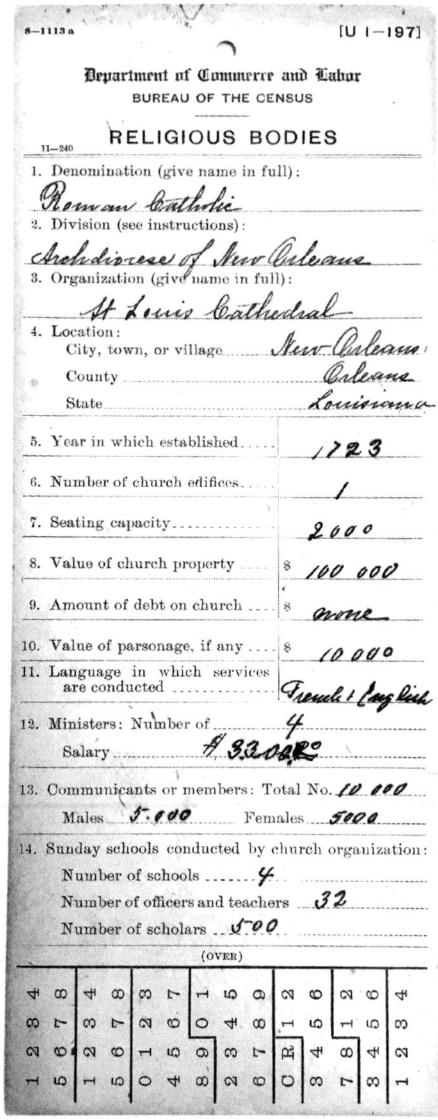

8—1113 a [U I—197]

Department of Commerce and Labor
BUREAU OF THE CENSUS

11—240 RELIGIOUS BODIES

1. Denomination (give name in full): Roman Catholic
2. Division (see instructions): Archdiocese of New Orleans
3. Organization (give name in full): St Louis Cathedral
4. Location:
City, town, or village .... New Orleans
County .... Orleans
State .... Louisiana

5. Year in which established.....	1723
6. Number of church edifices.....	1
7. Seating capacity............	2000
8. Value of church property	$ 100 000
9. Amount of debt on church	$ none
10. Value of parsonage, if any	$ 10 000
11. Language in which services are conducted	French & English

12. Ministers: Number of 4
Salary .... $ 3300.00
13. Communicants or members: Total No. 10 000
Males 5 000 Females 5000
14. Sunday schools conducted by church organization:
Number of schools 4
Number of officers and teachers 32
Number of scholars .. 500
(OVER)

Religious bodies census card, 1906, St. Louis Cathedral. (Courtesy of the Office of Archives and Records, Archdiocese of New Orleans.)

LANGUAGE USED IN THE SERVICE

The broadest and most fundamental data that could shed light on the parish linguistic situation at the time when the bulk of registers switched to English were extracted from the US Census of Religious Bodies. For example, one rough calculation of the percentage of Catholics living in the United States and in the state of Louisiana between 1906 and 1916 highlights the extent of Louisiana's Catholic identity compared to other states and, by extension, the importance of linguistic change in the Church with respect to that of the entire Louisiana population.

From 1906 to 1916, 60% of Louisianans were Catholics, whereas the percentage of Catholics in the United States did not exceed 3%. Dividing the state along the geographic borders of the dioceses, the Diocese of Natchitoches (the northern part of the state) and the Archdiocese of New Orleans (the southern part of the state), further illustrates the concentration of Catholics in south Louisiana. In the Archdiocese of New Orleans, more than 75% of the population was Catholic compared to roughly 20% of those living in the northern part of the state.

More critically, the census also collected information on the languages used in church services. Prior to changes made by the Roman Catholic Church in the 1960s, the mass was celebrated in Latin, but the homily was delivered in the vernacular. In the 1906 data cards the language of service was, not surprisingly, rarely noted as Latin. On 150 of the 160 cards (93.75%), the language used in the service was reported as English (29%) or French (26%), or a combination of English and French (38%). Other languages reported are in combination with English, such as English and German or English and Italian. One church reported a combination of English, Italian, and French, and in a unique case Hungarian was reported as the only language spoken. These data again indicate that the Church was making every attempt to accommodate its parishioners' language preferences.

Using these data to plot language usage on maps, first by individual church parish (fig. 6.1) and then by combining that information by civil

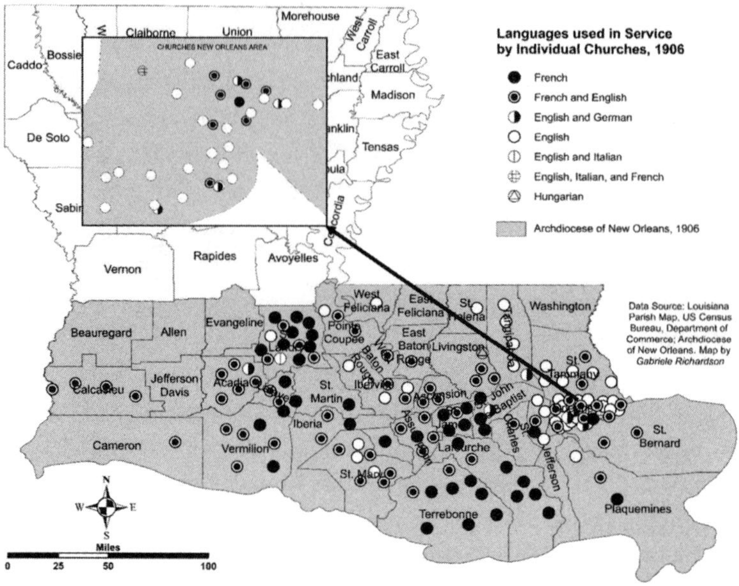

Figure 6.1. Languages used in services by individual churches, 1906

parish (fig. 6.2), illustrates the predominant use of English, French or English, and French across south Louisiana. First let us examine the data in figure 6.1.

The use of French exclusively is evident in the regions most identified with the Acadian culture—the civil parishes of St. Landry, St. Martin, St. James, St. John the Baptist, Lafourche, and Terrebonne. The use of English in New Orleans and the civil parishes nearest New Orleans is a clear indication of the city's change to English earlier than the rural areas. Iberville Parish appears to be a pocket of English surrounded heavily by French and French/English civil parishes. This scenario is consistent with the information found in the sacramental registers. Orleans and Iberville civil parishes have the earliest sacramental register switch dates of 1880 and 1887, respectively.

To illustrate the trend more clearly, in figure 6.2, languages are combined according to civil parish to further contrast the use of French and English.

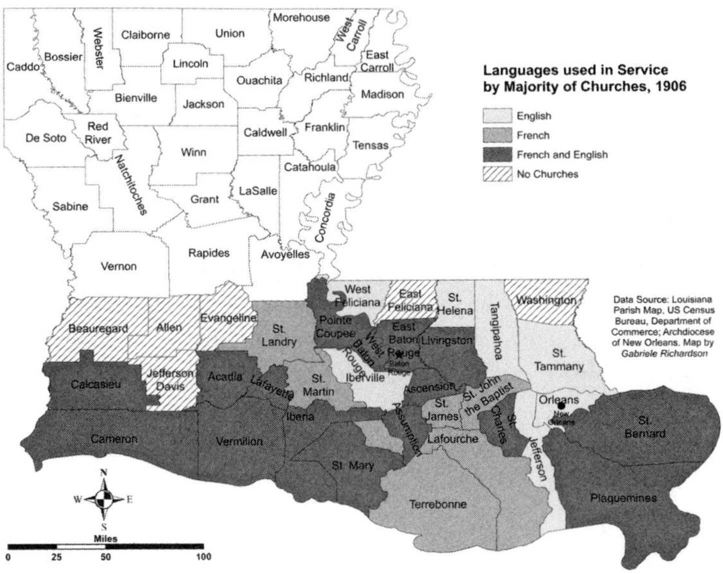

Figure 6.2. Languages used in services by majority of churches, 1906

If within the civil parish services were conducted at one church in English and another in French, the combination for that parish appears in dark gray as French and English. For example, in figure 6.1, in Plaquemines Parish, located in the southeast corner of the state, one church uses French, one church uses English, and one church uses French and English. Therefore, the color dark gray was assigned to Plaquemines Parish in figure 6.2.

Results clearly show the use of spoken French and English in Catholic Church services across the geographical region, further documenting the French and English bilingual practices in south Louisiana well into the twentieth century. Church services in French dominated in civil parishes alongside the Mississippi corridor from north to south. Bilingual church services were the norm in a majority of civil parishes from the west to the east of south Louisiana. From both the register entries and the 1906 census cards, it can be ascertained that many priests were comfortable in French as well as in English.

As revealing as the maps are, they immediately raise a number of questions of interpretation. What local factors could have compelled the churches to change their language practice? Was their impetus for change rooted in the linguistic use of their parishioners, as might be expected? Or did priests press upon their parishioners a language unwelcome within the church doors because of a perceived need to "Americanize" the Louisiana Church?

To answer these questions, another type of church documentation can be helpful, the parish visitation reports mentioned above, which were periodically prepared by the visiting bishop or priest with one copy to the chancery and one to the parish. These reports provide the contextual base of the parish case studies presented next, some of which offered unexpected results that add shading and sometimes surprise to our overall findings while generally confirming them.

PARISH VISITATION REPORTS: OLD AND NEW

The parish visitation reports record a variety of information, such as property, description of programs, parish profile, number of communicants, and so forth.[1] Early report forms, for example the 1885 form, were in French or English and captured such information as the number of Catholics (white and persons of color), number of schools and pupils, and number of sacraments. There was also a field to denote "language." It is regrettably not specified what the "language" field documented, whether it was the language of the parishioners, the priest, or the service. In 1889, the form switched to English and the language field was no longer included. Here information from the "language" field forms a small subset of the larger parish visitation report database as it is limited to the older churches and because many of these reports were not located.

Of the thirty-seven church parishes selected for the civil parish case studies, only fifteen reports from 1885 were located (table 6.1). In three civil parishes (Assumption, Lafourche, and Vermilion), no reports were found, while all nine (100%) of the reports were located for church parishes selected for the Orleans civil parish case study. These reports, while not providing enough information for a comparative analysis between civil parishes, are used for their metalinguistic value.

Table 6.1 combines the sacramental register switch date and the information collected from the 1885 parish report. Organizing the table chronologically by switch date enables us to see that the use of English in completing the form is evident in the first six churches where switches occurred before 1890. Aside from church parishes established for Italians and Germans, church services were provided in English as early as 1844 in some New Orleans church parishes.

In the later churches, eight of the nine churches used French to complete the form. Only at St. Gabriel Church, where the register switched in 1903, did the priest complete the form in English. The mean switch dates and the 1885 data for the churches in these three civil parishes are consistent with the trend in each of these localities: Orleans Parish—1880, Iberville Parish—1887, and St. James Parish—1930. Also of interest are the annotations from churches in New Orleans where the use of French, German, English, and Italian reflects the multiple languages actually spoken in the city, if not always used in the official documents.

The parish visitation reports become more useful for linguistic purposes in the new century. By 1912, the report noted the nationality of the Catholic parishioners and those who were unable to comprehend English. This field, "number who do not understand English," is consistent with the information gathered by the US Census of Religious Bodies. This information, which remained on the parish visitation report form until the 1950s, was collected from reports dated 1912 to 1954. Data elements included: the year of the parish report, the number of Catholics, Catholics of each nationality, those who did not understand English, number of non-Catholics, and observations/notes.

Despite the obvious value of such information, the visitation reports must be used with some caution. They were certainly not completed by trained sociolinguists and doubtless often relied on second-hand or impressionistic information from the local clergy. For example, visitation reports from one church described below claimed that in 1912 no parish-

TABLE 6.1. Metalinguistic comments from 1885 parish visitation reports

Register Switch Date	*Church Parish*	*City*	*Civil Parish*	*"Language/ Langage" Reported in 1885*
1844	St. Theresa of Avila (Irish)	New Orleans	Orleans	English
1856	St. Vincent de Paul	New Orleans	Orleans	English & French
1856	St. Anthony of Padua	New Orleans	Orleans	Italian
1867	St. John the Evangelist	Plaquemine	Iberville	chiefly English
1867	Holy Trinity (German)	New Orleans	Orleans	German
1880	Mater Dolorosa Church	New Orleans	Orleans	German
1890	St. Joseph	Grosse Tête	Iberville	français et anglais
1892	Annunciation (French)	New Orleans	Orleans	français, anglais, espagnol & italien
1901	St. Ann	New Orleans	Orleans	français
1903	St. Gabriel	St. Gabriel	Iberville	French with a mixture of English
1910	St. Louis Cathedral	New Orleans	Orleans	"tous de mixte"
1914	St. Michael the Archangel	Convent	St. James	français
1915	Our Lady of the Sacred Heart	New Orleans	Orleans	français & anglais
1935	Our Lady of Peace	Vacherie	St. James	français
1937	St. James	St. James	St. James	français

ioners spoke English, yet the next report seven years later claimed that *all* parishioners could speak English. In another case, a 1912 report claims all parishioners speak English, while a 1948 report says that only half can understand English, a possible but highly unlikely reversal of the trend in language fluency.

Parish visitation reports were found for 34 parishes, representing 91.89% of the total parishes (37) selected for case studies. A total of 159 reports were located, an average of 4.3 reports per church parish and 26 reports per civil parish. To supplement this information, significant language comments and content in parish files containing other historical information were sought as well as published and unpublished histories.

ASSUMPTION PARISH CASE STUDY

Assumption's history is rooted in its waterways. Bayou Lafourche, the main waterway, was a major route of transportation connecting the Mississippi River to the Gulf of Mexico. Large sugarcane plantations were established along the bayou, which was rich in alluvial soil. Under Spanish rule, during the last quarter of the eighteenth century, the area was also settled by Canary Islanders and Acadians. Spain established a military post along Bayou Lafourche, and Spanish officials promised to provide farming equipment, land, and a church in the center of the post.

The civil parish of Assumption was formed in 1807 as an original parish of the Louisiana Territory. It lies south of the civil parishes of Iberville, Ascension, and St. James. Assumption Parish was carved from the settlement of Lafourche and included one-half of the population of the settlement. This civil parish took its name from the church parish of the same name (Paroisse de l'Assomption). Today, the parish covers 338.7 square miles; the parish seat is Napoleonville.[2]

The first church, established in 1793 in the town of Plattenville, was dedicated under the title Assumption of the Blessed Virgin Mary. After Louisiana statehood, two more churches were established along the bayou: St. Elizabeth (1839) in Paincourtville and St. Philomena (1847) in Labadieville. During the second half of the nineteenth century, four more churches were built: two along Bayou Lafourche (St. Anne in 1874 in Napoleonville and St. Benedict the Moor in 1896 in Bertrandville) and two along other waterways (Immaculate Conception on Attakapas Canal in 1857 and St. Joseph in Pierre Part in 1858). Only one church, St. Jules, was established after 1900 along Bayou Lafourche (1911).

Twenty individual priests served in Assumption Parish from 1860 to 1920. Several priests appeared more than once, such as brother priests Fathers M. A. and J. B. Le Saicherre, and Father J. Bouchet, who appears five times, serving more than forty years at Assumption Church. Of these twenty priests, fifteen were born in France, two in Belgium, one in Canada, and one in Holland.[3] If one assumes that the priests from Belgium and Canada were French speakers, then 90% of the priests were native-born French speakers. None of the twenty priests were born in the United States, and it appears that none were born in a country where the first language was English, except perhaps Father L'Anglais from Canada.

Of the eight church parishes established before 1950, only two churches had registers that began in English: St. Jules in Belle Rose and St. Benedict the Moor. These two church parishes, however, were established by Archbishop Janssens to serve only African Americans, with Father Baast of Holland the first pastor for both of them, and thus are special if by no means unique cases.[4] The Assumption case study is therefore composed of six churches which had sacramental registers that switched from French to English, all switching after 1900, a time when the overall Catholic population of the parish (20,620) was estimated at 87%.

The earliest register switch—1905—appeared simultaneously in two churches. The first was St. Anne in Napoleonville, named after a saint to whom the parishioners had prayed for assistance during times of sickness. The second church was Immaculate Conception in Attakapas Canal, near Napoleonville. In both cases, a Belgian priest, Father E. de Wilde, maintained registers in French, but when Father L'Anglais was appointed to St. Anne, he switched registers to English (as his name might suggest). These two churches were not very far away from each other, hence the same pastor, and they share other data similarities. (Visitation reports were not found in either church for the years 1912, 1916, or 1934.) Interestingly, after the register switch, church services at both St. Anne and Immaculate Conception were kept in both French and English for an indeterminate period of time.[5] The 1948 report indicated 1,475 parishioners of St. Anne, all of them reported to understand English. As for the small population of 427 parishioners at Immaculate Conception, the local pastor reported that 90% of them could understand English.

Not long after the changes in Napoleonville, in 1910, language practices began changing in St. Philomena in Labadieville (formerly called Brule Labadie). In 1842 Father Menard, also known as "the Apostle of Bayou Lafourche," held a mission and later supervised the erection of the chapel. The parish rectory was completed in 1853, but registers were kept as early as 1847, the year when the work on the chapel began. Its first pastor was Father Cyprian Vennisat; French-born Father A. F. Ravoire also served St. Philomena. During his tenure, church services were provided in French, but in 1910 registers suddenly shifted to English. The 1912 report, sent two years after the switch, shows that less than half of the population was able to understand English, and a similar percentage is given in 1916. By 1934, however, the local priest wrote that many parishioners understood English, but he did not provide numbers.

Not much information can be obtained about St. Joseph the Worker in Pierre Part. Its registers changed from French to English in 1919, when a newly appointed priest from Spain, Father Juan de Diego Martinez, took over the church management after the departure of Father B. Branche, a French-born pastor. In 1906 church services were offered in French only. This should come as no surprise given the information found in the visitation reports: the 1916 report filed three years after the switch indicates that only 1% of the parishioners (eleven out of 1,100) could understand English. By 1934 this percentage increased only to 10%. One has to wait for the 1948 report to see a substantial number of parishioners comfortable in English.

Information is also missing for St. Elizabeth in Paincourtville. The church was built in 1838, thanks to a plot donated by Elizabeth Dugas. Parishioners had to rebuild the church after a fire devastated it in 1854.

Church services in 1906 were rendered in French. In 1912, only a small number of parishioners capable of understanding English are reported. The register switch, which happened in 1930, was due to a priest change, when Father William Parrot was replaced by Father Eudore Thériault. In 1948, 251 out of 1,005 faithful were still unable to comprehend English.

Plattenville is one of the earliest settlements in Assumption Parish, and its local church, Assumption of the Blessed Virgin Mary, also known as Assumption, is the oldest church for which data are found. The original church was built in 1793 during the Spanish regime, but the present facility dates from 1856. No data can be found on the language used in services. In 1912, the pastor reported two thousand Catholics. Out of these two thousand, 1,340 are estimated as having English comprehension. By 1916, the number of parishioners dropped to one thousand, but, by then, all were reported to be able to understand English. Nevertheless, the register switch originated from a priest change as late as 1948, that is, three decades after the parishioners supposedly knew English, when Father H. Holleman replaced French-born Father J. A. Francon.

The late change in Plattenville was the exception in this civil parish, however. Elsewhere, the switch to English church records appears somewhat ahead of the language practices of the parishioners. This is a pattern repeated in a number of the case studies.

IBERVILLE PARISH CASE STUDY

Iberville civil parish lies south of Pointe Coupée, West Baton Rouge, and East Baton Rouge parishes. Most of the parish is on the west bank of the Mississippi, with a small portion on the east bank. Bayou Plaquemine, which runs through Iberville Parish, was a common route from the Mississippi River to the interior of Louisiana. In 1768, Acadian exiles were sent by the Louisiana Spanish government to settle an area on the east bank of the Mississippi River below Bayou Manchac. This area became the community of St. Gabriel. Using cypress from the nearby swamps, the community built St. Gabriel Church in 1774–75, a building that still stands. It is the only Iberville church parish on the east bank, and for more than seventy-five years it was the only church in the parish. Eventually, between 1850 and 1883, four churches were erected on the west bank: St. John the Evangelist at Plaquemine, St. Paul at Bayou Goula, Our Lady of Prompt Succor at White Castle, and St. Joseph at Grosse Tête. No parishes were established after 1900. At the turn of the century, 75% of Iberville Parish's population was Catholic.

Compared to Assumption Parish, Iberville presents more linguistic variation with regard to the national origin of the eighteen priests who served the parish from 1860 to 1920. Of these eighteen priests, only half (nine) were born in France, three in Holland, two in Louisiana, and one each in Italy, Sicily, Ireland, and Belgium. Of the five church parishes established before 1950, all five had sacramental registers that switched from French to English.

The earliest switch happened in 1867 at St. John the Evangelist Church, built in Plaquemine in 1850. The first pastor was Father Charles Chambost from France, who also founded the College of the Immaculate Conception, a separate school for boys, and an academy for girls. In 1858, all buildings burned to the ground. The looming Civil War and its financial aftermath prevented Father Chambost from rebuilding and precipitated his departure from Louisiana. The current church is the third on its site. The change in language practices in 1867 originated from a newly appointed priest, Father V. D. C. d'Hémécourt from Louisiana, who took over the second church built after the Civil War. By 1906, church services had shifted from French to English. In 1912, all 350 parishioners reportedly could understand English, with the exception of a few Italians.

Three churches located on the west bank were established within a six-year interval, 1877–83. They all soon switched from French to English, at almost the same time. Registers at Our Lady of Prompt Succor switched in 1886, nine years after its erection, when an Irish scribe started to assist French-born pastor J. M. T. Massardier. In 1912, most of the three thousand parishioners understood English according to the visitation reports.

Both St. Joseph in Grosse Tête and St. Paul in Bayou Goula switched in 1890. In the case of St. Joseph Church, the switch was realized by Father E. D'Hommée, who took care of the vacant church from Lobdell a few years after Father J. M. T. Massardier left. No clue about the reason for the shift can be deduced from the registers. What is known, however, is that by 1906 church services were provided in English only, and only a few old Italian ladies were reported in 1912 as incapable of understanding English. Data for St. Paul are sparse since no visitation reports were found. The register shift followed the appointment of Father V. D. C. d'Hémécourt to St. Paul, years after his tenure at St. John the Evangelist. The French language, however, did not totally disappear from the parish after the switch in St. Paul and Our Lady of Prompt Succor since church services were available in French and English at both in 1906.

St. Gabriel Church goes back to the beginning of Iberville Parish in 1761. Built in 1769 under the supervision of Vicar-General Dagobert, it is believed to be one of the oldest wooden churches in the Louisiana Territory. Most of its exterior is made of cypress. Dedicated to St. Gabriel the Archangel, it was the pivot of the Catholic Church network of Iberville Parish. Registers started in 1773, when the church was dismantled and moved to its present location. The first baptism record is dated April 22, 1773, and the first marriage is from January 1, 1773. Father Valentin became its first resident pastor; Father Jean Marius Laval officiated at St. Gabriel from 1884 to 1890. He was succeeded by another French-born priest, Father A. M. Barbier, who was replaced in 1903 by an Irish pastor, Father Raymond, who switched registers to English and provided church services only in English. Perplexingly, the following priest who filed the visitation report in 1912 wrote that none of the nine hundred parishioners could understand English. By 1919 the congregation was in decline, and the visitation report sent that year indicates that by then all parishioners understood English. This is a case where the records are more obfuscating than enlightening. Did the parishioners of 1912 rush to learn to speak English by 1919? Did all the French speakers move to another church by 1919 while a group of English speakers took over? Are one or both of the visitation reports simply wrong? Unfortunately, only the third case seems likely.

LAFOURCHE PARISH CASE STUDY

Lafourche civil parish is located south of St. James, St. Charles, and Jefferson civil parishes. At the southern end of the parish, Bayou Lafourche empties into the Gulf of Mexico. With sixty-five miles of farms and homes fronting Bayou Lafourche, from Thibodaux (the parish seat) to Leeville, Lafourche Parish is considered to have the longest line village in the world because of so many successive villages. It is one of the largest parishes in square-mile area. Settlers and immigrant populations were comprised of French, Acadian exiles, and Canary Islanders. In 1822, Lafourche was divided to form two civil parishes: Lafourche and Terrebonne. We focus here on the area established as Lafourche Parish in 1822, which is also its current area. In 1900 the Lafourche population was 28,882, with 91% of its residents Catholics.

The first church, St. Joseph, was originally a mission of Assumption Parish. Once established as a church parish in 1817, St. Joseph became the mother church of the surrounding area. In 1842, Father Charles Menard became the pastor of St. Joseph. For the next fifty-six years, he worked tirelessly, establishing dozens of parishes, missions, and schools. Four of the churches in this study were established through his missionary work: St. Mary's Nativity in Raceland, Holy Savior in Lockport, Our Lady of the Rosary in Larose, and Our Lady of Prompt Succor in Chackbay.[6]

Five churches were established in Lafourche Parish before 1900 (St. Joseph and Menard's churches), and four after 1900. Of the nine parishes, Chackbay (Our Lady of Prompt Succor) is the only community that does not lie along the banks of Bayou Lafourche. Seven churches had sacramental registers that switched from French to English. The only two churches with records that began in English, St. Charles Borromeo (1912) and St. John the Evangelist (1919), were both established in Thibodaux.

However, the end of the nineteenth century does not represent a cut-off period in Lafourche for registers in French. Two churches established well after 1900 started their records in French: Our Lady of Prompt Succor in Golden Meadow (1916) and Sacred Heart in Cut-Off (1923). One reason is the origins of the priests: of the twenty-four priests identified as serving in Lafourche from 1860 to 1920, twenty (83%) were born in France, two in Louisiana, and two in Canada.

Father Menard built Our Lady of Prompt Succor in Chackbay in 1873 on land bought from Jean Baptiste Benoit. Prior to the construction of a chapel, religious services were conducted in private homes. Our Lady of Prompt Succor Parish was established in 1892 by Archbishop Janssens with Alexander Juille as its first pastor. Father Charles Tessier succeeded him in 1895. Eight years later (1903), a Louisiana-born priest, Father J. Schmitt, took the reins of the parish and switched registers from French to English, although church services continued exclusively in French at least until 1906. In his 1912 visitation report, the new resident priest, Father Chapon, reported 2,500 parishioners, all of whom knew only French. In his 1948 report, Father Sebastian Arjonilla listed a similar number of parishioners, but according to his evaluation only half of the congregation understood English.

Although different in size and in date of establishment, two church parishes switched in 1911. The first was St. Joseph, the oldest church parish in Thibodaux (1817). When Father Alexandre Barbier was appointed to the church in 1911, after the tenure of another French-born pastor, registers were kept in English. A year later, he listed approximately seven thousand parishioners and estimated that 85% of these could understand English. This high assessment of English proficiency may explain why church services at St. Joseph were already performed in 1906 in both languages.

The second switch in 1911 was Our Lady of the Rosary Church (1873) in Larose, a small town named after a local druggist who had a post office in his store. Father Hyacinthe Brindejone, its first pastor, served three hundred parishioners until 1876. Many French-born priests were successively appointed to the church, notably Father Alexander Juille, who served Our Lady of the Rosary from 1906 to 1912, the year of his death. He conducted church services only in French. During the last year of his tenure, a French-born priest, Father Jan, who succeeded him a year later, changed the church's administrative language practice and started to write registers in English. Unlike St. Joseph, however, Our Lady of the Rosary's congregation dwindled over the next decades. According to the 1912 visitation report, only a third of the congregation (4,500 parishioners) could understand sermons in English.

St. Mary's Nativity in Raceland and Holy Savior Church in Lockport were established in 1850. St. Mary's Nativity was originally dedicated under the title of the Nativity of the Blessed Virgin Mary. Its first resident pastor was Father Amédée Beccard. Holy Savior began as a mission church. It was reconstructed in 1916 after the original building was destroyed by a hurricane. These small parishes present many similarities. First, the language shift in registers happened late in both parishes, with St. Mary's first in 1926 during Father Peter Nies's tenure, followed by Holy Savior in 1932 during J. Boudreaux's tenure. Second, their congregations must have been French-dominant at the beginning of the twentieth century since church services were provided only in French in 1906. For both churches, a book change coincided with the switch in church services. Despite these similarities, their parishioners differed in their language practices. Almost all Holy Savior parishioners reportedly could understand English at the time of the shift, but only 50% could do so at St. Mary's during the same period; the elderly there still did not understand English in 1948 and 1954.

The two church parishes established after 1900, Our Lady of Prompt Succor in Golden Meadow (1916) and Sacred Heart in Cut-Off (1923), were chapels released from the church parish in Larose, where numerous monolingual French-speaking parishioners lived. Visitation reports filed after their establishment show a high number of parishioners who did not grasp the English language. When registers switched at Sacred Heart Church in 1949, under Father F. D. Barbier, only half of the adult congregation could understand English, whereas "the children speak English." The same linguistic situation occurred at Our Lady of Prompt Succor, where Father W. Breault initiated the language shift in 1954, despite the fact that 50% of his parishioners, "overwhelmingly native born French Acadians," were monolingual in French.

ORLEANS PARISH CASE STUDY

Orleans Parish and the city of New Orleans are synonymous for our purposes since they share the same territory, so simply "New Orleans" instead of "Orleans Parish" or "Orleans civil parish" will be used in this section. New Orleans has had an important church practically since its founding in 1718. St. Louis Cathedral, itself a symbol of New Orleans, stands in the same location as when it was established in 1720. It was the only church in the city for more than one hundred years. On March 31, 1807, the city of New Orleans with all its precincts became the first civil parish of Louisiana.

During the nineteenth century, new Catholic churches were established in the area largely due to Irish and German immigration to the city. Table 6.2 lists the church parishes created before 1950 in New Orleans.[7] From 1833 to 1860, under Archbishop Blanc's administration, twenty new church parishes were founded. From the end of the Civil War until the turn of the century, nine more churches were added. Overall, twenty-nine churches were established before 1900 and twenty-eight more churches by 1950, for a total of fifty-seven churches established before 1950.

A number of the earlier churches naturally started with French registers, but after 1880 none of the newly founded churches started registers in French.[8] Thus of the churches established before 1880, only nine churches had sacramental registers that switched from French to English. The country of origin and native language for sixty-five of the seventy-four priests who served in these nine parishes from 1860 to 1920 can be established from the records.[9] Out of these sixty-five priests, 36% were from France, 20% were from English-speaking countries (England, United States, Ireland), 13% were from German-speaking countries (Bavaria, Germany, Prussia), and a few priests were from Spain (seven), Italy (three), and Holland (three). By the turn of the twentieth century, Catholics represented 80% of New Orleans's population.

Let us now look at the change in language practices in these nine church parishes. Three churches—St. Theresa of Avila, St. Anthony of Padua, and St. Vincent de Paul—had a register change that occurred a few years after their founding in the early 1840s. In each case, the language change was

TABLE 6.2. Church parishes in New Orleans, 1720–1949

Year of First Entry	*Church*	*Year of First Entry*	*Church*
1720	St. Louis Cathedral	1897	St. Cecilia
1833	St. Patrick	1905	Our Lady of Lourdes
1839	St. Vincent Chapel	1907	Our Lady of the Rosary
1838	St. Vincent de Paul	1909	St. Joan of Arc
1840	St. Theresa of Avila	1912	Our Lady Star of the Sea
1840	Holy Trinity	1915	Blessed Sacrament
1841	St. Anthony of Padua	1915	St. Anthony of Padua
1842	St. Augustine	1916	Corpus Christi
1844	Annunciation	1916	Holy Ghost
1845	St. Joseph	1919	Holy Redeemer
1845	St. Mary	1919	All Saints
1848	Mater Dolorosa	1920	St. James Major
1848	Sts. Peter and Paul	1920	St. Leo the Great
1850	Immaculate Conception	1920	St. Matthias
1851	St. John the Baptist	1920	St. Peter Claver
1852	St. Ann	1921	St. Rita
1853	St. Alphonsus	1922	Incarnate Word
1856	St. Henry	1924	St. Dominic
1857	St. Rose of Lima	1924	St. Monica
1858	St. Mary's Assumption	1925	St. Mary of the Angels
1858	Notre Dame de Bon Secours	1927	St. Raymond
1869	St. Michael	1929	St. Theresa of the Child Jesus
1871	St. Boniface	1937	St. David
1878	Our Lady of the Sacred Heart	1947	St. Christopher the Martyr
1879	Sacred Heart of Jesus	1947	St. Louis King of France
1886	Holy Name of Jesus	1947	St. Paul the Apostle
1886	St. Francis de Sales	1947	St. Raphael the Archangel
1887	Our Lady of Good Counsel	1948	Epiphany
1895	St. Katherine	1949	St. Philip the Apostle

triggered by the arrival of a new priest, although the origin of the priests who changed the churches' language practice is unknown. Records were kept in French for four years (1840–44) at St. Theresa of Avila, fifteen years (1841–56) at St. Anthony of Padua, and eighteen years (1838–56) at St. Vincent de Paul. The 1912 and 1934 visitation reports from St. Theresa of Avila and St. Vincent de Paul indicate that all parishioners understood English and church services were already rendered only in English in 1906. Unfortunately, no visitation reports are available from St. Anthony of Padua. Since church services were provided in French, English, and Italian in 1906, the number of French monolinguals was probably still significant four decades after the register change.

Priests from three churches in New Orleans felt the need to switch registers to English before the end of the nineteenth century. The earliest shift happened at Holy Trinity (1867), under Father M. Schifferer, but no justification can be surmised from the church records. Parishioners in 1906 could attend church services in both English and German, but almost all were reported understanding English in 1912. Language practices at Mater Dolorosa (1880) follow the same pattern. A few Italian parishioners still did not comprehend English in 1912, but all did after 1919. Interestingly, it was a French-born priest, Father Vallée, who changed the church's language practice to English in 1880. Annunciation's first register entry is dated in 1844. When the resident priest, Father G. A. Rouxel, started a new year register in 1892, he chose to write in English. But a decade later, Annunciation parishioners could still attend church services in French along with English. Most of them could understand English by 1919.

In 1906, church services at St. Ann, St. Louis Cathedral, and Our Lady of the Sacred Heart were provided in both French and English. St. Ann, however, switched five years (1852–1901) before the 1906 census was conducted, when Holland native Father J. B. Bogaerts took the place of French-born pastor Father J. A. Thébault. At the time of the shift, "very few" parishioners could understand English.

Language practices changed a few years after the census at St. Louis Cathedral (1720–1910) and Our Lady of the Sacred Heart (1878–1915) but for different reasons. The resident pastor at St. Louis Cathedral, Father J. M.

Laval, waited until January 1, 1910, to start writing registers in English. The 1912 visitation report is missing, but the 1919 report indicates that 95% of the parishioners understood English. By contrast, language change at Our Lady of the Sacred Heart Church was triggered in 1915—the same year that the church was destroyed by the Great Hurricane—by the replacement of a French-born pastor, Father W. J. P. Vincent, by a Dutch native, Father P. Wynhoven. In 1912, Father Vincent wrote in French that he knew no parishioners who could understand English, whereas the new priest in 1919, in charge of a community that probably had to meet in other church buildings, declared that almost all parishioners could do so. Once again, neither scenario seems probable in New Orleans at this late date.

ST. JAMES PARISH CASE STUDY

St. James civil parish is located midway between New Orleans and Baton Rouge. It lies south of Ascension Parish and north of Lafourche Parish. The parish is divided by the Mississippi River, which was the "highway" for all commercial traffic between New Orleans and Baton Rouge, an English-speaking town, during the eighteenth and nineteenth centuries.

Lillian Bourgeois recounts the history of the parish in her book *Cabanocey,*[10] the term first used for the area. In 1764, Jacques Cantrelle moved to the area, receiving a large land grant from the Spanish government. As the Acadians began arriving in 1765, Cantrelle agreed to settle them in the area, and it became known as the First Acadian Coast. In 1767, a French Capuchin priest, Father Barnabe, traveled upstream from Destrehan to the west bank of the Mississippi to serve the settlers at the newly established military post. The church parish of St. James was established shortly thereafter (1770). As settlements grew on both sides of the river, the community on the east bank needed a church to serve its inhabitants. St. Michael the Archangel was established in 1809. These two churches served the Catholics of the parish for many years. During the last half of the nineteenth century, four new parishes were established, two on the west bank in the town of Vacherie (Our Lady of Peace in 1856 and St.

Philip in 1873) and two on the east bank in the towns of Paulina and Union (St. Joseph in 1882 and St. Mary in 1887).

Five of the six churches had sacramental registers that switched from French to English. The registers of St. Joseph in Paulina were destroyed in 1921 when the church, rectory, and church hall burned. Although all early records of the parish were lost, it is likely that the language used in the registers was French since twenty-three (85%) of the twenty-seven priests who served from 1860 to 1920 in St. James civil parish were born in France, while one each was born in Louisiana, Ireland, Spain, or Holland. The registers of St. James Church remained in French even though the pastor in 1860, Father Lecuru, was Irish.

French-written registers from all these church parishes changed to English in the first half of the twentieth century. During this period, Catholics represented 88% of the civil parish population (21,238).[11] Language practices first started to change at St. Michael's in Convent in 1914, when French-born pastor Father A. Simon began a new register book in English. No visitation reports are found before 1934 (when 80% of the parishioners are reported as being capable of understanding English). Nevertheless, eight years before the switch occurred, church services were offered only in French to a population composed of approximately 2,600 faithful. Then, the register language switch occurred in 1918 at St. Mary in Union when a new scribe was assigned to the pastor who attended to the church. At the time of the register switch, however, less than 50% of the eight hundred parishioners could understand English.

The first register entry at St. James Church in St. James civil parish is dated 1770. French was maintained as the register language until 1937 when the resident priest, Father J. Coulombe, started a new year register in English. No visitation reports are available during the 1920s, 1930s, and 1940s, but the 1912 report points to a high number of parishioners who could understand English with the exception of "but a few old ones." Already in 1906, church services were delivered in both French and English. This leads us to believe that English as a language practice within the St. James church parish started decades before the register switch.

In contrast, the churches in Vacherie remained resolutely French until the 1950s. The source of change at Our Lady of Peace (1935), where Father A. Delnom was assigned, is undetermined. Data from the census and visitation reports show that the French language was very much alive during the first half of the twentieth century. Church services in 1906 were conducted only in French; among the 1,800 parishioners in 1912, only a few could understand English, and half of them still could not do so in 1934. The same language practices are found for St. Philip Church (1873–1947) in Vacherie. Two decades before the switch, Father B. Fontaine reported that no more than 150 out of 1,500 parishioners could understand English. In 1934, old parishioners hardly understood a sermon in English, a linguistic reality that persevered in the 1948 and 1954 visitation reports.

VERMILION PARISH CASE STUDY

Situated in the southwest portion of the state, Vermilion civil parish is located south of the civil parishes of Acadia and Lafayette. Bordering the Gulf of Mexico, the southern portion of the parish is coastal marsh, while the north is prairie land. The histories of the parish seat of Abbeville and St. Mary Magdalen Church (the oldest church) are intertwined. As pastor of the church in Lafayette, Father Megret visited the outlying sections of his church parish. These areas were too distant from Lafayette, so Father Megret bought property on the Vermilion River to build a chapel. The adjoining property was laid out in squares and lots, thus beginning the town of Abbeville. When the Louisiana legislature decided to divide Lafayette Parish in 1844, Vermilion Parish was formed and Abbeville later became its parish seat.[12] For a long time, agriculture (rice, sugarcane, beef cattle) was the only economic resource of the parish. Today, oil, gas, and related industries play a major role.

At the close of the nineteenth century, when 91% of Vermilion's population (20,705) was Catholic, five new church parishes were established: St. Alphonsus in Maurice, Our Lady of the Most Holy Rosary in Kaplan,

Our Lady of the Lake in Delcambre, St. John in Henry, and Our Lady of Prompt Succor in Bancker. Only the first four had sacramental registers that switched from French to English. From 1900 to 1950, seven more church parishes were founded, but all had registers that began in English. Fifteen priests served Vermilion church parishes from 1860 to 1920. A majority of them (ten, or 66%) were born in France; two pastors each were from Holland and Canada and one from Louisiana. Fathers Alexander Marie Mehaut and J. A. Maltrait served in the area for more than twenty years in the church parishes of St. Mary Magdalen and Our Lady of the Holy Rosary respectively.

Vermilion's oldest church, St. Mary Magdalen, was the first to shift its language practice in 1907, fifty-six years after its establishment. Regrettably, visitation reports could not be found. Other reports show that the resident priest, Father F. Laforest, and his Holland-born assistant, Father F. Rombouts, offered church services in French and English in 1906. But a year later, they both began writing registers in English.

Two church parishes, Our Lady of the Lake in Delcambre and Our Lady of the Holy Rosary in Kaplan, switched approximately twenty-five years after their erection, 1914 and 1918 respectively. Before the register change, French was the language in which services in both church parishes were performed. Our Lady of the Lake and Our Lady of the Holy Rosary shared another similarity. At the time of the switch, most of their parishioners did not understand English. Only 10% of the faithful population in Kaplan did; 25% of Delcambre's congregation could do so. However, the context in which the linguistic change took place was not the same. Our Lady of the Holy Rosary's pastor, Father A. van de Bilt, started a new year register book in English, while the arrival of a new Louisiana-born priest, Father L. P. Castel, triggered the shift in Delcambre.

The next two church parishes to switch were St. Alphonsus in Maurice in 1928 and St. John in Henry in 1941, the last standing church with French registers in Vermilion Parish. What is notable about these two parishes is that church services were already offered in both French and English as early as 1906. This time period of bilingual practices (services and registers) lasted twenty-two years for St. Alphonsus and an astonishing thirty-five years for St. John. When language shift happened in the registers of both parishes, almost all parishioners understood English. Conversely, French-language record preservation in St. John can be partly explained by the fact that only 30% of its parishioners could understand English in 1919. In spite of their similar environment, what prompted register changes in these two church parishes came from different factors. At St. Alphonsus, its French-born pastor, Father F. A. Buquet, suddenly began writing entries in English in the 1928 register book (at the first of the year) whereas an incoming priest, Father A. Verheem, is responsible for the 1941 switch in St. John registers, maintained until then in French by Father Raphael Gauthier.

WHAT DO WE LEARN FROM THE PARISH CASE STUDIES?

Perhaps the most important fact revealed by the parish visitation reports is that the civil parish boundaries do not present distinct patterns of register switch. Highly variable linguistic behaviors are found within each civil parish. Most church parishes show a unique pattern, with the exception of those churches served by the same priest; this is further proof that individual churches mark the smallest community of practice in the Louisiana church structure.

Another significant fact is the time span of language switch, the length of time during which the French and English languages shifted back and forth in church registers. This factor does not seem to be correlated with linguistic resistance to written English. As mentioned, changes first happened in Orleans Parish, triggered by the newly established Irish churches (1844); paradoxically, the parish visitation reports show that New Orleans had the longest time span of language change (seventy-one years). In other words, civil parishes that switch earlier do not show, as might be expected, a shorter time span in switching entirely to English.

Two categories of civil parish (if one leaves Orleans Parish aside) emerge from the parish visitation reports. First, there are the civil parishes with a shorter time span; St. James (33 years/first switch in 1914); Vermilion (34 years/ first switch in 1907); Iberville (36 years/first switch in 1867). Then, there are those with the lengthiest resistance to linguistic conformity: Assumption (43 years/first switch in 1905); Lafourche (51 years/first switch in 1903).

Accounting for the divergent time span in switching to English is difficult. Factors such as a high or low supply of priests, the origins of the priests, and the language used for sermons sometimes might help explain the speed of change. For example, Iberville and (to a lesser degree) Vermilion, which shows a shorter time span of change, also happen to have had a higher number of English-speaking priests who served in local churches. In contrast, almost all priests officiating in churches in Assumption and Lafourche were native-born French speakers from France. Their registers not only switch from French to English much later in time; the change was initiated by the arrival of a new French-speaking or bilingual priest and, later on, the beginning of a new register. Not surprisingly, the homogenous French environment in these churches seems to have strengthened the continued use of registers written in French while an increase in linguistic diversity appear to accelerate the rate of change. However, these factors do not play a role in New Orleans and in St. James. Despite its most diverse linguistic environment, New Orleans kept registers in French for the longest time (as well as sermons provided in both French and English). However, the size and diversity of population in New Orleans were surely factors for both the preservation of French registers and services and for the early English-language registers. In other words, New Orleans had enough churches to accommodate numerous language groups. As for St. James, although it had a linguistic environment similar to Assumption and Lafourche, register changes took place promptly. If the two churches in Vacherie (St. Philip and Our Lady of Peace) are put aside, however, St. James shows a shorter time span of change.

These results therefore show that linguistic resistance or conformity was localized but could happen on two different scales. Sometimes it occurred at a macro or civil parish level when several local churches experienced similar conditions, especially the spread of Protestant churches in the parish. At other times it was situated at the church level, with each local church in the parish having a distinctive experience (arising from factors such as the number and origin of priests, the language of the service, or the parishioners' language behavior). In that case, each church parish represents a unique religious community of practice.

Let us delve deeper into the language practices of the parishioners as indicated by the parish visitation reports. Can a direct correlation between a priest's decision to switch the language of his register and the reported linguistic behavior of his parishioners be observed? Yes and no. What emerges from the data are three language-change scenarios, each scenario matching a similar number of churches from the six selected civil parishes (table 6.3).

TABLE 6.3. Switches to English

Civil parish	*Switches when almost all parishioners understood English*	*Switches when half of the parishioners understood English*	*Switches when few parishioners understood English*
Lafourche	St. Joseph Cathedral, Thibodaux P*: 1911	Our Lady of Prompt Succor, Golden Meadow B†: 1954	Our Lady of Prompt Succor, Chackbay P*: 1903
	Holy Savior, Lockport B†: 1932	Sacred Heart, Cut Off B†: 1949	Our Lady of the Rosary, Larose P*: 1911
St. James	St. James, St. James B†: 1937	St. Mary, Union P*: 1935	St. Michael, Convent B†: 1914
	St. Philip, Vacherie P*: 1947	Our Lady of Peace, Vacherie Impossible to determine: 1935	
Vermilion	St. Alphonsus, Maurice B†: 1928		Our Lady of the Holy Rosary, Kaplan B†: 1918
	Our Lady of Prompt Succor, Henry P*: 1941		Our Lady of the Lake, Delcambre P*: 1914

(*continued*)

TABLE 6.3. Switches to English (*continued*)

Civil parish	*Switches when almost all parishioners understood English*	*Switches when half of the parishioners understood English*	*Switches when few parishioners understood English*
Assumption	Assumption, Plattenville P*: 1948	St. Elizabeth, Paincourtville P*: 1930 St. Philomena, Labadieville B†: 1910	St. Joseph the Worker, Pierre Part P*: 1919
Iberville	St. Gabriel, St. Gabriel P*: 1903 St. John the Evangelist, Plaquemine P*: 1867 Our Lady of Prompt Succor, White Castle P*: 1886		
Orleans	St. Louis Cathedral, New Orleans B†: 1910	St. Vincent de Paul, New Orleans P*: 1856 Annunciation, New Orleans B†: 1892 Our Lady of the Sacred Heart, New Orleans P*: 1915	St. Ann, New Orleans P*: 1901

P*: priest change
B†: Book change

Interestingly, these scenarios are not conditioned by location or whether a switch corresponds to a change of priest or a change to a new register. In the first scenario, a switch occurred when most of the French-speaking parishioners (from 80% to 100%) sufficiently understood spoken English. There is thus a strong and expected correlation between the number of bilingual speakers and the priest's apparent motivation for changing the register. The second scenario is similar to the first, but the correlation is less robust since a switch is realized when half of the parishioners (more or less 50%) understood spoken English. In the third scenario, priests initiated changes when none or very few parishioners reportedly understood English; that is, when the local language preferences apparently did not warrant a switch from French to English in terms of the sheer number of English speakers.

Although the data sources used above are both incomplete and sometimes contradictory, the data supports nevertheless the previous contentions and conclusions that: (1) priests of all language origins generally understood that English was now the language of Catholicism in America; (2) the Church would make whatever linguistic accommodation it felt necessary to retain the faithful, and (3) parish priests rarely if ever imposed language changes upon their parishioners. Instead, they quietly helped bring to an end a bilingual practice that was already fading in the spoken language among the faithful.

Two other nonquantifiable observations are critical to understanding the Church's reaction to the growing strength of English. First, the very fact that the visitation reports tried to determine, however amateurishly, the linguistic make-up of the parishes and their churches demonstrates that the diocesan authorities were keeping a cautious watch on language changes and preferences among the parishioners in order to assign priests who could accommodate for the language needs of those parishioners. But "nationalism" was the underlying ideology behind the US government's census initiative. Census cards exposed clearly where cultural diversity stood out and which religious organizations did not reflect the ideology of "one nation, one language" (i.e., English), Louisiana being one place, the Louisiana Catholic Church being one organization. The desire of some priests to conform to this Americanist ideology or, more likely, to disguise nonassimilation could explain why some local priests would overestimate the use of English as the language of service or underestimate the use of French. Other priests did not seem to care, and hence the wild swings of estimated proportional language use in the same parish over the years.

The visitation reports show that priests were willing to hold multilanguage services to satisfy both major language groups, and earlier chapters have shown that the Church was willing to replace francophone priests with multilingual priests to assure that all parishioners could hear a sermon in their preferred language (except, perhaps, a few unfortunate Italian ladies who keep surfacing in the cards). The ability simply to understand English does not mean that a parishioner wished to hear a sermon delivered in it, and the church higher-ups seemed to want to keep an eye on what language would best keep the parishioners in their pews.

Second, the information above makes us strongly suspect, although we cannot empirically prove, that the Louisiana Catholic Church associated the spread of English with the threat of Protestantism. Since there is a direct parish-based correlation between the switch of the registers to English and the encroachment of Protestant churches into the parishes (chapter 5), these register switches to English in French-dominant parishes with francophone priests suggest that, except in the most remote parishes, priests understood that English must be the language of American Catholicism at some point. We also saw in the Redemptorist parishes of New Orleans the need for English to be used with the young. The older generation would stay in the pews, but the younger generation who wanted to fit in with the Americans were learning English and were drawn to the Protestant churches. For fear of losing the younger generation and its future parishioners, the Church followed that lead. It certainly did not try to convert its francophone parishioners to English sermons and, as shown earlier, local priests were sometimes unhappy about having to give sermons in English. We have also shown, however, that they were generally willing to change the most important parish records into English when the time or occasion seemed right, even when English was a distinctly minority local language and their sermons were still given in French. It is as if the priests were consciously preparing for the Americanization of the Louisiana Church, keeping a close watch on the Baptists and Methodists whose churches were increasingly appearing in their own or nearby parishes.

7

MAJOR FINDINGS AND CONTEXTUALIZATION

This study documents the shifting grounds of language change and maintenance over 250 years in the history of the Louisiana Catholic Church, both at different levels of its organization and at different levels of its participants. It relies heavily on sacramental registers, which record the major events in the religious life of the faithful. These registers were not written for the public and consequently could as well have been written in Latin, the traditional language of the Church. But Louisiana priests chose to work in the vernacular of the people. These records show that from the late eighteenth through the nineteenth centuries, language diversity within the Louisiana Church was a given; no one was confused about it, questioned it, or insisted on a practice of uniformity. What language to use, when to use it, with whom, and for what purpose were decisions made more on a basis of local perceptions, sensitivities, and assumptions than on a basis of formal church procedures and pronouncements.

From the early stages of language change in Louisiana to the post–Civil War social pressures that shaped its later transformations within the Church, language shift in the registers did not take a straightforward path. Changes followed a variety of patterns: swift language changes, ones that took decades to happen, numerous back-and-forth language switches over an extended period, politically driven (Spanish during the colonial period, "English-for-Americans" on the other end) or circumstantial administrative shifts (new year, new book).

The Church's strategies to accommodate the advance of English within Louisiana society differed according to the structural level (archdiocesan administrators, local priests), location (urban centers or rural settings), and priests' and parishioners' origins. Language choice in written records and in church services was also influenced by ideology (US nationalism) and religious competition (Protestantism). Sometimes, shifts can be explained by the priests' language abilities. In other times, we can clearly tell that the bilingual priest wrote in the language of the person receiving the sacrament—Murphy in English, Boudreaux in French.

The case studies show that language diversity among parishioners was reflected in parish registers. Outside New Orleans, parish priests usually accelerated the rate of change when the level of bilingualism was high. When French was predominant in the parish, even bilingual priests naturally chose to maintain French registers. A few priests, however, changed to English even when the majority of their parishioners did not understand English. All these tactics indicate the complicated nature of what was taking place on the ground.

In the investigation of language shift over time, Wenger's concept of community of practice has proved to be a useful interpretive framework. We have characterized the Louisiana Church as a network of distinct communities of practices sharing an overriding mutual engagement: the practice, spread, and preservation of the Catholic faith and its teaching among Louisianans. By separating the central ecclesiastical authority in New Orleans from the peripheral communities of practices, that is, the church parishes, it has been possible to determine who made language choices, at what point in time, and at which level within this "society of unequals." Through this approach, the Louisiana Church's implicit conventions and assumptions about language accommodation have become apparent, allowing better tracking of the multiple directions of language changes and what possibly triggered them.

Register changes are not isolated events, but part of the broader and holistic context of Louisiana, world history, and social change. The language itinerary of the Louisiana Church was also pushed by macro processes at work on a much broader level. It is not too much to say that the complexity of local forces that promoted or deterred the use of French or bilingualism in favor of English drew their origin from confrontations at a global level that sometimes reached back long before the Louisiana Purchase—colonialism most of all, but more specifically the Seven Years' War, the French Revolution, the Napoleonic Wars, the continuing strife between England and Ireland, and many other international factors. From the beginning to the end of the eighteenth century, colonization and Christianization in Louisiana did not happen in a vacuum. The rise and fall of the Catholic imperial enterprises in North America inversely mirrored those of their common European rivals, the British, who were not just distant enemies but a nearby colonial rival in the Caribbean, on the Gulf Coast, and even in northern Louisiana.

Powerful concentric waves of a strategic repositioning by competing powers began in Europe and moved inexorably to New France. In many ways Louisiana's real "mother country" in the early colonial period, Quebec endured serious conflict through much of the eighteenth century, and its transference to Great Britain in 1763 effectively cut off the last New France political ties with Louisiana. It was through the same conflict that Louisiana itself became part of the Spanish empire at about the same time, albeit without much enthusiasm on either side. In these colonial dramas, Louisiana was not a site of major armed conflict (with the exception of the Battle of New Orleans in 1815), but it was a major port city controlling the mouth of the Mississippi River and, as a result, an economic center and strategic port of entry for immigrants, many fleeing the above-mentioned European and colonial conflicts. Its culture, one of the most distinctive and unique among the American states, was therefore formed by shock waves from distant events and shores. Likewise, the early nineteenth-century political chessboard changed with the emergence of the United States (and New Orleans) as a new economic world force and, with the Louisiana Purchase and statehood, the final and complete severance of the Louisiana Church from the European secular powers that had fostered it. Finally, there was the American Civil War and its aftermath, creating forces which unleashed much long-term violence in Louisiana and then pulled

Louisiana powerfully into "America." These waves all guided the rhythms of the history of the French language in Louisiana.

As this book illustrates, the Louisiana Church adapted linguistically to locally driven demographic and cultural changes, and also adjusted to these great socioeconomic realities at a macro political level. Over time, the cumulative effect of its responses affected the vitality and furthered the decline of the French language, especially after the Civil War. There was neither an open nor a hidden language policy within the Louisiana Church. Its linguistic adjustments at different church levels were made primarily to protect its spiritual investments and, jointly, to secure its future in a predominantly Protestant nation. The Louisiana Church changed as Louisiana changed, but in many ways it cannily anticipated these changes as a measure of self-protection and to preserve the essentials of the faith at the expense of the tangential, such as the French language.

The word "accommodation" has been used many times in this study because it is the key to our overarching story of the decline of the French language in Louisiana. Let us first consider the many stages that the Louisiana Church went through. The essentials of Louisiana colonization were, to a large extent, no different from those involved in other colonial enterprises. The expansion of the king's territory and God's kingdom went hand in hand. Whatever lip service was paid to the propagation of the faith by colonial French officials, the Church was unmistakably a subordinate agent of social control in Louisiana, and its development—such as it was—was deeply tied to the Crown's financial successes or misfortunes. During the French colonial regime, the Louisiana Church consisted of a loose network of independent religious orders with no other superseding authority than the bishop of Quebec. As a community of practice, the Louisiana Church was in its infancy—one might go so far as to say it was intentionally "infantilized" by the secular authorities. The success of its evangelization mission was measured by the number of conversions, the number of recruited missionaries, and the number of parish churches. The French language was part and parcel of the identity and culture of the incoming colonists and the Church. To this extent, Louisiana was like the "mother country," Quebec.

But the types of the "French" language that survived the journey from France or Quebec were varied and sometimes almost mutually incomprehensible in Louisiana colonial times. There was no standardized form except in the official written communications of the secular and ecclesiastical rulers. Writing and reading were luxuries that only the civil and religious elite could afford, and a rudimentary religious education, when possible, was the only option for the rest of the population, an option recognized and passed on chiefly by women. So from the beginning, the Louisiana Church had to accommodate a challenging mix of regional varieties of French, not to mention the Native American languages learned by missionaries and the African languages that came with slavery. The necessity of accepting linguistic variety was a key factor in maintaining ties with the colonists, who were spread thinly across a hostile and decidedly un-French terrain and were not particularly inclined toward religious devotion to begin with.

Next, when Spain created a formal local diocesan structure in 1793, it also tried to lay the foundations of a hierarchy composed of Spanish administrators directing Spanish priests and those French missionaries left behind. The relative efficiency of the Spanish administration gave the Louisiana Church an opportunity to focus its mission on something besides mere survival and bickering over scraps handed down from the French authorities and elite. For the first time, the Louisiana Church stood out as a separate local institution or community of practice. Under the Spanish, the Church could focus its full energy on its primary mission: to spread and preserve the Catholic faith and its teaching among the local people. With the new colonial ruler came a new clerical vernacular. For the new Spanish-speaking religious hierarchy, the establishment of written and spoken Spanish among its local officials was a mission requirement. Yet the realities of the sparsely populated colony, with its mostly francophone people separated by swamps, rivers, and other physical barriers, made it highly unlikely that Louisiana would ever have a truly Spanish-speaking church. Thus the dispersal of Spanish church records into rural parishes where most of the French-speaking population was located was less successful. The geographical distance and poor transportation between local parishes and the diocesan seat in New Orleans left local priests to their own modest devices. As a result, church survival strategies and community practices prevailed over the development of a shared (Spanish) way of doing things—notably the continued use of French in sermons and other sacramental services, despite a number of register switches to Spanish, especially under direct pressure from Bishop Peñalver after 1795.

With the Louisiana Purchase in 1803, the Louisiana Church's ecclesiastical power veered back into the hands of French clerics and priests as the relatively few Spanish clergy decamped. Yet the Purchase set afoot forces that would eventually undermine the power of French culture and language. Statehood in 1812 happened at a time when American political figures were beginning to assume that the nation's economic potential was in territorial development and with the dissemination of an anglophone culture. Within a few short decades, the francophone population, which had accommodated forty years of Spanish rule without really changing much, now had to share social power with people having different cultural and linguistic assumptions, and most of them were Protestants. And of course whereas Spain was on a distant continent, the United States was a large nation contiguous to and physically inseparable from Louisiana. National forces thus turned the Louisiana political landscape wobbly. Church officials had to foster relations with different branches of a Protestant local and regional power at a time when anti-Catholicism was fashionable and politically potent in many parts of the United States, especially from the 1820s on. At first the Church chose to focus its mission on its native and newly arrived French-speaking members, of whom there were many in the earlier nineteenth century. This focus on Francophones caused not only a continuation of French registers but also a rise in the number of new churches with registers in French. But sociolinguistic trends too important to ignore propelled both the archdiocesan administration and the parish priests to negotiate new markers of identity (language, ethnicity, and status). As a consequence of this negotiation, the Louisiana church parishes—operating independently according to local conditions—changed their linguistic practices. Starting with the first register switch in 1844 for an Irish church, many registers switched from French to English from 1881 to 1901 throughout south Louisiana. Most registers became bilingual, with entries written in French and in English (and sometimes another language) depending on several factors. As we have shown, the register switches appear to correspond with the changes in actual language practices within the church parishes, although in an inconsistent way, which suggests that priests understood that English was the incoming standard and the Church was becoming "American."

What were these local trends that the religious reacted to over the nineteenth century? First, in many church parishes the traditional French parishioners became a minority, despite the number of French-speaking immigrants in the earlier part of the century. The religious activism and fervor of the Catholic Irish from the 1830s on were rewarded by grateful francophone prelates, and soon the Irish were not only able to speak to their God in English, but could write to Him too, introducing the use of English-only church records. Next, after statehood, Louisiana's upper class became more diversified, with English and French planters and merchants intermingling. For them, economic and political interests overrode linguistic and ethnic considerations. As the financial backbone of the Louisiana Church, this elite's bilingualism was a reality that was reflected in church records. The different language choices (French or English) made by mixed families are frequently displayed in registers, and we have seen the vigilant Archbishop Blanc searching Ireland and the United States for bilingual priests. Finally, successive waves of vocal English-speaking Catholic immigrants and up-for-grabs foreign-born Europeans without strong religious preferences likewise tipped the antebellum church's record practices toward bilingualism. For the church hierarchy, these immigrants represented not only a bulwark against the rapid development of Protestant institutions but also effective instruments of spiritual promotion. What was once a small, highly centralized spiritual nucleus holding a nebulous sway over multitudes of lukewarm nominal Catholics gave way to an ethnically diversified joint enterprise with a multilingual membership.

Consequently, as an accommodating strategy, what we have called "collective bilingualism" allowed the Louisiana Church to both serve its traditional francophone population and become "American" at the same time, at least for much of the nineteenth century. In fact, from Archbishop Blanc to the nomination of Archbishop Blenk, written French and English cohabited within the Archdiocese of New Orleans for an impressive time span of seventy-five years.

Nevertheless, bilingualism eventually became a social liability in most parishes. The bulk of language changes in church records happened from 1888 to 1935, with 78% of the parish registers switching to English, with a variable average switch date according to locality. From that time, writing registers in French was plainly in steady decline. Even more significant is that the use of French after 1888 was considered less and less necessary by the archdiocesan administration and parish priests. This relatively quick change in language practices highlights the central role that the parish priests played as agents of change. Switching registers to English was a bottom-up rather than a top-down change process. Half of the register switches coincided with a priest change. For sociopolitical reasons rooted in Europe (especially World War I), French-born priests were unavailable, and even before the Civil War bilingual native-born priests were seen as valuable. True, the ordination of newly accepted native-born Louisianans kept the French language as an option. However, the arrival of English-speaking priests had an important impact on the ethnic composition of the priest population.

The fact that some American-born and/or Louisiana-born priests felt more comfortable writing registers in English is only natural. But many signs that strong pressures were at play were uncovered in this study: some Irish priests' negative attitudes toward the francophone Catholics; the desire expressed in writing by English-speaking parishioners, and even some French priests, in the Antebellum Correspondence that the Church tacitly ratify English as its institutional language; register changes made by some priests when the linguistic composition of their parishioner population did not warrant it; the fact that many local priests waited for the "right" moment (change in book format, new year, a bishop's visit) to move toward monolingualism in English.

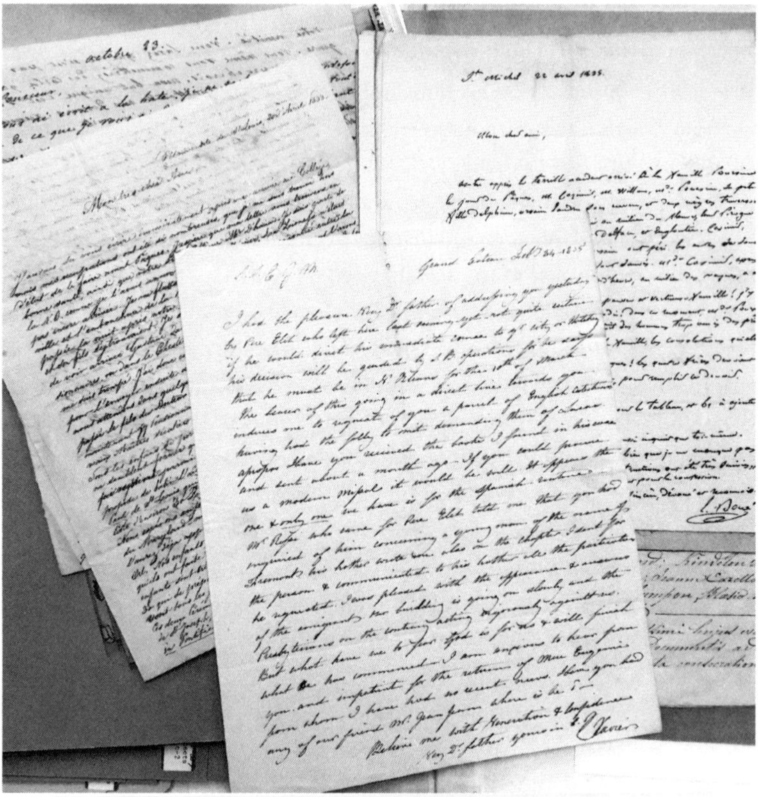

Pages from the Antebellum Correspondence in the Archives of the Archdiocese of New Orleans. (Courtesy of the Office of Archives and Records, Archdiocese of New Orleans.)

So there is no single, easily identifiable local social change which by itself tipped the balance, no "smoking gun." Taken together, these cultural forces slowly but surely pressured each religious community of practice in south Louisiana to use English-only records. It is no surprise that the extensive time span of register changes in south Louisiana paralleled the economic and political ascension of the United States and the slow decline of a Europe weakened by wars. Adding to this was the national desire for conformity and assimilation as the only way to prove a true American identity, a tendency on the ascendant after the Civil War, and finally driven home on a local level by the rise of the oil industry and its hard-cash jobs in south Louisiana.

Also locally, the post–Civil War priests' actions responded to the unspoken but strongly implied wishes and practices of the church hierarchy. One unmistakable signal sent by church officials was writing the parish reports and publishing the preprinted registers in English. Between 1911 and 1920, the archdiocesan administration changed its bilingual practices (its meeting minutes, its pastoral letters, and its newspaper) and started writing and publishing only in English. The linguistic practice of a growing and vocal Catholic English-speaking majority could not be ignored, while the dwindling numbers of young French speakers left little need for bilingualism. Registers in highly populated centers (more than two thousand inhabitants) switched to English earlier to accommodate their higher number of English-speaking people. Demands for official English-language copies of important personal documents sped up the switch for churches, especially those in financial straits.

A new key factor influencing the parish priests' attitudes toward the maintenance of the French language can be identified statistically: the increasing establishment of Protestant churches in previously French-dominant parishes. As the Antebellum Correspondence reveals, this development generated high anxiety among Catholic English speakers, who conveyed their apprehension to their parish priest, who, in turn, was compelled to linguistic conformity with "the Americans."

The case studies show that each parish church represented a unique religious community of practice; highly variable linguistic behaviors are found within each. Nonetheless, there are strong overall tendencies. With the exception of New Orleans and St. James Parish, a higher number of English-speaking priests sped up the move to monolingualism and shortened the switch's time span. Parishes with French-born priests showed the lengthiest resistance to monolingualism. Not surprisingly, there is a strong correlation between register switches to English and the linguistic behavior of parishioners. In other words, local priests ceased bilingual practices when it was already fading within the church parish. Sometimes, the switch to English in church records is ahead of the language practices of the parishioners. By the beginning of the twentieth century, bilingualism was still a daily practice in some farming and fishing localities, the few which had stayed very French-dominant. For these people, language change must have appeared abrupt. Local priests started to deliver sermons, write registers, and conduct church affairs mainly in English, while French-dominant parishioners were left behind.

In summary, the Louisiana Church has held a constant focus on the language needs of its members from the earliest colonial days until now; this study has tried to analyze the varied ways the Church's written records show that it was deeply concerned with language issues despite its formidable French-speaking façade and hierarchy throughout most of its history. Measuring both local and macro responses adds new data and nuance to the relationship of French and English in south Louisiana. It can truly be said that the story of the Louisiana Church represents three hundred years of language accommodation. Today, the Archdiocese of New Orleans conducts services in English, Vietnamese, Spanish, and sign language. Sacramental registers are kept in English. Most correspondence is written in English. The archdiocesan newspaper, the *Clarion Herald,* is published in English and Spanish. The archdiocese continues to minister to its faithful by accommodating the language needs of all of God's people. It is not far-fetched to imagine a near future in which a long-serving New Orleans priest echoes to his parishioners what Father Subileau, who opened this study, sadly said a century before: "I am getting too old for my words to have any weight with you. What I say, instead of sinking in, slides off, leaving no impression. I deem it necessary that a younger man take charge of you, and perhaps his word may have more effect than mine." Only in this scenario the priest is an English speaker, and his parishioners are Hispanic.

NOTES

INTRODUCTION

1. The *Times-Democrat* published in New Orleans in 1913.

2. Dolan, "A Critical Period in American Catholicism," 526.

3. Fishman, *Reversing Language Shift*, 6.

4. The terms "language shift," "language switch," and "language change" will be used interchangeably in this book although there may be subtle nuances in the definitions.

5. Many nineteenth-century travel accounts exist, including Robin, *Voyages dans l'intérieur de la Louisiane* (1807); Clapp, *Autobiographical Sketches and Recollections* (1857); Castellanos, *New Orleans as It Was* (1895). For studies on the nineteenth-century New Orleans elite, see Cable, *The Creoles of Louisiana* (1884; rpr. 1970); Crété, *La vie quotidienne en Louisiane* (1978); Blassingame, *Black New Orleans* (1973).

6. For readers who would like to have an overview of recent linguistic studies on language issues in Louisiana, we refer to four edited collections of essays from the most prolific scholars in linguistics: Valdman, *French and Creole in Louisiana;* Valdman, Auger, and Piston-Hatlen, *Le français en Amérique du Nord;* Papen and Chevalier, *Les variétés de français;* Picone and Davies, *New Perspectives on Language Variety in the South.*

7. With the exception of August Rubrecht's PhD dissertation research carried out in the early 1970s, the introduction and development of English in Louisiana have not been, to our knowledge, the focus of any extensive empirical study: see Rubrecht, "Regional Phonological Variants in Louisiana Speech." Recent studies by Michael Picone and Connie Eble on nineteenth-century plantation French written by the elite (white Creoles or Creoles of color), as well as those pertaining to Cajun English and Creole African American English by Sylvie Dubois and Barbara Horvath, have provided a sociolinguistic frame of analysis that deserves to be emulated by linguists working on other ethnic varieties in Louisiana and elsewhere. See Picone, "Anglophone Slaves," 404–33; Eble, "The Loss of French," 91–98;

Dubois and Horvath, "When the Music Changes," 287–313, and "The English Vernacular," 255–88.

8. Beers, *French and Spanish Records of Louisiana.*

9. Dulles, *Models of the Church,* 38.

10. Wenger, *Communities of Practice.*

11. This definition is taken from Eckert and McConnell-Ginet, "Think Practically and Look Locally," 464. It is reiterated in Meyerhoff, "Communities of Practice," 526–48.

1. THE CHURCH, LANGUAGE, AND POLITICS IN COLONIAL LOUISIANA, 1718–1803

1. There are several nineteenth-century studies and countless recent books on regional and local history. The most often cited pioneer works are Le Page Du Pratz, *The History of Louisiana* (1774); Martin, *The History of Louisiana from the Earliest Period* (1829); Gayarré, *Louisiana: Its History as a French Colony* (1854); Bunner, *History of Louisiana, from Its First Discovery and Settlement to the Present Time* (1855); Fortier, *A History of Louisiana* (1904).

2. Archives Nationales–Archives Coloniales (henceforth AN-AC), C13A-119, June 29, 1716, Decree from the French Council of the Navy.

3. AN-AC, C13A-134, February 26, 1708, Letter from d'Artaguiette; C13A-457, March 1, 1714, Letter from La Mothe-Cadillac; C13A-351 (no date) 1713, Letter from Father Hidalgo.

4. Codignola, "Les premiers pas de l'Église Catholique en Acadie et au Canada," 45–60.

5. Nolan, *History of the Archdiocese of New Orleans,* 16.

6. O'Neill, *Church and State in French Colonial Louisiana,* 52.

7. Hardy, "Church and State in French Louisiana," 88.

8. AN-AC, C13A-43, January 19, 1732, Letter from Perier; AN-AC, C14A-143, April 23, 1735, Letter from Bienville.

9. Census data are taken from many studies: Beer, *Early Census Tables of Louisiana;* Voorhies, *Some Late Eighteenth-Century Louisianians;* Allain, "French Emigration Policies: Louisiana," 39–46; Denuzière, *Je te nomme Louisiane;* Brasseaux, *A Refuge for All Ages.*

10. Hall, *Africans in Colonial Louisiana;* Berlin, *Many Thousands Gone.* Christianization went along with the learning of the French language (and later on Spanish). The Church was therefore a powerful (if impoverished) linguistic and cultural assimilator that extended even to African and Native American slaves. Close contact with a population (living with them or closely working with them) offered a better language learning environment that allowed slaves to develop closer approximations, if not a perfect command, of different varieties of French, while lack of contact favored rudimentary forms of learning. See studies done by linguists on Louisiana Creole French: Valdman, *French and Creole in Louisiana;* Klingler, *If I Could Turn My Tongue like That;* Neumann-Holzschuh, "Restructuration dans un créole conservateur," 382–407.

11. AN-AC, G1-464, January 1, 1726, *Recensement des habitations et des habitants de la colonie de la Louisiane.* The number of slaves in Bienville's concession and the nearby Tchoupitoulas and Cannes Brulées plantations is included in New Orleans city area.

12. It is fitting to recall that in France itself during this era speakers from the north of France or even the Ile-de-France but living outside of Paris were considered to be dialect speakers. Lodge, *French: From Dialect to Standard;* Ayres-Bennett, *A History of the French Language through Texts.*

13. Rickard, *A History of the French Language,* 121.

14. Usner, *Indians, Settlers, and Slaves,* 23–30.

15. Dubois, "Autant en emporte la langue," 155–78.

16. Chaudenson, *Creolization of Language and Culture.*

17. After Spain snatched control of the Gulf Coast out of the hands of Britain in 1783, the local Spanish officials in New Orleans tolerated illicit trade with them.

18. Data taken from the 1785 New Orleans census.

19. Lemmon, "Spanish Louisiana," 16–29. Like the French Crown, the Spanish royal authorities did try to control the expansion of the Church (for example, the suppression of the French Capuchins' slave plantation in 1784) and deny the right of local priests to meddle in what were considered by the Crown as civil matters only. One example is the Spanish imperial decree of 1776, which prohibited unequal unions (marrying beneath one's own class or outside one's own race) and required parental consent for all people below the age of twenty-five. Also see Gutiérrez, *When Jesus Came.*

20. Charles Nolan discussed these changes in *History of the Archdiocese of New Orleans,* 16–20.

21. *Catholic Encyclopedia,* http://www.newadvent.org/cathen/11005b.htm.

22. Nolan, *History of the Archdiocese of New Orleans,* 20.

23. Dispensations are permissions granted to relax ecclesiastical laws—e.g., the prohibition to marry a person of different religion or a first-degree cousin—either for legitimizing marriages already contracted or permitting others about to be contracted. But second- and third-degree consanguinity—cousins as well as affinity or related by marriage—gave other reasons to ask for a dispensation. A typical example is Joseph Villars, a New Orleans native and son of the commissary of the army, who wished to marry Maria Eulalia Livaudais, his second cousin. Since they were poor, he asked for a matrimonial dispensation in 1802. Matrimonial dispensation petitions represent half of the nine thousand preserved letters of the Antebellum Correspondence between 1780 and 1860.

24. Louisiana historians have written profusely on both groups, notably Carl Brasseaux, Thomas Fiehrer, and Gilbert Din. The two groups established themselves along the Mississippi River and Louisiana bayous.

25. The consequences of the Saint Domingue revolt (1791–1804) and outmigration to Louisiana will be discussed in the next chapter.

26. For details about Spanish administrators' accommodation to local culture, see Gayarré, *Louisiana* 3:310–11; Miller, "Bourbon Social Engineering," 261–90.

27. Dubois, "Letter-Writing in French Louisiana," 68.

28. The facts about education are taken from David Bjork, "Documents relating to the Establishment of Schools in Louisiana," 561–69.

29. AN-AC, C13A-43, January 19, 1732, Letter from Perier. He mentioned the education of girl orphans so that they could be trained in silkworm farming.

30. AN-AC, C13A-399, May 15, 1725, and C13A-38, March 12, 1726, Letters from Father Raphael to l'Abbé Raguet.

2. TENDING TO MULTIETHNIC CATHOLIC FLOCKS IN A PROTESTANT NATION, 1812–1861

1. Paris was the official crossroads of missionary relations for the Society for the Propagation of the Faith. The society was in charge of France, Quebec, the United States, China, Cayenne, the Antilles, and Senegal. Information about missionary works in those territories resumed after the Napoleonic period in 1814, but Paris never recovered its central role. See Codignola, "La bureaucratie romaine," 61–72.

2. Smith-Thibodeaux, *Les francophones de Louisiane,* 3.

3. Ingersoll, *Mammon and Manon in Early New Orleans,* 244–47.

4. Letter dated April 2, 1814, from John Cravath May Windship to his friend William Plumer Jr., in Brown, "Letters from Louisiana, 1813–1814," 575. Paul Lachance also wrote about this issue in "Intermarriage and French Cultural Persistence," 59.

5. Gray, *A Short History of Louisiana,* 143. For more details about the influx of Anglo-Americans, see Wall, *Louisiana: A History,* 7.

6. The 1805 census data are reported in Hanger, *Bounded Lives, Bounded Places,* 22. The 1805 census numbers are taken from Paxton, *The New-Orleans Directory and Register,* 112.

7. Data taken from Spletstoser, "Back Door to the Land of Plenty," 299. The Irish and Germans began arriving in 1820. Articles about these two populations are found in Brasseaux, *A Refuge for All Ages.*

8. Fiehrer, "From La Tortue to La Louisiane," 1–30.

9. Brasseaux, *The "Foreign French."* Marriage records show that, from 1790 to 1830, 24% of these new French migrants were from Aquitaine, 28% were from other Atlantic regions, and 25% were from southern regions of France. Hirsch and Logsdon, *Creole New Orleans: Race and Americanization,* 109–12.

10. Dominguez argues that the planter class has French ancestry, Catholic religion, and French language as crucial denominators. Dominguez, *White by Definition,* 104.

11. Numbers are taken from two studies: Roussève, *The Negro in Louisiana,* 44; Brasseaux, "Creoles of Color," 67–86. The wealth of Creoles of color is discussed in Fairclough, *Race and Democracy.* More information can be found in Hanger, "Origins of New Orleans's Free Creoles of Color," 1–27.

12. One of the letters is from Jean Baptiste Blanc, brother of Bishop Blanc, who served in the Barrens in 1826. It is addressed to the vicar-general of the Lyon Diocese. *Annales de l'Association de la Propagation de la Foi* (hereafter VANT-PF *Annales*), 1826, Tome 2 (Paris: Librarie ecclésiastiques de Rusand).

13. Archdiocese of New Orleans–Antebellum Correspondence (hereafter AANO-AC), June 10, 1803, Letter from Father Hassett to the clergy.

14. The six out of twenty-one nuns who stayed behind were French nuns. See Heaney, "A Century of Pioneering"; Clark, *Masterless Mistresses*, 227.

15. In his letter written in Italian to the Secretariat of State, the secretary of the Propaganda Fide gave his views on the Ursulines' demand. VANT-PF 1406, vol. 296: fols. 340–41, September 26, 1815. Four months later, the same secretary wrote to the Ursulines a letter in Latin in which he paid tribute to their religious and educational achievements and exhorted them to persist in their efforts. VANT-PF 1406, vol. 297: fols. 1rv, January 5, 1816.

16. The originals are in the archives of the Ursuline Community of New Orleans. Copies are in the Archdiocese Antebellum Correspondence. AANO-AC, March 21, 1804, Letter from Mother St. Xavier Fargeon to Thomas Jefferson; AANO-AC, May 15, 1804, Letter from Thomas Jefferson to Mother Therese de St. Xavier Farjon.

17. Three years later, Bishop Dubourg was appointed bishop of the diocese. Melville, *Louis William Dubourg.*

18. Bishop Rosati became coadjutor in 1823 with the understanding that when the diocese was divided in two, he would become bishop of one of the new dioceses.

19. Pasquier, "*Les confrères et les pères:* French Missionaries and Transnational Catholicism," 154–55.

20. Ibid., 156.

21. AANO-AC, February 6, 1825, Letter from Father Dubourg to Father Brute.

22. VANT-PF 264, fols. 231–32, February 22, 1793, Letter to the secretary of the Propaganda Fide. His exact terms in Latin are "*a provinciis americanis expectamus solacium.*" Also mentioned in Codignola, "La bureaucratie romaine," 68.

23. Nolan, *A Southern Catholic Heritage*, 2.

24. Ibid., 5.

25. Letter quoted ibid., 25.

26. Spear, *Race, Sex, and Social Order in Early New Orleans*, 97–99.

27. Anonymous report in VANT-PF *Annales*, 1830, Tome 4 (Paris: Librarie ecclésiastiques de Rusand).

28. Dawdy, *Building the Devil's Empire*, 227.

29. University of Notre Dame Archives online. *Catholic Encyclopedia*, http://archives.nd.edu/mano/neworlea.htm.

30. Greene, *Antoine Blanc*, 2008.

31. Our translation. AANO-AC, August 12, 1835, Letter from Father Alaux to Bishop Blanc.

32. AANO-AC, February 25, 1850, Letter from Father Blin to Bishop Blanc.

33. AANO-AC, February 24, 1850, Letter from Father Chambodut to Father Rousselon.

34. AANO-AC, February 25, 1850, Letter from Bishop Portier to Father Rousselon.

35. Niehaus, *The Irish in New Orleans,* 50.

36. Barry, *The Catholic Church and German Americans,* as cited by Niehaus in "Catholic Church in Louisiana," 51.

37. According to Giordano, *The Italians of Louisiana.*

38. Karnes, *Tropical Enterprise,* 297.

39. The Chapel of the Resurrection and St. Anthony of Padua (today Our Lady of Guadaloupe) were the first churches to serve the Italian immigrants. St. Mary's records begin in 1803. It was established as a church parish in 1840.

40. Niehaus, *The Irish in New Orleans,* 57.

41. AANO-AC, November 18, 1844, Letter from William G. Read to Bishop Blanc.

42. Baudier, *The Catholic Church in Louisiana,* 415.

43. Vecoli, "Prelates and Peasants," 217–267.

44. Doorley, "Irish Catholics and French Creoles," 41.

45. Niehaus, *The Irish in New Orleans,* 51.

46. Reinders, *End of an Era: New Orleans,* 102.

47. Evidence of this demand can be found in several letters addressed to Bishop Blanc: AANO-AC, December 2, 1835, Letter from Caroline Hall and others; AANO-AC, October 2, 1837, and March 20, 1840, Letters from John Joseph and others; AANO-AC, April 22, 1847, Letter from Robert Sewall; AANO-AC, February 2, 1846, Letter from Muli Milites, Army of Occupation, Corpus Christi.

48. Letters addressed to Bishop Blanc, unless indicated. AANO-AC, February 8, 1836, and January 29, 1838, Letters from B. Gravet; AANO-AC, March 1847 and January 9, 1852, Letters from Father Dufour; AANO-AC, August 4, 1840, Letter from Father Armengol mentioning Father Abbadie; AANO-AC, January 22, 1841, Letter from Father Jouanneault; AANO-AC, February 25, 1850, and March 25, 1851, Letters from Father Blin; AANO-AC, August 17, 1847, Letter from Father Lavadiere; AANO-AC, December 28, 1848, Letter from Sister Ste. Therese (Carmelite); AANO-AC, January 6, 1850, Letter from Sister Emily (Sister of Charity) to Father Rousselon.

49. Father Gache's role as Jesuit chaplain is described in Buckley, *A Frenchman, a Chaplain, a Rebel.*

50. VANT-PF *Annales,* Tome 4, January 25, 1830, Letter from Father Blanc to the vicar-general of the Lyon Diocese.

51. AANO-AC, January 6, 1850, Letter from Maria B. Williams to Bishop Blanc.

52. AANO-AC, July 2, 1835, Letter from Father Beauprez to Bishop Blanc.

53. See Dubois, "Autant en emporte la langue," 198–232.

54. The embryonic state system was hampered by underfunding and a lack of support. Although newly established Protestant churches provided education in English, the educational level was as rudimentary as in the Catholic churches. See Suarez, "Chronicle of a Failure," 109.

55. Lachance, "The 1809 Immigration of Saint-Domingue Refugees to New Orleans"; Brasseaux, *A Refuge for All Ages,* 258–86.

56. Kara VanDam, who studied two West Michigan Dutch Calvinist communities, has written about the need of bilingual priests in immigrant settings. VanDam, *A Study of Language Identity and Shift.*

57. AANO-AC, October 26, 1840, Letter from Father Rousselon to Bishop Blanc.

58. AANO-AC, November 9, 1840, Letter from Father Rousselon to Bishop Blanc.

59. AANO-AC, February 18, 1850, Letter from Father Pitrat to Bishop Blanc.

60. AANO-AC, (no date) 1840, Letter from Father Lafranc to Bishop Blanc.

61. AANO-AC, July 26, 1844, Letter from Bishop Loras to Bishop Blanc. His negative learning experience may explain why he, a French-born priest, persistently wrote to Bishop Blanc in English, as illustrated in table 2.1.

62. Only one priest, Father Blin, mentioned a priest's financial advantage to preaching in both French and English. According to Blin, a bilingual priest could double his fee. AANO-AC, February 25, 1850, Letter from Father Blin to Bishop Blanc; AANO-AC, July 9, 1853, Letter from Bishop Odin to Father Rousselon; AANO-AC, December 21, 1849, Letter from Father Martin to Bishop Blanc; AANO-AC, (no date) 1845, Letter from Bishop Flaget to Bishop Blanc.

63. These priests later served as bishops. Perché was archbishop of New Orleans from 1870 to 1883; Martin became bishop of the newly formed diocese of Natchitoches (1853–75); Odin was nominated bishop of Galveston, Texas (1847–61), then archbishop of New Orleans (1861–70). He followed Bishop Blanc and was the second archbishop of New Orleans.

64. AANO-AC, July 7, 1847, Letter from Sister Marie Hall (S.C.) to Bishop Blanc; AANO-AC, July 26, 1847, Letter from Sister Marie de St. Stanislas (R.U.) to Bishop Blanc; AANO-AC, September 26, 1847, Letter from Sister St. Arsene (R.U.) to Bishop Blanc.

65. As an example, in 1846 Father Victor Blanc wrote about St. Patrick's priest's efforts in learning French. AANO-AC, (no date) 1846, Letter from Father V. Blanc to Bishop Blanc.

66. AANO-AC, November 25, 1839, Letter from Father Point to Bishop Blanc.

67. AANO-AC, July 22, 1841, Letter from Father Armengol to Bishop Blanc.

68. AANO-AC, April 20, 1844, Letter from Father Priour to Bishop Blanc.

69. AANO-AC, no date, Letter from William Lowndes to Bishop Blanc.

70. AANO-AC, (no date) 1854, Letter from Father Stephane Henriot to Bishop Blanc. His letter sent from Cleveland, Ohio, is marked with Blanc's corrections.

71. AANO-AC, November 14, 1835, Letter from Mother Julie Bazire to Bishop Blanc.

72. AANO-AC, March 4, 1859, Letter from Carrollton parishioners to Bishop Blanc.

73. AANO-AC, July 19, 1847, Letter from Father Tumoine to Bishop Blanc.

74. Miller, "A Church in Cultural Captivity," 31.

75. Redemptorists' Provincial Archives, Denver, Colorado: House Files, New Orleans, June 3, 1854, Letter from Father Rulland.

76. Pasquier, "*Les confrères et les pères:* French Missionaries and Transnational Catholicism," 37.

3. THE REGISTERS SPEAK: THE RISE AND FALL OF LOUISIANA BILINGUALISM AND THE LUCK OF THE IRISH

1. See Gitlin, *The Bourgeois Frontier*, 166.

2. Data elements for each church parish include several variables: year of first entry, church parish, city, civil parish, current diocese, switch date, possible cause of switch (priest change, new book, etc.), and observations. We primarily used the baptism register to document the switch. When that was not clear, we reviewed the marriage and death registers. Not all churches were consistent. As an example, the St. Louis Cathedral baptism registers switched in 1911 (with a few stragglers after that) while the marriage register was bilingual (some in English and some in French) until 1919, when it abruptly switched to English.

3. We originally identified 252 church parishes, but we eliminated eight parishes from the study due to the absence of earlier records that were destroyed by fire. We also put aside three parish registers that include the interjection of Latin as a third language. In each case, the language switched from French to Latin for a period of years, before switching to English, making a clear date of switch impossible to calculate. We speculate that the priest was delaying the use of English by selecting Latin, the universal language of the Catholic Church at the time. Registers where entries are recorded in German or Italian were not part of our focus due to the complexities involved in adding another language to the study.

4. "Compendium of the Catechism of the Catholic Church," accessed May 10, 2013. http://www.vatican.va/archive/compendium_ccc/documents/archive_2005_compendium-ccc_en.html.

5. Since death is not a sacrament, death registers are not strictly speaking sacramental registers. For our purposes, we treat them as a type of sacramental register, since, in its everyday nomenclature, the Catholic Church includes them in this collection.

6. Bruns, "Annotating for Posterity," 349–59.

7. Ibid., 349.

8. Ibid., 350.

9. AANO-AC, January 12, 1790, Decree from Cirilo Sieni of Barcelona written by notary Estevan Quinones.

10. Most of these pioneer churches were short-lived. Three still exist today: St. Louis Cathedral, St. Charles Borromeo, and St. Francis of Pointe Coupée (now St. Mary, New Roads). We have one early register from St. Charles Borromeo, which started in 1723. In 1877, a fire destroyed the rectory and the records. Only one early register survived and is located in the archives: St. Charles Borromeo: Baptisms, Marriages and Deaths, 1739–55. Records from Natchitoches exist, but since it is not part of the geographic area of our study, we did not use them.

11. In all church registers, we have entries written in Spanish. Ascension of Our Lord Church in Ascension Parish and St. Bernard Church in St. Bernard Parish even have entries written in Latin. It is worth noting that St. Louis Cathedral is the only church parish that

switched exclusively to Spanish from 1775 to 1805; however, Pere Antoine continued to write his entries in Spanish until his death in 1829.

12. This switch is partly due to Baton Rouge being under British control from 1763 to 1779, when the Spanish gained control during the Battle of Baton Rouge. English-speaking inhabitants were allowed to stay in the area, thus the need for English, especially in the St. Francisville area.

13. Audisio, "Crisis in Baton Rouge," 347.

14. This period corresponds to what Dubois has called the "ethnic period," when bilingualism (French and English) in Louisiana ceased to be desirable and beneficial. The "ethnic period" is the third of four chronological periods (a historical categorization essentially based on sociolinguistic distinctions), which allow an interpretation of language diversity and change in Louisiana from the colonial times to the present. Dubois, "Autant en emporte la langue," 155–78.

15. By the early 1800s, the shift to English in Ireland was extensive except in the west, an area divided in four provinces of relatively equal size. Mandatory English education was established in 1831, and the use of Irish by church personnel had become the exception in this period (Wolf, "The Irish-Speaking Clergy," 62). By the time of the major immigration to Louisiana, both educated and working-class Irish originating from the west provinces spoke English as a second language, albeit sometimes begrudgingly. These probably considered English as a compromise language in the Louisiana Church.

16. Niehaus, "The Irish and Their Church," 429–41.

17. AANO-AC, May 5, 1847, Letter from Father Mullon to Bishop Blanc.

18. AANO-AC, October 10, 1856, Letter from Father Mullon to Bishop Blanc.

19. AANO-AC, May 10, 1839, Letter from Father Walsh to Father Rousselon. Rousselon's reply is written on the back of Father Walsh's letter; May 17, 1839, Letter from Bishop Blanc to Father Rousselon.

20. Doorley, "Irish Catholics and French Creoles," 34–54, 42.

21. Niehaus, "The Irish and Their Church," 437.

22. Doorley, "Irish Catholics and French Creoles," 41.

23. Niehaus, "The Irish and Their Church," 429.

24. Doorley, "Irish Catholics and French Creoles," 28.

25. Ibid., 38.

26. AANO-AC, January 11, 1844, Letter from Bishop Purcell of Cincinnati.

27. *Le Propagateur Catholique,* November 18, 1843, quoted in Niehaus, "The Irish and Their Church," 436.

28. *L'Orléanais,* March 31, April 27, 1852, quoted in Doorley, "Irish Catholics and French Creoles," 39.

29. Reinders, *End of an Era.*

30. Spletstoser, "Back Door to the Land of Plenty."

31. Robert Maguire has described this exodus in "Hustling to Survive."

32. Dubois and Horvath, "The English Vernacular," 253–86.

33. Shugg, *Origins of Class Struggle in Louisiana,* 45–50.

34. Virginia Dominguez has described the multiple definitions that the label "Creole" acquired over time in Louisiana. During the ethnic period, being Creole usually meant being a Louisiana-native Francophone. As such, many racial populations could claim this label. However, white Creoles, fearing being associated with the nonwhite Creoles, argued that people of color and blacks could not be identified as such. Dominguez, *White by Definition.* See also Dubois and Melançon, "Creole Is, Creole Ain't," 237–58.

35. Hirsch and Logsdon, *Creole New Orleans.*

36. Holt, *The Rise and Fall of the American Whig Party.*

37. Dubois, "Autant en emporte la langue," 166.

38. Many scholars have described this period of linguistic nationalism: Fass, "The IQ," 432–48; Rury, "Race, Region, and Education," 51–65; Krashen, *Condemned without a Trial.*

39. Dubois, "Autant en emporte la langue."

40. Dominguez, *White by Definition,* 145.

41. Dubois and Horvath, "When the Music Changes," 287–313. See also Dubois and Horvath, "Creoles and Cajuns," 253–86.

42. See Bernard, *The Cajuns,* for a description of the Cajun revival in Louisiana.

43. Nolan, *History of the Archdiocese of New Orleans,* 50.

4. LANGUAGE PRACTICES OF THE ARCHDIOCESAN ADMINISTRATION, 1861–1917

1. The decree stipulated that there should be six, or at least four, diocesan consultors, half to be appointed by the bishop and the other half to be appointed after nomination by the clergy. Office was held for three years, but consultors could be reappointed or selected at the expiration of each term.

2. The Third Plenary Council also recommended that bishops appoint deans and vicars "forane," i.e., district officials who aid in the administration of parishes in a certain vicinity. Fanning, "Plenary Councils of Baltimore."

3. Nolan, *History of the Archdiocese of New Orleans,* 40.

4. A half-dozen Louisiana clergy served as Confederate chaplains; sisters from different orders served in hospitals and buildings transformed as such, assisting war victims.

5. In his letter written in English and dated September 1864, Archbishop Odin describes Louisiana's sad condition to Archbishop Purcell of Cincinnati: "For want of hands, its crops are almost an entire failure. All horses and mules have been taken by the government. People apprehend that all Catholic schools will be closed by military authority." AANO-AC, September 24, 1864, Letter from Archbishop Odin to Archbishop Purcell.

6. Odin successfully "guided the affairs of the Archiepiscopal See through difficult times: the conflict of 1861–1865 and the Reconstruction Period." Wight, "A Letter from the Archbishop of New Orleans," 129.

7. The archdiocese was not the only Louisiana institution crippled with debt; the city and the state were also near bankruptcy. The end of the Civil War did not stop the political and social disruptions, which continued and even intensified during the following decades. They plunged Louisiana into profound distress, and the terrible flood of 1874 completed its economic ruin.

8. AANO-AC, February 11, 1879, Letter from Father Ferreol Girardey to James Alphonsus McMaster.

9. Archbishop Perché solicited financial aid from the Holy See, but the Franco-Prussian War in Europe prevented him from receiving additional funds. In a letter dated February 19, 1871, addressed to all priests of his diocese, Archbishop Perché recommended putting an emphasis on the Easter and Christmas collections, suspending any dispensations from these collections, due to the state of affairs in France and in Europe. AANO-AC, February 4, 1871, Letter from Archbishop Perché. While he imposed upon the archdiocesan priests a 10% tax on their receipts, archdiocesan expenses kept exceeding revenues and creditors grew restless. Very soon the corporation was contemplating judicial liquidation.

10. AANO-AC, September 10, 1876, Letter from Bishop William Henry to Archbishop Perché.

11. The Catholic lawyers were of the opinion that liquidation should be ordered and the Corporation of the Diocese of New Orleans dissolved to protect French and American creditors equally. While Father Leray declined to join the corporation as president, he refused nonetheless to liquidate it. Instead he worked tirelessly to repay its debt.

12. See the website of the Diocese of Alexandria: http://diocesealex.org/about-diocese-alexandria.

13. His letter was written in English, but this expression was in French. Kasteel, *Francis Janssens,* 173.

14. Niehaus, "Catholic Church in Louisiana."

15. See Kasteel, "Archbishop Francis Janssens," 156–69.

16. US Census population of 1887.

17. Archdiocese of New Orleans–Administrative Business Records (hereafter AANO-ABR), September 16, 1888; Redemptorists' Provincial Archives, Denver, Colorado, *Annales* 1847–1890.

18. As quoted in Ellis, *Documents of American Catholic History,* 529–30.

19. Chapelle's new functions are described in the section "Louisiana" on the *Catholic Encyclopedia* website, accessed September 19, 2013, http://www.newadvent.org/cathen/09378a.htm. See also Niehaus, "Catholic Church in Louisiana," 819.

20. AANO-ABR, January 10, 1898, Archiepiscopal Council Minutes.

21. AANO-ABR, September 26, 1899, Archiepiscopal Council Minutes.

22. Georgelin, *The Catholic Church in Algiers, Louisiana,* 47.

23. Niehaus, "Catholic Church in Louisiana," 819.

5. PARISH PRIESTS AS AGENTS OF LINGUISTIC CHANGE: ANALYZING THE DATA

1. The *Official Catholic Directory* collection (1836–2017) includes the *Official Catholic Directory* as well as the same serial under its previous names. The directories provide detailed profiles of each (arch)diocese, listing its parishes, schools, convents, orphanages, hospitals, and other institutions. It also lists the current and former (arch)bishops, administrators, and secular and religious-order priests, including the parishes or institutions in which they served. To capture a detailed snapshot of the parish priests and their countries of origin, we gathered information from the *Official Catholic Directory* for the years 1860, 1870, 1880, 1890, 1900, 1910, and 1920. These years were used because they matched the dates for the US Census (with the exception of the missing 1890 Census), and with this information it was possible to determine country of origin for each of the priests serving in the parishes during that year. Archbishop Janssens recorded in his diary the status of the priests in the archdiocese, including date of birth, country of birth, date and place of ordination, and arrival in the archdiocese. Due to the unavailability of the 1890 US Census, the diary is invaluable. In 1921, many of the original 1890 Census records were destroyed by fire. Few fragments remain.

2. AANO-ABR, December 6, 1914, Burial register from St. Peter Church in Reserve in St. John the Baptist Parish.

3. Of the 1,043 entries, country of origin was not determined for seven priests: two in 1860; one in 1880; and four in 1920. The country of origin for each priest was given in the US Census. Although today many of these countries do not exist (i.e., Alsace, Bavaria, Prussia, and Sicily), they are identified as the country of origin.

4. A minor seminary was a boarding school for teenage boys that prepared students for the major seminary, a higher education institution. Baudier, *The Catholic Church in Louisiana,* 495–99.

5. AANO-AC, March 22, 1915, Pastoral letter from Archbishop Blenk to the clergy and laity.

6. Another interesting situation is the switch to Latin in many church registers in New Orleans as a neutral language in the tumultuous linguistic climate of the Civil War.

7. Archdiocese of New Orleans—Dioceses of Lafayette, Baton Rouge, Lake Charles, Houma-Thibodaux Church Parish Records and Reports (hereafter AANO-DD), May 17, 1889, Burial register from St. Paul Church in Bayou Goula.

8. AANO-DD, May 17, 1889, Burial register from St. Raphael Church in West Baton Rouge Parish.

9. Britain, "Space and Spatial Diffusion," 603–37.

10. In an earlier study on the archdiocese, Dubois, Leumas, and Richardson (2007) tested the efficacy of three explanatory spatial models within the field of social geography. Their basic approach was inspired by sociolinguists such as Britain (2002) and Horvath and Horvath (2001 and 2003), who expanded earlier work in sociolinguistic dialect geography done by Trudgill (1986) and Chambers (1995). All these scholars have provided key studies on the spatial distribution of linguistic forms across a range of localities (cities, regions, and countries). The study done by Dubois and colleagues, in contrast, analyzes diffusion of a language practice over space *and* time. Dubois, Leumas, and Richardson, "Spatial Diffusion," 51–64; Horvath and Horvath, "A Multilocality Study," 37–57, and "A Closer Look," 143–70; Trudgill, *Dialects in Contact;* Chambers, *Sociolinguistic Theory.*

11. Britain, "Space and Spatial Diffusion," 623.

12. Ibid., 623.

13. During this period, the number of urban centers was low and some of them saw their population dwindling during the Depression (e.g., Donaldsonville and Napoleonville as sugarcane centers). Given the agricultural economy, the number of villages is much higher than cities and towns.

14. Britain, "Space and Spatial Diffusion," 625.

15. Cited ibid.

16. To transfer the continuous gravity index into a nominal variable, we used a percentile calculation.

17. We also calculated the gravity index for Baton Rouge as a diffusion center, excluding cities near New Orleans. The assumption was that this urban center could have influenced cities in southwest Louisiana, where many Acadians lived (e.g., Opelousas, Lafayette, Breaux Bridge). None of the geographical models had a significant effect. We also tested Thibodaux and Opelousas as diffusion centers in their own geographical locations. No correlation was found.

18. Dubois and Horvath. "The English Vernacular," 255–88.

19. The presence of English in French communities in Louisiana is reported in several studies. We list here only a representative sample of academic works: Smith, "A Recording of English Sounds"; Scott, "Cajun Vernacular English"; Walton, "Flat Speech and Cajun Ethnic Identity"; Lambert, "The R-ful Truth of the Matter"; Cheramie, "Cajun Vernacular English"; Fontenot, "Cajun English"; Emmitte, "Un Cadjin qui dzit Cher bon dieu!"

20. Brasseaux, "Creoles of Color," 74.

21. Milroy and Milroy, "Linguistic Change," 375.

22. Our translation. Anonymous report in VANT-PF *Annales,* 1830, Tome 4 (Paris: Librarie ecclésiastiques), 655.

23. The ideal calculation would have been the proportion of Protestant churches versus Catholic churches in each city at the same period. However, attempts to access these data from Protestant organizations were unsuccessful.

24. AANO-AC, August 14, 1844, Letter from Maria B. Williams to Bishop Blanc.

25. Connor, "The Protestant Church."

26. Duncan, *Diocese of Louisiana,* 79–80.

6. THE LANGUAGE PRACTICES OF PRIESTS AND PARISHIONERS: CASE STUDIES, 1885–1954

1. These reports were collected prior to an episcopal visit by the ordinary. The archbishop/bishop is required to visit each parish usually every three years. The report allowed him to know the parish a little better before his visit and to be able to address certain issues of importance.

2. "County-Parish Boundaries in Louisiana," prepared by the Historical Records Survey Division of Professional and Service Projects Works in 1939, provided the information and dates. The 2006–7 *Louisiana Almanac* provided the data size, parish seat, other towns, significant waterways, agriculture, and industry. See Calhoun, *Louisiana Almanac.* For histories of the case-study churches located in the Diocese of Baton Rouge, see Leumas and Richard, *Roots of Faith.*

3. The country of birth for Father Juan de Diego Martinez is unknown, but judging from his last name one can assume he was of Hispanic origin.

4. Why Archbishop Janssens assigned English-speaking priests or priests more comfortable in English to African American churches is a question that archival material does not allow us to answer.

5. We could not determine from the visitation reports when French services actually stopped. It is quite possible the services were conducted in French and English well after 1950.

6. St. Joseph became a co-cathedral when the diocese of Houma-Thibodaux was established in 1977. Information taken from Aguirre, *Celebrating Faith along the Bayous,* 87.

7. To construct this table, we obtained information provided by all the dioceses to the archdiocese.

8. It should be noted that several parishes kept records in languages other than French. These languages included German, Italian, and Latin. Churches where registers switched from French to Latin before switching to English are not part of this study.

9. There were five priests whose country of origin was determined to be Alsace-Lorraine, Belgium, or Switzerland. These countries are not included in the calculations because French or German may have been the native language. If German is the language, the percentage of German-speaking priests increases to 20.27%.

10. *Cabanocey* is an Indian word meaning "duck's roosting." Bourgeois, *Cabanocey.*

11. 1916 Religious Bodies Census.

12. Baudier, *The Catholic Church in Louisiana,* 358.

BIBLIOGRAPHY

ARCHIVAL RECORDS

Archdiocese of New Orleans (AANO)

Antebellum Correspondence (AC), 1803–1860

Archbishop Janssens' diary

Archdiocesan administrative business records (ABR)

Archiepiscopal Council Minutes, 1858–1921

Catholic directories (published annually)

Dioceses of Lafayette, Baton Rouge, Lake Charles, Houma-Thibodaux Church Parish Records and Reports (DD)

New Orleans Church Parish Records and Reports

Pastoral Letters, 1844 to 1934

Archives Nationales de France (AN)

Fonds des Colonies (Colonial Archival Collection, or AC): Correspondance à l'arrivée en provenance de la Louisiane, 1678–1807. C13-A. Centre des archives d'outre mer in Aix-en-Provence, France.

Official Catholic Directory for the years 1860, 1870, 1880, 1890, 1900, 1910, 1920

Redemptorists' Provincial Archives, Denver, Colorado

Provincial *Annales,* 1847–1890

Sacred Congregation of the Propaganda Fide

Annales de l'Association de la Propagation de la Foi, 1816–1830, Vols. I–IV (VANT-PF *Annales*)

Series Congressi America-Canada of the Propaganda Fide (VANT-PF)

OTHER REFERENCES

Aguirre, Louis G., ed. *Celebrating Faith along the Bayous: The Churches of the Diocese of Houma-Thibodaux.* Schriever, LA: H-T Publishing Co., 2002.

Allain, Mathé. "French Emigration Policies: Louisiana, 1699–1715." In *Proceedings of the Fourth Meeting of the French Colonial Historical Society,* edited by Alf Heggoyand and James Cooke, 39–46. Washington, DC: French Colonial Historical Society, 1984.

Audisio, Gabriel. "Crisis in Baton Rouge, 1840–1860: Foreshadowing the Demise of Louisiana's French Language?" *Louisiana History* 29 (1988): 343–63.

Aycock, Joan Marie. "The Ursuline School in New Orleans, 1727–1771." In *Cross, Crozier, and Crucible: A Volume Celebrating the Bicentennial of a Catholic Diocese in Louisiana,* edited by Glenn R. Conrad, 203–18. New Orleans: Archdiocese of New Orleans in cooperation with the Center for Louisiana Studies, 1993.

Ayres-Bennett, Wendy. *A History of the French Language through Texts.* London: Routledge, 1996.

Barry, Colman. *The Catholic Church and German Americans.* Notre Dame, IN: University of Notre Dame Press, 1953.

Baudier, Roger. *The Catholic Church in Louisiana.* New Orleans: A. W. Hyatt, 1939.

Beer, William. *Early Census Tables of Louisiana.* New Orleans: Louisiana Historical Society Publications, 1911.

Beers, Henry Putney. *French and Spanish Records of Louisiana: A Bibliographical Guide to Archive and Manuscript Sources.* Baton Rouge: Louisiana State University Press, 1989.

Berlin, Ira. *Many Thousands Gone: The First Two Centuries of Slavery in North America.* Cambridge, MA: Belknap Press of Harvard University Press, 1998.

Bernard, Shane K. *The Cajuns: Americanization of a People.* Jackson: University Press of Mississippi, 2003.

Bjork, David. "Documents relating to the Establishment of Schools in Louisiana, 1771." *Mississippi Valley Historical Review* 11, no. 4 (1925): 561–69.

Blassingame, John W. *Black New Orleans, 1860–1880.* Chicago: University of Chicago Press, 1973.

Bourgeois, Lillian C. *Cabanocey: The History, Customs, and Folklore of St. James Parish.* New Orleans, LA: Pelican Publishing Co., 1957.

Brasseaux, Carl A. *The "Foreign French": Nineteenth-Century French Immigration into Louisiana.* 3 vols. Lafayette: Center for Louisiana Studies, University of Southwestern Louisiana, 1990.

———. "Creoles of Color in Louisiana's Bayou Country, 1766–1877." In *Creoles of Color of the Gulf South,* edited by James H. Dormon, 67–86. Knoxville: University of Tennessee Press, 1996.

———, ed. *A Refuge for All Ages: Immigration in Louisiana History.* Lafayette: Center for Louisiana Studies, University of Southwestern Louisiana, 1996.

Britain, David. "Space and Spatial Diffusion." In *Handbook of Language Variation and Change,* edited by J. K. Chambers, Peter Trudgill, and Natalie Schilling-Estes, 603–37. Oxford: Blackwell, 2002.

Brown, Everett. "Letters from Louisiana, 1813–1814." *Mississippi Valley Historical Review* 11, no. 4 (1925): 570–79.

Bruns, J. Edgar. "Annotating for Posterity: The Sacramental Records of Father Antonio de Sedella." In *Cross, Crozier, and Crucible: A Volume Celebrating the Bicentennial of a Catholic Diocese in New Orleans,* edited by Glenn R. Conrad, 349–59. New Orleans: Archdiocese of New Orleans in cooperation with the Center for Louisiana Studies, 1993.

Buckley, Cornelius M., ed. and trans. *A Frenchman, a Chaplain, a Rebel: The War Letters of Pere Louis-Hippolyte Gache, S.J.* Chicago: Loyola University Press, 1981.

Bunner, E. *History of Louisiana, from Its First Discovery and Settlement to the Present Time.* New York: Harper & Brothers, 1855.

Cable, George Washington. *The Creoles of Louisiana.* 1884; rpr. New York: Garrett Press, 1970.

Calhoun, Milburn, ed. *Louisiana Almanac, 2006–2007 Edition.* Gretna: Pelican Publishing Co., 2006.

Castellanos, Henry C. *New Orleans as It Was: Episodes of Louisiana Life.* 1895; rpr. Baton Rouge: Louisiana State University Press, 2006.

Catholic Encyclopedia. http://www.newadvent.org/cathen/09378a.htm.

Chambers, J. K. *Sociolinguistic Theory: Linguistic Variation and Its Social Significance.* Oxford: Blackwell, 1995.

Chaudenson, Robert. *Creolization of Language and Culture.* London: Routledge, 2001.

Cheramie, Deany. "Cajun Vernacular English and the Influence of Vernacular on Student Writing in South Louisiana." PhD diss., University of Southwestern Louisiana, Lafayette, 1999.

Clapp, Theodore. *Autobiographical Sketches and Recollections during a Thirty-Five Years' Residence in New Orleans.* Boston: Phillips & Sampson, 1857.

Clark, Emily. *Masterless Mistresses: The New Orleans Ursulines and the Development of a New World Society, 1727–1834.* Chapel Hill: University of North Carolina Press, 2007.

Codignola, Luca. *Guide des documents relatifs à l'Amérique du Nord française et anglaise dans les archives de la Sacrée Congrégation de la Propagande à Rome.* Canada: Archives Nationales, 1990.

———. "La bureaucratie romaine face à la crise de la fin du XVIIIe siècle." In *Le Saint-Siège, le Canada et le Québec: Recherches dans les Archives Romaines,* edited by Luca Codignola, Giovani Pizzorusso, and Matteo Sanfilippo, 61–72. Viterbo, Italy: Sette Città, 2011.

———. "Les premiers pas de l'Église Catholique en Acadie et au Canada." In *Le Saint-Siège, le Canada et le Québec: Recherches dans les Archives Romaines,* edited by Luca Codignola, Giovanni Pizzorusso, and Matteo Sanfilippo, 45–60. Viterbo, Italy: Sette Città, 2011.

"Compendium of the Catechism of the Catholic Church." Accessed May 10, 2013. http://www.vatican.va/archive/compendium_ccc/documents/archive_2005_compendium-ccc_en.html.

Connor, Robert. "The Protestant Church and Its Effect on Language Shift in Louisiana." MS, Louisiana State University, 2006.

Crété, Liliane. *La vie quotidienne en Louisiane, 1815–1830.* Paris: Hachette, 1978.

Dawdy, Shannon Lee. *Building the Devil's Empire: French Colonial New Orleans.* Chicago: University of Chicago Press, 2008.

Denuzière, Maurice. *Je te nomme Louisiane: Découverte, colonisation et vente de la Louisiane.* Paris: Éditions Denoël, 1990.

Din, Gilbert C. *The Canary Islanders of Louisiana.* Baton Rouge: Louisiana State University Press, 1999.

"The Diocese of Alexandria." Accessed August 8, 2013. http://diocesealex.org/about-diocese-alexandria.

Dolan, Jay P. "A Critical Period in American Catholicism." *Review of Politics* 35 (1973): 526.

Dominguez, Virginia. *White by Definition: Social Classification in Creole Louisiana.* New Brunswick, NJ: Rutgers University Press, 1986.

Doorley, Michael. "Irish Catholics and French Creoles: Ethnic Struggles within the Catholic Church in New Orleans, 1835–1920." *Catholic Historical Review* 87 (2001): 34–54.

Dorian, Nancy C. *Language Death: The Life Cycle of a Scottish Gaelic Dialect.* Philadelphia: University of Pennsylvania Press, 1981.

Dormon, James H., ed. *Creoles of Color of the Gulf South.* Knoxville: University of Tennessee Press, 1996.

Dubois, Sylvie. "Letter-Writing in French Louisiana: Interpreting Variable Spelling Conventions, 1685–1840." *Journal of Written Language and Literacy* 6, no. 1 (2003): 31–70.

———. "Autant en emporte la langue: La saga louisianaise de la langue française." In *Globalization and the French Language*, edited by Salikoko Muwfene and Cécile Trépanier, 155–78. Paris: Odile Jacob, 2014.

Dubois, Sylvie, and Barbara M. Horvath. "When the Music Changes, You Change Too: Gender and Language Change in Cajun English." *Language Variation and Change* 11 (2000): 287–313.

———. "Creoles and Cajuns: A Portrait in Black and White." *American Speech* 15 (2003): 253–86.

———. "The English Vernacular of the Creoles of Louisiana." *Language Variation and Change* 15 (2003): 255–88.

Dubois, Sylvie, and Emilie Leumas. "Language Practices in Louisiana: The Switch from Written French to Written English within the Catholic Church." *LACUS Forum 35: Language and Linguistics in North America, 1608–2008: Diversity and Convergence* (2009): 31–44.

Dubois, Sylvie, Emilie Leumas, and Malcolm Richardson. "Spatial Diffusion of Language Practices within the Catholic Church in Louisiana." *University of Pennsylvania Working Papers in Linguistics* 132 (2007): 51–64.

Dubois, Sylvie, and Megan Melançon. "Creole Is, Creole Ain't: Diachronic and Synchronic Attitudes toward Creole Identity in Southern Louisiana." *Language in Society* 29 (2000): 237–58.

Dulles, Avery, S.J. *Models of the Church.* GardenCity, NY: Doubleday & Co., 1974.

Duncan, Herman C. *The Diocese of Louisiana.* New Orleans: A. W. Hyatt, 1888.

Eble, Connie. "The Loss of French in Antebellum Louisiana: A Social Network Perspective." *LACUS Forum 32: Networks* (2006): 91–98.

Eckert, Penelope, and Sally McConnell-Ginet. "Think Practically and Look Locally: Language and Gender as Community-Based Practice." *Annual Review of Anthropology* 21 (1992): 461–90.

Ellis, John Tracy, ed. *Documents of American Catholic History.* Volume 2, 1866–1966. Wilmington, DE: Michael Glazier, 1987.

Emmitte, Aaron. "Un Cadjin qui dzit Cher bon dieu! Assibilation and Affrication in Three Generations of Cajun Male Speakers." PhD diss., Louisiana State University, Baton Rouge, 2013.

Fairclough, Adam. *Race and Democracy: The Civil Rights Struggle in Louisiana, 1915–1972*. Athens: University of Georgia Press, 1995.

"Faith and Action." Congregation of Notre Dame, accessed July 21, 2013. http://www.archivesvirtuelles-cnd.org.

Fanning, William. "Plenary Councils of Baltimore." In *The Catholic Encyclopedia New Advent*. Accessed October 27, 2015. http://www.newadvent.org/cathen/02235a.htm

Fass, Paula. "The IQ: A Cultural and Historical Framework." *American Journal of Education* 88 (1980): 432–48.

Fiehrer, Thomas. "From La Tortue to La Louisiane: An Unfathomed Legacy." In *The Road to Louisiana: The Saint-Domingue Refugees, 1792–1809*, edited by Carl A. Brasseaux and Glenn R. Conrad, 1–30. Lafayette: Center for Louisiana Studies, University of Southwestern Louisiana, 1992.

Fishman, Joshua A. *Reversing Language Shift: Theoretical and Empirical Foundations of Assistance to Threatened Languages*. Clevedon, UK: Multilingual Matters, 1991.

Fontenot, Leigh Ann. "Cajun English: A Study of Monothongization." Honors thesis, Louisiana State University, Baton Rouge, 2003.

Fortier, Alcée. *A History of Louisiana*. 4 vols. New York: Manzi, Joyant & Co., 1904.

Gayarré, Charles. *Louisiana: Its History as a French Colony*. 3 vols. New York: Redfield, 1854.

Georgelin, J. Francis. *The Catholic Church in Algiers, Louisiana (1848–1948): The Marist Fathers and the Holy Name of Mary Church*. New Orleans: privately printed, 1949.

Giordano, Paul Anthony. "The Italians of Louisiana: Their Cultural Background and Their Many Contributions in the Fields of Literature, the Arts, Education, Politics, and Business and Labor." PhD diss., Indiana State University, 1978.

Gitlin, Jay. *The Bourgeois Frontier: French Towns, French Traders, and American Expansion*. New Haven, CT: Yale University Press, 2010.

Gray, Noel. *A Short History of Louisiana*. Dubuque, IA: Brown Co., 1960.

Greene, William Lemuel. *Antoine Blanc, 1792–1860: Fourth Bishop and First Archbishop of New Orleans*. Baton Rouge: Claitor's, 2008.

Gutiérrez, Ramón A. *When Jesus Came, the Corn Mothers Went Away: Marriage, Sexuality, and Power in New Mexico, 1500–1846*. Stanford, CA: Stanford University Press, 1991.

Hachard, Marie Madeleine de St. Stanislaus. *Relation du voyage des Ursulines de Rouen à la Nouvelle Orléans*. Rouen: Antoine Le Prevost, 1872.

Hall, Gwendolyn Midlo. *Africans in Colonial Louisiana: The Development of Afro-Creole Culture in the Eighteenth Century.* Baton Rouge: Louisiana State University Press, 1992.

Hanger, Kimberly S. "Origins of New Orleans's Free Creoles of Color." In *Creoles of Color in the Gulf South,* edited by James H. Dormon, 1–27. Knoxville: University of Tennessee Press, 1996.

———. *Bounded Lives, Bounded Places: Free Black Society in Colonial New Orleans, 1769–1803.* Durham, NC: Duke University Press, 1997.

Hardy, James D. "Church and State in French Louisiana: An Essay Review." *Louisiana History* 8, no. 1 (1967): 85–95.

Heaney, Jane Frances. "A Century of Pioneering: A History of the Ursuline Nuns of New Orleans, 1727–1827." PhD diss., St. Louis University, 1949.

Hernández-Campoy, Juan M. "Geolinguistic Models of Analysis of the Spatial Diffusion of Sociolinguistic Innovations." *Studia Anglica Posnaniensia* 34 (1999): 7–42.

Hirsch, Arnold R., and Joseph Logsdon, eds. *Creole New Orleans: Race and Americanization.* Baton Rouge: Louisiana State University Press, 1992.

Holt, Michael F. *The Rise and Fall of the American Whig Party: Jacksonian Politics and the Onset of the Civil War.* New York: Oxford University Press, 1999.

Horvath, Barbara, and Ronald Horvath. "A Multilocality Study of a Sound Change in Progress: The Case of /l/ Vocalization in New Zealand and Australian English." *Language Variation and Change* 13, no. 1 (2001): 37–57.

———. "A Closer Look at the Constraint Hierarchy: Order, Contrast, and Geographical Scale." *Language Variation and Change* 15, no. 2 (2003): 143–70.

Ingersoll, Thomas N. *Mammon and Manon in Early New Orleans: The First Slave Society in the Deep South, 1718–1819.* Knoxville: University of Tennessee Press, 1999.

Karnes, Thomas L. *Tropical Enterprise: The Standard Fruit and Steamship Company in Latin America.* Baton Rouge: Louisiana State University Press, 1978.

Kasteel, Annemarie. *Francis Janssens, 1843–1897: A Dutch-American Prelate.* Lafayette: Center for Louisiana Studies, University of Southwestern Louisiana, 1992.

———. "Archbishop Francis Janssens and the Americanization of the Church in Louisiana." In *Cross, Crozier, and Crucible: A Volume Celebrating the Bicentennial of a Catholic Diocese in New Orleans,* edited by Glenn R. Conrad, 156–69. New Orleans: Archdiocese of New Orleans in cooperation with the Center for Louisiana Studies, 1993.

Klingler, Thomas A. *If I Could Turn My Tongue like That: The Creole Language of Pointe Coupee Parish, Louisiana.* Baton Rouge: Louisiana University Press, 2003.

Krashen, Stephen. *Condemned without a Trial: Bogus Arguments against Bilingual Education.* Portsmount, NH: Heinemann, 1999.

Lachance, Paul F. "Intermarriage and French Cultural Persistence in Late Spanish and Early American New Orleans." *Histoire Sociale/Social History* 15, no. 29 (1982): 47–81.

———. "The 1809 Immigration of Saint-Domingue Refugees to New Orleans." In *A Refuge for All Ages: Immigration in Louisiana History,* edited by Carl A. Brasseaux, 258–86. Lafayette: Center for Louisiana Studies, University of Southwestern Louisiana, 1996.

Lambert, Sage. "The R-ful Truth of the Matter: An Analysis of the Constriction of /r/ in Mississippi and Louisiana." PhD diss., University of Memphis, 1995.

Lemmon, Alfred E. "Spanish Louisiana: In the Service of God and His Most Catholic Majesty." In *Cross, Crozier, and Crucible: A Volume Celebrating the Bicentennial of a Catholic Diocese in Louisiana,* edited by Glenn R. Conrad, 16–29. New Orleans: Archdiocese of New Orleans in cooperation with the Center for Louisiana Studies, 1993.

Le Page Du Pratz, Antoine-Simon. *The History of Louisiana, or of the Western Parts of Virginia and Carolina.* London: T. Becket, 1774.

Leumas, Emilie Gagnet. "'*Mais,* I sin in French, I gotta go to confession in French': A Study of the Language Shift from French to English within the Louisiana Catholic Church." PhD diss., Louisiana State University, Baton Rouge, 2009.

Leumas, Emilie Gagnet, and Renée B. Richard. *Roots of Faith: History of the Diocese of Baton Rouge.* Strasbourg: Editions du Signe, 2009.

Lodge, Anthony. *French: From Dialect to Standard.* London: Routledge, 1993.

Maguire, Robert E. "Hustling to Survive: Social and Economic Change in a South Louisiana Black Creole Community." PhD dissertation, McGill University, Montreal, 1989.

Martin, François Xavier. *The History of Louisiana from the Earliest Period.* New Orleans: Penniman & Co., 1829.

Melville, Annabelle M. *John Carroll of Baltimore, Founder of the American Catholic Hierarchy.* New York: Scribner, 1955.

———. *Louis William DuBourg: Bishop of Louisiana and the Floridas, Bishop of Montauban, and Archbishop of Besançon, 1766–1833.* Chicago: Loyola University Press, 1986.

Menier, Marie-Antoinette, Etienne Taillemite, and Gilberte de Forges. *Inventaire des Archives Coloniales: Correspondance à l'arrivée en provenance de la Louisiane.* 2 vols. Paris: Imprimerie Nationale, 1976.

Meyerhoff, Miriam. "Communities of Practice." In *Handbook of Language Variation and Change,* edited by J. K. Chambers, Peter Trudgill, and Natalie Schilling-Estes, 526–48. Oxford: Blackwell, 2002.

Miller, Gary M. "Bourbon Social Engineering: Women and Conditions of Marriage in Eighteenth-Century Venezuela." *America* 46 (1990): 261–90.

Miller, Randall M. "A Church in Cultural Captivity: Some Speculations on Catholic Identity in the Old South." In *Catholics in the Old South: Essays on Church and Culture,* edited by Randall M. Miller and Jon L. Wakelyn, 11–52. Macon, GA: Mercer University Press, 1983.

Milroy, Leslie, and James Milroy. "Linguistic Change, Social Network, and Speaker Innovation." *Journal of Linguistics* 21 (1985): 339–84.

Neumann-Holzschuh, Ingrid. "Restructuration dans un créole conservateur: Le cas du créole louisianais." In *Degrees of Restructuring in Creole Languages,* edited by Ingrid Neumann-Holzschuh and Edgar W. Scheider, 382–407. Amsterdam: J. Benjamins, 2000.

"New Orleans Catholic Encyclopedia." University of Notre Dame Archives, accessed May 19, 2013. http://archives.nd.edu/mano/neworlea.htm.

Niehaus, Earl. "Catholic Church in Louisiana." In *The Encyclopedia of American Catholic History,* edited by Michael Glazier and Thomas J. Shelley, 816–21. Collegeville, MN: Liturgical Press, 1997.

———. *The Irish in New Orleans.* New Orleans: Pelican Publishing Co., 1997.

———. "The Irish and Their Church, 1830–1862." In *Religion in Louisiana,* edited by Charles E. Nolan, 429–41. Lafayette: Center for Louisiana Studies, University of Louisiana at Lafayette, 2004.

Nolan, Charles E. *A Southern Catholic Heritage.* New Orleans: Archdiocese of New Orleans, 1976.

———. "Historians and Diocesan Archives: A View from New Orleans." *U.S. Catholic Historian* 16 (1998): 73–83.

———. *A History of the Archdiocese of New Orleans.* Strasbourg: Éditions du Signe, 2000.

The Official Catholic Directory. New Providence, NJ: P. J. Kenedy & Sons, 2004.

The Official Catholic Directory, Almanac and Clergy List. Milwaukee: M. H. Wiltzlus Co., 1900.

O'Neill, Charles Edwards. *Church and State in French Colonial Louisiana: Policy and Politics to 1732.* New Haven, CT: Yale University Press, 1966.

Papen, Robert, and Gisèle Chevalier, eds. *Les variétés de français en Amérique du Nord: Evolution, innovation et description.* Special number of *Revue Canadienne de Linguistique Appliquée* 9, no. 2 (2006).

Pasquier, Michael. "*Les confrères et les pères:* French Missionaries and Transnational Catholicism in the United States, 1789–1865." PhD diss., Florida State University, 2007.

Paxton, John Adams. *The New-Orleans Directory and Register; containing the names, professions, & residences, of all the heads of families, and persons in business, of the city and suburbs. . . .* New Orleans: Benjamins, Levy & Co., 1823.

Picone, Michael D. "Anglophone Slaves in Francophone Louisiana." *American Speech* 78, no. 4 (2003): 404–33.

Picone, Michael D., and Catherine Evans Davies, eds. *New Perspectives on Language Variety in the South: Historical and Contemporary Approaches.* Tuscaloosa: University of Alabama Press, 2015.

Poche-Frilot, Donna, and Petra Munro Hendry. "Whatever Diversity of Shade May Appear: Catholic Women Religious Educators in Louisiana, 1727–1862." *Catholic Southwest* 20 (2010): 34–62.

Reinders, Robert C. *End of an Era: New Orleans.* New Orleans: Pelican Pub., 1964.

Rickard, Peter. *A History of the French Language.* 2nd ed. London: Routledge, 1989.

Robin, Charles-César. *Voyages dans l'intérieur de la Louisiane, de la Floride occidentale, et dans les isles de la Martinique et de Saint-Domingue, pendant les années 1802, 1803, 1804, 1805 et 1806. . . .* 3 vols. Paris: F. Buisson, 1807.

Roussève, Charles Barthelemy. *The Negro in Louisiana: Aspects of His History and His Literature.* New Orleans: Xavier University Press, 1937.

Rubrecht, August. "Regional Phonological Variants in Louisiana Speech." PhD diss., University of Florida, Gainesville, 1971.

Rury, John. "Race, Region, and Education: An Analysis of Black and White Scores on the 1917 Army Alpha Intelligence Test." *Journal of Negro Education* 57 (1988): 51–65.

Scott, Ann Marie. "Cajun Vernacular English: Informal English in French Louisiana." PhD diss. University of Southwestern Louisiana, Lafayette, 1992.

Shugg, Roger. *Origins of Class Struggle in Louisiana: A Social History of White Farmers and Laborers during Slavery and After, 1840–1875.* Baton Rouge: Louisiana State University Press, 1939.

Smith, Harley. "A Recording of English Sounds at Three Age Levels in Ville Platte, Louisiana." PhD diss., Louisiana State University, Baton Rouge, 1936.

Smith-Thibodeaux, John. *Les francophones de Louisiane.* Paris: Editions Entente, 1977.

Spear, Jennifer M. *Race, Sex, and Social Order in Early New Orleans.* Baltimore: Johns Hopkins University Press, 2009.

Spletstoser, Frederick. "Back Door to the Land of Plenty: New Orleans as an Immigrant Port, 1820–1860." PhD diss. Louisiana University Press, Baton Rouge, 1978.

Suarez, Raleigh. "Chronicle of a Failure: Public Education in Antebellum Louisiana." *Louisiana Historical Journal* 12, no. 2 (1971): 109–22.

Tranchepain, Marie de St. Augustin. *Relation du voyage des premières Ursulines à la Nouvelle Orléans et de leur établissement en cette ville.* Paris: Cramoisy de J. M. Shea, 1859.

Trudgill, Peter. *Dialects in Contact.* New York: Basil Blackwell, 1986.

"The United States Census Population of 1887." US Census Bureau, accessed July 15, 2013. http://www.census.gov.

Usner, Daniel H., Jr. *Indians, Settlers, and Slaves in a Frontier Exchange Economy: The Lower Mississippi Valley before 1783.* Chapel Hill: University of North Carolina Press, 1992.

Valdman, Albert, ed. *French and Creole in Louisiana.* New York: Plenum Press, 1997.

Valdman, Albert, Julie Auger, and Deborath Piston-Hatlen, eds. *Le français en Amérique du Nord: État présent.* Saint Nicolas, QC: Presses de l'Université Laval, 2005.

VanDam, Kara H. "A Study of Language Identity and Shift: The Calvinist Dutch of West Michigan." PhD diss., University of North Carolina, Chapel Hill, 2007.

Vecoli, Rudolph. "Prelates and Peasants: Italian Immigrants and the Catholic Church." *Journal of Social History* 2 (1969): 217–67.

Voorhies, Jacqueline K., trans. and comp. *Some Late Eighteenth-Century Louisianians: Census Records, 1758–1796.* Lafayette: University of Southwestern Louisiana, 1973.

Wall, Bennett H., ed. *Louisiana: A History.* 2nd ed. Arlington Heights, IL: Forum Press, 1990.

Walton, Shana. "Flat Speech and Cajun Ethnic Identity in Terrebonne Parish, Louisiana." PhD diss., Tulane University, 1994.

Wenger, Etienne. *Communities of Practice: Learning, Meaning, and Identity.* Cambridge: Cambridge University Press, 1998.

Wight, William. "A Letter from the Archbishop of New Orleans, 1862." *Journal of the Louisiana Historical Association* 3, no. 2 (1962): 129–30.

Wolf, Nicolas. "The Irish-Speaking Clergy in the Nineteenth Century: Education, Trends, and Timing." *New Hibernia Review* 12, no. 4 (2008): 62–83.

INDEX

Index